Running

Microsoft®
Works 3
for the PC

Charles Rubin

Second Edition

The Authorized Edition

PUBLISHED BY
Microsoft Press
A Division of Microsoft Corporation
One Microsoft Way
Redmond, Washington 98052-6399

Library of Congress Cataloging-in-Publication Data
Rubin, Charles, 1953–
    Running Microsoft Works 3 for the PC / Charles Rubin. -- 2nd ed.
       p. cm.
    Includes index.
    ISBN 1-55615-509-3 : $24.95 ($32.95 Can.)
    1. Integrated software. 2. Microsoft Works. I. Title.
QA76.76.I57R83 1993
005.369--dc20   92-41058
                                         CIP

1 2 3 4 5 6 7 8 9 FFG 8 7 6 5 4 3

Distributed to the book trade in Canada by Macmillan of Canada, a division
of Canada Publishing Corporation.

Distributed to the book trade outside the United States and Canada by
Penguin Books Ltd.

Penguin Books Ltd., Harmondsworth, Middlesex, England
Penguin Books Australia Ltd., Ringwood, Victoria, Australia
Penguin Books N.Z. Ltd., 182–190 Wairau Road, Auckland 10, New Zealand

British Cataloging-in-Publication Data available.

Acquisitions Editor: Marjorie Schlaikjer
Project Editor: Tara Powers-Hausmann
Manuscript and Technical Editors: Editorial Services of New England

Contents

APPENDIXES

Acknowledgments

I've written fifteen books over the past nine years, and I've never worked with a more conscientious and helpful group of people than those I worked with on this one. In particular, I want to thank:

- Rob Armstrong and the Works development team at Microsoft for staying on schedule

- Polly Kornblith, my technical editor, for dozens of helpful suggestions and corrections to my manuscript

- Michelle Neil, my production editor at Editorial Services of New England, for never dropping the ball

- Justin Cuyler of Editorial Services of New England for many screen dump edits

- Mary DeJong at Microsoft Press for helping out with beta releases and overcoming some technical problems

- Tara Powers-Hausmann at Microsoft Press for managing the whole process

Thank you one and all. It has been a privilege.

Introduction

This book is for anyone who wants to learn to get the most out of Microsoft Works version 3.0 for MS-DOS. You can learn how to use Works from the program's printed and on-line documentation, but this book contains many techniques, tips, and shortcuts that will help you use Works to its best advantage. As you learn, you'll discover how to apply the Works Word Processor, Spreadsheet, Database, and Communications tools to data-handling tasks in your daily life.

Most computer manuals do a good job of explaining which keys to press to operate a program. The manuals and on-line documentation provided with Works are no exception. For most of us, though, knowing how a program works doesn't help much unless we also know how to apply that knowledge. Everybody knows how to use a hammer, for example, but few people know how to build a table. This book will show you not only how to use Works but also what you can do with it.

WHY WORKS WORKS

Microsoft Works for MS-DOS has long been a best-selling program because it's both easy to use and powerful. Many software programs sacrifice ease of use for power, but Microsoft Works version 3.0 offers most of the power that most people need for most of the things they do, and it does so in a way that's easy to learn and understand.

There are, of course, some fancy features that Works doesn't have, but if you're a typical computer user, you'll rarely miss them. After a while, if you find that one of the Works tools simply doesn't have the power you need, you can always buy a more sophisticated word processor, spreadsheet, database, or communications program for that particular application and continue to use Works for your other tasks. Particularly if you're new to computers, Works is a good choice because it provides an easy and useful introduction to the four most common computer applications in one low-cost package.

One of the major reasons people choose Works is that it combines, or integrates, four applications. Rather than having to buy separate programs for word processing, spreadsheet and chart creation, database management, and communications, and then learn to use each of those programs, Works gives you all these tools in one program. Many of the commands in Works are the same for each tool, so you only have to learn them once, and all the Works tools have the same basic interface — the way you choose commands and view or manage data on the screen is the same in every situation.

Another benefit of having four integrated application tools is that you can easily move data from one tool to another. You can work with the data using the tool that you need at the time. If you calculate a lot of numbers with the Spreadsheet tool, for example, and you then want to apply some fancy formatting to them, you can easily copy the numbers to a Word Processor document and use that tool's formatting features.

Finally, Microsoft Works is popular because it's easy to learn. Works comes with an extensive on-line Help file and the Learning Works tutorial program, which you can use either to look up instructions for specific procedures or to practice procedures using simulated Works screens. You can access these facilities while you use the program. For example, you can pause and learn about Word Processor formatting while you work on a Word Processor document. By following the lessons in the Learning Works tutorial, you can learn all the basic operations of the program in a few hours. Later, when you need help with a particular command or procedure, Works' on-line Help file is like having a Works expert beside you.

WHAT'S NEW ABOUT MICROSOFT WORKS VERSION 3.0

Version 3.0 of Microsoft Works incorporates many suggestions from Works users about extra capabilities they wanted in the program. When adding new features, Microsoft was careful to avoid making the program harder to use. The following are some of the new features that have been added in Works version 3.0. You'll discover other enhancements as you explore this new version of Works. In every case, Works' power has been improved without diminishing its ease of use.

Microsoft WorksWizards

WorksWizards are a new, automated feature in Works version 3.0 that handle five tasks quickly and easily. By following on-screen directions and answering a few simple questions, you can use WorksWizards to

- Make a Database file for addresses

- Create mailing labels

- Produce customized form letters

- Select specific sets of records in a Database file

- Search for a specific document

Each of these tasks is only a few keystrokes away with WorksWizards.

The Calendar

More than simply an enhancement to the collection of accessories included in Works version 2, the Calendar is a complete productivity tool that lets you schedule appointments on any day at any time, make notes about each appointment, and then manage appointments by displaying specific days or searching for blocks of free time. You can even set Works to remind you about appointments by beeping at the appropriate time.

Toolbars

Toolbars in each of the four Works tools and the Calendar now offer more mouse support than ever before. Simply click the mouse on items in the toolbar to quickly handle common tasks.

Templates

Works now offers a wide selection of ready-made Word Processor, Spreadsheet, and Database documents to suit many common business and personal computing needs.

Word Processor Graphics

You can now use graphics to dress up Word Processor documents, including drawings in headers, footers, or the main body of a document. Works 3 comes with a selection of clip-art files you can use, or you can draw your own graphics with a graphics program and then paste them into a Works Word Processor document.

Spreadsheet Links in the Word Processor

When you insert Spreadsheet data into a Word Processor document, you can now link the data to the original Spreadsheet document. When values in the Spreadsheet document change, those changes are reflected in the copy you've inserted in the Word Processor document.

Footnotes and Word Counts in the Word Processor

You can now place footnotes at the end of the page on which they occur, rather than only at the end of the document. Also, there's a new word count feature that is invaluable when you're trying to prepare a document to fit a specific length requirement.

Simplified Database Reports

Preparing Database reports is now simpler than ever with the new report generator. After choosing New Report from the Database View menu and typing a report title, you can create a Database report simply by selecting field names and calculations.

More Spreadsheet Power

The Microsoft Works 3 Spreadsheet is now larger, with 16,384 rows, and it is simpler to use as well as more powerful. The new Autosum feature automatically sums values in a column, and the Best Fit formatting option automatically sets a column's width to accommodate its widest entry. Also, the Spreadsheet now supports text functions so you can manipulate text with calculation formulas, and it also lets you enter fractions as numerators and denominators (1/2) instead of only as decimal numbers.

More Flexible Communications

The Communications tool now supports XModem, YModem, ZModem, and Kermit protocols. You can now record more activities while communicating, and you can edit recorded scripts.

HOW TO USE THIS BOOK

Microsoft Works comes with an excellent disk-based tutorial and a large on-line Help file along with its printed manual. This book is intended to supplement these learning aids. Although many parts of the book provide step-by-step instructions for completing a procedure, you'll also be referred to Works' Help file to learn more on your own.

Rather than reiterating the contents of the printed manual and the Help and tutorial files, this book focuses on explaining Works' concepts and techniques in a way that might make more sense to you. We'll try to anticipate questions that Works' own documentation doesn't answer and show you how to use Works in practical ways.

How This Book Is Organized

Chapter 1 discusses basic Works techniques. You'll learn how to move around in the Works screen, choose commands, and create and manage files. You'll also learn about Works' user aids: the Help and tutorial files, WorksWizards, the Works accessories, and the Calendar tool. Finally you'll learn how to change Works' settings and use Works' built-in macro feature. These Works techniques are explained in overview fashion; the goal is to help you understand how each fits in the Works program and your daily use of Works. When a Help file explanation would be beneficial, this book directs you to it.

Chapters 2 through 10 cover the Word Processor, Spreadsheet, and Database. The first chapter about each tool is an overview in which you'll do some quick exercises to learn the basics of using the tool. Unlike the Learning Works tutorial, these exercises emphasize a broader understanding of each tool's capabilities and how the tools relate to the rest of the program. The exercises also help you learn and practice the most efficient ways to issue commands. The second chapter about each tool contains general tips for using the tool to its best advantage. The final chapter about each tool contains business and personal projects that show you how to use Works' power to simplify your life. These projects include a form letter, an address book, a budget, an amortization table, and an expense and income tracking system.

Finally, Chapters 11 and 12 show you how to use the Communications tool and then all the Works tools together. Each of these chapters contains an overview, tips, and practical projects you can complete.

If you've never used Works before, read Chapter 1. Then focus on the chapters that describe the tool you want to learn about first.

If you have used Works before, you might want to skim Chapter 1 to pick up some new techniques for performing basic tasks. Then you can continue to the chapters that describe the individual tools. If you need help with a specific subject, check the index for related information.

Following Mouse and Keyboard Instructions

Although you can use either the mouse or the keyboard to issue Works commands, we'll assume you'll use the mouse most of the time. As we explain various Works features, we'll ask you to click or drag items on the screen or choose a command name from a certain menu.

- "Click" means to point to the item using the mouse and then click the left mouse button.

- "Double-click" means to point to the item using the mouse and then click the left mouse button twice, quickly.

- "Drag" means to point to an item, hold down the left mouse button, and then move the mouse pointer.

- "Choose a command" means to point to the menu name and hold down the left mouse button, point to the command name, and then release the mouse button to select the command.

You'll find lots of special mouse tips throughout the book.

Many keyboard commands in Works require that you press two keys at the same time or press a key or two and then immediately press a third key. In this book, these keystroke shortcuts are indicated with all the keys together, separated by hyphens. For example,

- If you're supposed to hold down the Alt key and then press the F key, you'll be told to press Alt-F.

■ To choose the Create New File command from the File menu, you must first display the File menu by pressing Alt-F, and then you must press the N key by itself. In this case, you'll be asked to press Alt-F-N.

In most cases, the keyboard alternate for choosing a command is shown in parentheses following the command instruction. There are also special keyboard tips throughout the book.

For more on choosing commands in Works, see "Choosing Menu Commands" and "Using Dialog Boxes" in Chapter 1.

Getting Started

To use this book, you'll need an IBM PC, PC/XT, PC/AT, PS/2, or 100 percent compatible computer with at least two floppy disk drives (a hard disk is strongly recommended). You'll also need a copy of PC-DOS or MS-DOS version 3 or later, and a copy of the Microsoft Works version 3 program.

If you haven't yet installed Works, see the instructions in Appendix A. This appendix also contains tips for installing Works on a laptop computer.

Microsoft Works is an easy program to learn, but mastering any computer program requires some effort and concentration. You'll benefit most from this book if you can set aside an hour or so each time you want to learn something and devote that hour exclusively to Works. Everybody makes mistakes when learning, so don't get frustrated when you do. You cannot possibly press a key that will damage your computer while running Works, and if you're about to do something — such as erasing a file — that you might later regret, Works alerts you with clear warnings.

Although learning to use any computer program is difficult at times, it's also rewarding. Few experiences can match the satisfaction you'll get from learning something new and then using the knowledge to improve your life. You're at the beginning of such an experience now.

1

Basic Microsoft Works Techniques

Before you begin using each of the Microsoft Works tools, you'll need to learn some basic techniques for using the program in general. In this chapter, we'll look at the fundamentals that are common to using every Works tool. These basics include:

- Using the Microsoft Works interface
- Working with files
- Using templates
- Using Microsoft WorksWizards
- Running other programs
- Using on-line help
- Using accessories
- Using the Calendar
- Customizing Microsoft Works' settings
- Using macros

In this chapter, you'll practice these techniques. The printed *Microsoft Works User's Guide* and the on-line help and tutorials each cover these topics in detail.

USING THE MICROSOFT WORKS INTERFACE

The Microsoft Works interface consists of the Works screen and the elements of the screen that let you control the program. Whenever you're using Microsoft Works, several elements of the Works interface appear on the screen at all times. Let's start Works, open a new word processor document, and look at a typical screen.

Creating a New File

1. Type *works* to start Works from the floppy or hard disk directory where the program is installed. (See Appendix A for more information on starting Works.) The Works Quick Start dialog box is displayed, like this:

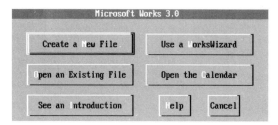

2. Click the Create a New File button. Works displays the Create New File dialog box, like this:

   Here, you choose the type of document you want to create by clicking the appropriate button at the left (or typing *W, S, D,* or *C*), and then you choose whether you want to open a new, blank document or a custom-formatted template. (See "Using Templates," later in this chapter, for more on templates.)
   Works has already selected the Word Processor document type, and it has also selected the Standard/Blank template option at the right.

3. Click the OK button. Works displays a new, blank word processor document on the screen, as in Figure 1-1.

4. Press Alt-F or click the word *File* at the top of the screen to display the File menu.
   This screen now includes the interface features that are common to every screen in Works.

2

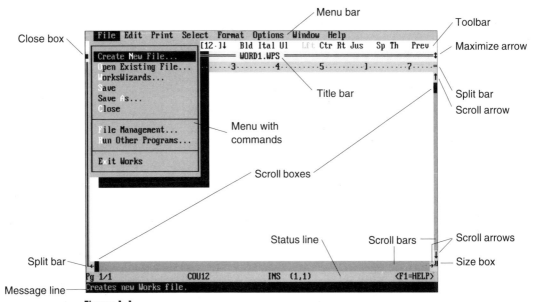

Figure 1-1.
A typical Works screen.

KEYBOARD TIP: Whenever a button in a dialog box has a double outline around it, like the OK button in the Create New File dialog box, you can press the Enter key to select it rather than clicking the button with the mouse.

Every Works screen has a menu bar at the top, a toolbar beneath the menu bar (if you've chosen to display it), a message line at the bottom, and a status line above the message line.

- The menu names showing in the menu bar change, depending on whether or not you have a document open and, if so, whether it's a word processor, spreadsheet, database, or communications document.

- The commands showing on the displayed menu let you perform specific program functions.

- The toolbar displays abbreviated names of commonly used commands. You can click these commands with the mouse to choose them in the toolbar, instead of having to find them on a menu.

(If the toolbar is not visible on the screen, click Options, Show, Show toolbar, OK — or press Alt-O-H-B — to display it.)

- The message line at the bottom of the screen suggests which key you should press next to issue a command, or it provides a brief description of what the currently selected command does.

- The status line shows the cursor's current location in a document (which is the current page number of a word processor document, for example, or the active cell of a spreadsheet). This line also shows other information specific to the Works document you're working on, such as the font, size, and style and the current cursor position in a word processor document, or the number of records in a database file.

These interface features let you issue program commands or get information about what you're doing in Works.

Working with a Document Window

The menu bar and status line appear on the screen whenever Works is running, whether you have a document open or not. Each time you open a document, Works opens a window that fills the area between the menu bar and the status line.

NOTE: *For basic instructions on using the mouse, see "Following Mouse and Keyboard Instructions" in the Introduction.*

A window always starts at its full size (as shown in Figure 1-1), but you can move a window around on the screen or change its size using either the keyboard or the mouse. Each window also has interface features that let you control which part of a document is displayed in it at any given time. All windows have the following:

- A *title bar*, which shows the name of the document. You can move a window around the screen by dragging it by its title bar.

- A *close box*, which closes the window when you click it with the mouse.

- A *maximize button*, which changes the size of a window quickly when you click it. (If you've made the window smaller than full size, clicking the maximize button makes it full size. If the window is already full size and you made it smaller earlier, clicking the maximize button makes the window smaller again.)

- A *split bar,* which lets you split a window into two or four parts, each of which can be independently scrolled so that you can view two or four different parts of a document on the screen at one time. The word processor has only a vertical split bar, but the spreadsheet and the database list view have both vertical and horizontal split bars. (The Communications windows do not have a split bar.) To split a window, drag the split bar in the appropriate scroll bar to the place where you want the document split, and then release the mouse button. Works then splits the window into two panes. (In the spreadsheet or the database list view, you can drag the split bars in both scroll bars to split the window into four panes.)

- *Scroll bars* and *scroll boxes,* which let you display different parts of a document. Drag the scroll box up or down, left or right to scroll the screen proportionally, or click in the scroll bar above or below the scroll box to scroll one screen at a time. You can also click in a scroll bar and hold down the mouse button to scroll continuously.

- *Scroll arrows,* which scroll the document up, down, left, or right in smaller increments. Click an arrow once to scroll one line, character, spreadsheet row or column, or database field or record at a time, or click an arrow and hold down the mouse button to scroll continuously.

- A *size box,* which lets you change the size of a window. Drag the box up and to the left to make a window smaller, or down and to the right to make a window larger.

 MOUSE TIP: You can also choose commands from the Window menu to move, resize, maximize, or split windows in the Word Processor, Spreadsheet, or Database; but if you're using the mouse anyway, it's much faster to simply click or drag the appropriate part of a window itself.

KEYBOARD TIP: If you don't want to take your hand off the keyboard to use the mouse to manipulate a document window, use these keyboard shortcuts to choose commands from the Window menu.

Alt-W-M chooses the Move command. When you type this, Works selects the window border, and you can then move the whole window left, right, up, or down by pressing the arrow keys.

Alt-W-S chooses the Size command. When you type this, Works selects the window border, and you then press the arrow keys to resize the window.

Alt-W-X chooses the Maximize command, resizing a window quickly to either its maximum size or to the size you last selected using the Size command or the Size box.

Alt-W-T chooses the Split command. When you type this, Works displays a split bar across the window. Press the Up and Down arrow keys to move the split bar up and down the screen. When the bar is where you want it, press the Enter key to split the window. (To eliminate the split, choose the Split command again and move the split bar back to its original location.)

PgUp and *PgDn* scroll the contents of a window up or down one screen at a time.

Arrow keys move the cursor up, down, left, or right one line, character, database field, or spreadsheet cell at a time.

Arranging Windows

You can have up to eight different documents open at one time in Works (six if you're using a WorksWizard). As you open each document, Works places its window on top of the windows of any other open documents. Only one document window can be *active* at a time in Works.

To activate a particular document, choose its name from the Window menu. That document's window moves to the top of the stack of open windows so that you can work on it. (If part of the window you want to work with is showing behind the currently active one, you can also click that part of the window with the mouse to activate it and bring it to the top of the stack.)

When you have more than one window open, you can use the Arrange All command on the Window menu to change the sizes of all the open windows and arrange them so that you can see part of every window at the same time, like this:

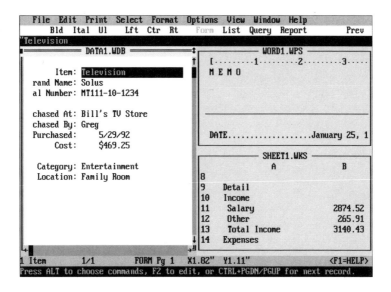

After Works arranges the windows this way, you can click in any window to make it active and then click the window's Maximize button (Alt-W-X) to expand it to full screen size.

Choosing Menu Commands

You can display any menu by pointing to its name in the menu bar and clicking the left mouse button. When Works displays the menu, click the command name you want. To choose a command in one smooth motion, simply point to the menu name, hold down the mouse button, drag the pointer to the command name, and then release the mouse button.

If you're using the keyboard, press the Alt key to activate the menu bar. After you press Alt, Works highlights one letter from each menu and selects the File menu's name. To display a menu, either press the highlighted letter key, or press the Left or Right arrow keys to select the desired menu name, and then press the Down arrow key to display the menu.

After Works displays a menu, it highlights one letter in each command name on the menu. To select a command, either press the highlighted letter key, or press the Up or Down arrow key to select the command you want, and then press the Enter key.

Some commands, such as Save, execute immediately when you choose them. Other commands offer more than one option for accomplishing a task. On the menus, these command names are always followed by an ellipsis (. . .), and choosing them always produces a dialog box, such as the Indents & Spacing dialog box shown in Figure 1-2 on the next page.

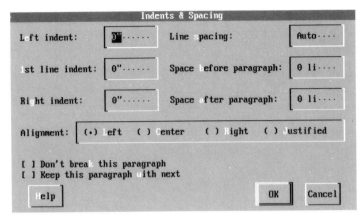

Figure 1-2.
Dialog boxes contain several options.

 WORKS TIP: You can cancel any dialog box by pressing the Esc key. In fact, you can cancel just about any Works operation by pressing Esc.

Using Dialog Boxes

When Works displays a dialog box, you can select options with either the keyboard or the mouse. If you have a mouse, simply click the options you want to select. From the keyboard, hold down the Alt key and press the letter key for the option you want to select, or press the Tab key to advance the cursor to the next set of options.

 **KEYBOARD TIP:** In dialog boxes where there are no text entry areas (such as the Works Quick Start dialog box, shown at the beginning of this chapter), you can simply press the letter key alone to choose a command without the Alt key.

Some dialog boxes have only a set of buttons you click to select options. In others, like the one in Figure 1-2, you must select an option and then type in text or a value. When you're finished typing an entry for a particular option, there are three ways to select the next option in the same dialog box.

- Click any other option to select it. If the option has a text box, click the text box, not the description of the text box.

- Press the Tab key to move to the option following the one you're currently on.

- Hold down the Alt key and press the highlighted key to select any other option. (In some cases, such as bullets or checkboxes, simply press the highlighted key to select another option.)

Most dialog boxes have a Cancel option that you select to tell Works to close the dialog box without changing any options. You can select this from the keyboard by pressing the Esc key.

Also, most dialog boxes have an OK button that you press to carry out the command using the options you've selected. Usually, the OK option in the dialog box has a double outline, so you can select it simply by pressing the Enter key.

 KEYBOARD TIP: You might get into the habit of pressing Enter whenever you finish typing a line of text, but be careful in dialog boxes. Sometimes after you enter text — such as a filename — in a dialog box, you might want to change other options in the dialog box. However, if you press Enter, Works closes the dialog box and accepts the current options. Be sure you don't press Enter when you're in a dialog box until you've selected all the options you want.

WORKING WITH FILES

Whichever Microsoft Works tool you're using, you'll use the same commands on the File menu to create, save, open, and close files and to run WorksWizards. Other File menu commands let you manage files, disks, and directories; temporarily quit Works and run another program; and exit the Works program.

About New Files

If you followed the exercise at the beginning of this chapter, you've already used the Create New File command (Alt-F-N) to make a new Word Processor file. Every file you create begins with a generic name that indicates which Works tool you used to create it and how many new files you have created with that tool during the current Works session. If the new Word Processor file was the first file you created in Works this session, Works named it WORD1.WPS. (The only exception to this is the Calendar document, which is always named CALENDAR.) The filename appears in the title bar at the top of the document window.

Every file named by Works has a three-letter extension that identifies the Works tool that created the file. The extensions are WPS for the Word Processor, WKS for the Spreadsheet, WDB for the Database, WCM for the Communications tool, and CAL for Calendar documents.

Works stores newly created files only in your computer's active memory, so if you exit Works or shut off your computer without saving these files, they can be lost. If you want to keep a file so that you can work with it later, you must save it on disk. (See "Saving Files," later in this chapter.)

Opening Existing Files

When you choose the Open Existing File command from the File menu, Works displays a dialog box, like this:

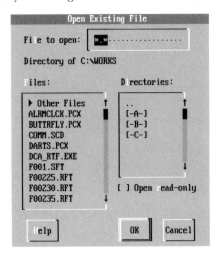

Using this dialog box, you select the name of the file you want to open and then press Enter.

The Directory Of line shows the directory from which you loaded Works. Because you will probably store your data files in a different directory, you must specify the directory that contains the file you want. To indicate a different directory, you have two options:

- If you want to open a file from a different directory but you don't want to change the current directory, you can type the directory name in front of the filename in the File To Open text box. For example, if the current directory is C:\WORKS and you want to open a file called BUDGET from the directory named BIZ, you would type *\biz\budget* in the File To Open box. Works would open the file, but the current directory would remain C:\WORKS.

- If you're opening the first of a series of files that are all located in a different directory, you can change the current directory itself. Either type only the directory name in the File To Open box (type *\biz* and press Enter to switch to the BIZ directory, for example) or use the Directories box. To change the current directory using the Directories box, simply double-click the name of the directory you want. You can also change the directory by using the arrow keys to highlight the directory you want and then pressing Enter.

Initially, the list of directories contains only disk drive names. If you want to select a directory that's on the same disk as the current directory, do the following:

1. Highlight the two dots at the top of the Directories list, and press Enter or double-click the two dots to move up one level to your root directory. Works displays all the directory names at the same level as the Works directory. (Usually, all your directories are on the same level in the main directory of the disk, so selecting the two dots will show you all the directories on your disk.)

2. Select the directory you want (or double-click the directory name), and press Enter to change to another directory. The new directory name appears in the Directory Of line.

After you change to the directory from which you want to open the file, the list of files contained in that directory appears in the Files list box at the left. Notice that Works groups files in the list by their type: Word Processor, Spreadsheet, Database, Communications, and Other Files. You can either type the filename you want in the File To Open text box or select the filename from the Files list box.

Works lets you use three different methods to select a file from the list and open it:

- Double-click the filename with the mouse. Use the scroll bar to find the file if the list box contains many names.

- Move to the Files list box and press the Down arrow key until the filename is selected, and then press Enter to open the file.

- Type the first letter of the filename to select the first filename in the list beginning with that letter, press the Down arrow key to select the specific file you want, and then press Enter. Typing the first letter of the filename is particularly handy when the Files list box contains many names. The selection jumps right to the first group of files beginning with that letter. This way, you don't have to do so much scrolling to find the file you want.

Saving Files

Two commands on the File menu allow you to save files: Save and Save As. When you choose the Save command to save a file that has been saved on disk before, Works simply saves the file again at the same location with the same name, without presenting a dialog box. If you choose the Save command to save a newly created file, however, Works presents the Save As dialog box, because you must name a new file before you save it. When you choose the Save As command, Works displays a dialog box similar to the Open Existing File dialog box. The dialog box lets you enter a different filename or choose a different disk or directory in which to save the file. It also includes a few other options. The Save As dialog box looks like this:

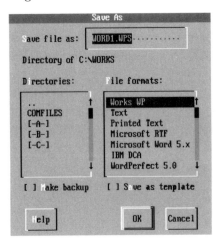

12

To save a new file or save a file under a new name, type the name of the file in the Save File As box. (If you're saving a new file, the name that Works has given it so far is something like WORD1.WPS. When you begin typing, this name disappears.) If you're saving an existing file under a new name, the current filename will appear here.

The Directory Of line below the filename shows the current disk directory. As with opening a file, the current directory might not be the one in which you want to save the file. For example, if you start Works by switching to the WORKS directory and typing *works,* the current directory shown when you choose the Save As command will be WORKS. You shouldn't save your data files in that directory because it contains dozens of Works program files, and it might be hard to find your own data files among them. To save the file in a directory other than the current one, you'll have to select a new directory.

After you select a directory and type a filename, you can save the file and exit the dialog box by pressing Enter. You might, however, want to select one of the other options in this dialog box before leaving it.

The File Formats list box lets you save the file in a format that can be used by other programs. The default option here is Works WP, Works SS, Works DB, or Works CM (depending on which type of document you're saving), which means that if you save the file in this format, you can open the file only by using the Works tool that created it. If you select another option, you'll be able to open the file with another Works tool or with another program entirely. (See Chapter 12 for more information on file formats.)

Selecting the Make Backup option tells Works to save your file two times: once with the usual extension (WPS, WKS, etc.) and once with a backup extension (BPS, BKS, etc.) so that you can tell the two files apart in a file listing. Making a backup copy is a precautionary measure you can take so that you'll always have an extra copy of a file in the event that the one you normally work with is damaged or erased. When you select this option, Works will always save a backup copy each time you save the file, overwriting any previously created backup file.

The other option in the Save As dialog box is Save As Template. We discuss templates in "Using Templates," later in this chapter.

Closing Files

To close a file, you can either click the close box in the upper-left corner of the document window or choose the Close command from the File menu (Alt-F-C). If you try to close a file that has been changed since you opened it, Works displays a dialog box that asks whether or not you want to save the changes to the file.

Managing Files

You might want to perform some MS-DOS–related functions while you run Works, such as formatting a new floppy disk, making a new disk directory, or deleting a file from a disk. The File Management command (Alt-F-F) gives you access to these functions. When you choose the File Management command, Works displays a dialog box listing different file management functions, like this:

After the box is displayed, you can select a function by double-clicking the name of the function you want to perform, or pressing the Down arrow key to highlight it and then pressing the Enter key.

NOTE: *You can't copy, delete, or rename a file when it is open.*

 KEYBOARD TIP: When you press the first letter of a function name in the File Management dialog box, the selection jumps to that function name. For example, each time you press the letter *C,* the selection jumps from one function beginning with that letter to the next.

After you select a function, Works displays a dialog box in which you can enter the name of the file to be copied, deleted, or renamed; the name of the directory to be created or removed; the new date and time you want to set; or the floppy disk to be formatted or copied. (For more information on these options, click the Help button in the File Management dialog box.)

After you enter the correct information in the function's dialog box, press the Enter key to carry out the function. (In the Remove Directory dialog box, press Enter if necessary to change to the directory you want to remove, and then click the Remove button.) In contrast to most dialog boxes, however, the list of file-management functions doesn't disappear after you carry out an operation. You have to click the Cancel button or press Escape to remove the list from your screen and return to the last Works screen.

USING TEMPLATES

Templates are special files you can create to store and easily reuse custom settings or information for new documents. Once you store a template, you can open it as if you were creating a new document and then save it under a different name. In the Word Processor, for example, new documents have a 1.3-inch left margin and are single-spaced. If you change the format settings of a document to a 1-inch left margin and double-spacing and then save that document as a template called *MYDOC*, every new Word Processor document you create from that template will have a 1-inch left margin and will be double-spaced.

Templates are handy when you don't like the Standard/Blank document settings in a Works tool and you want to be able to open a new document that has different settings.

In addition to format settings, templates can store text, such as the return address in a letterhead; data, such as field names in a database or row or column titles in a spreadsheet; or other information, such as telephone numbers or custom connection setups in communications documents.

You can create and save as many template files as you like by using the Save As Template option in the Save As dialog box. When Works saves a template, it stores the file with the name "Template *XX*," where *XX* is the number that follows the number of the last template stored. (If you choose the Open Existing File command, select the WORKS directory, and look under Other Files in the Files list, you'll see several numbered template files there.)

It's pretty difficult to tell which template is which when each template has only a number to identify it, so when you save a file as a template, Works lets you give it a more descriptive name. When you select the Save As Template option and click OK, Works displays a dialog box, like this:

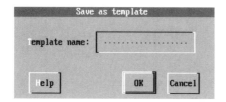

In this dialog box, you type a descriptive name for the template and then click OK or press Enter.

Opening Templates

After a template is stored on disk, the descriptive name appears in the Available Templates list in the Create New File dialog box. Since a template file opens as a new, untitled document, you use the Create New File command (not the Open Existing File command) to open a template file. Try opening some of the templates that come with Works for more ideas about templates you might create on your own.

Changing Templates

To change a template, you must use the Open Existing File command, locate the template by its number, and then open it. The descriptive names for templates don't appear in the list of files when you use the Open Existing File command.

When you open a template file from the Open Existing File dialog box, the document opens with its template number name rather than with a new document name. If you make changes to the template and save it with the Save command, Works saves the changes to that template and will alter accordingly any new documents you create with it.

 WORKS TIP: To save some disk space, check out the templates that were installed with Works, and delete the ones you don't want. Because templates are stored with numbers, you must open each template file with the Open Existing File command. The document window has the template's number in it (rather than WORD1 or something like that), so you can tell which template number is which.

USING MICROSOFT WORKSWIZARDS

WorksWizards let you accomplish a complex series of tasks by answering some simple questions on the screen. Microsoft Works version 3 comes with five WorksWizards:

- Address Book, which automatically creates a database where you can store names and addresses

- Form Letters, which creates custom form letters by merging data from an existing Database file into a Word Processor document

- Mailing Labels, which creates a mailing label document in the Word Processor using data merged from an existing Database file

- File Finder, which helps you locate and open a file on your disk if you don't remember its full name or directory

- Data Finder, which selects a subset of records from a Database file

To access these WorksWizards, do the following:

1. Choose the WorksWizards command on the File menu (Alt-F-W), or click the Use a WorksWizard button in the Works Quick Start dialog box. You'll see a dialog box, like this:

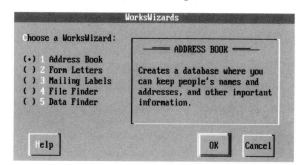

2. Click the name of the WorksWizard you want to use. A description appears in the space at the right.

3. Click OK or press Enter. Works then displays an introduction to the WorksWizard you chose. Next follow the directions on the screen to answer the questions, or type the information Works needs to know.

If you're using the Address Book, Form Letters, or Mailing Labels WorksWizards, you'll end up with a new Word Processor or Database document you can then save to your disk. Once a WorksWizard has created such a file, and you've saved it on disk, you can open, modify, and save it in the same way as you would any other Works file.

We'll see WorksWizards in action as we create word processing and database projects in Chapters 4 and 10.

RUNNING OTHER PROGRAMS

Works is a full-featured productivity program, but you'll probably want to use other programs on your personal computer for specific tasks. The Run Other Programs command on the File menu lets you exit Works temporarily and run another program. When you quit the other program, return to the MS-DOS prompt, and type *exit*. Works starts up again, and the files you had open when you chose Run Other Programs appear as they were.

When you choose the Run Other Programs command (Alt-F-R), Works displays a dialog box, like this:

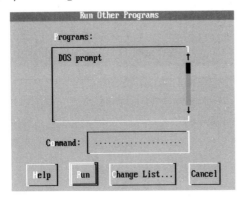

To run another program, double-click the program's name or press the Down arrow key to select the program name and then press Enter. Works displays a message telling you that you're about to exit the program. Click OK or press Enter again, and the other program will run.

When you first install Works, the MS-DOS prompt is the only "other program" in the list. You can add new programs, however, by clicking the Change List button in this dialog box. When you do, the Change List dialog box appears, like this:

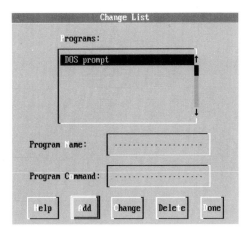

Click the Program Name box and type the name of the program you want to add, and then click the Program Command box and type the MS-DOS command you would enter at the MS-DOS prompt to run this program. After you've typed all the correct information, click the Add button to add the program to the list, and then click the Done button to close the dialog box.

WORKS TIP: A small part of your computer's memory stores Works when you run another program. If the program you're trying to run is very large, you might get a message saying that there's not enough memory to run it. If so, you must exit Works (using the Exit command from the File menu) to free up as much memory as possible.

You can also change programs in the Change List dialog box by selecting the program name, typing new information in the Program Name or Program Command boxes, and then clicking the Change button. To delete a program from the list, select the program name and click the Delete button.

For more information on running other programs, click Help in the Run Other Programs dialog box.

USING ON-LINE HELP

The extensive on-line help and tutorial facilities in Microsoft Works are a great source of quick information as you work with this program.

Most dialog boxes in Works have a Help button you can click to access the on-line Help file. You will be referred to the Help file for further information about Works procedures throughout this book.

You can also use the Learning Works tutorial to learn more about the Works techniques explained in the preceding sections. Both the on-line help and tutorial options are available from the Help menu in Works.

The Learning Works Tutorial

The Learning Works tutorial is a series of lessons that can teach you about the basic Works functions and how to use each Works tool. You can access the tutorial from inside Works any time you need it, so you can easily learn about and practice a specific group of procedures if you're not familiar with them.

The tutorial program automatically loads when you choose the Learning Works Tutorial command from the Help menu (Alt-H-L). Let's start up the tutorial now and take a quick tour.

1. Start the Works program if it isn't running. (See Appendix A if you need help.)

2. Choose the Learning Works Tutorial command (Alt-H-L) from the Help menu. The first time you use the Learning Works tutorial, you will see a welcome screen in which you enter your name. Next Works displays the Learning Works menu, like this:

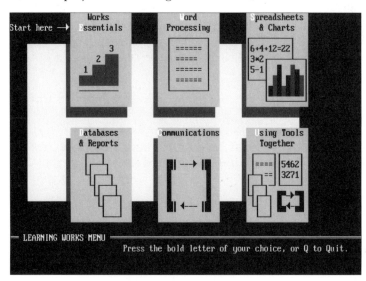

This screen shows the tutorial's six sections. You select a section by pressing the highlighted letter key in the section's name — you can't use the mouse to make these choices.

■ Press E to display the Works Essentials section.

After you select a tutorial section, Works displays a list of several lessons, each of which shows you how to perform a particular Works activity, such as entering Word Processor text or entering Spreadsheet formulas. The list of lessons for the Works Essentials section looks like this:

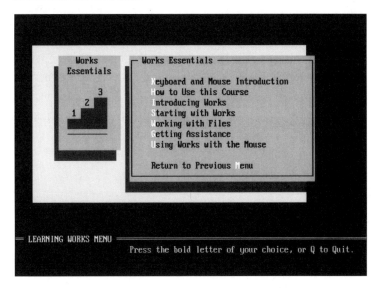

The name of each lesson contains one highlighted letter. To select a lesson, press the letter key that matches the highlighted letter in the lesson's name.

■ Press H to select How To Use This Course.

When you select a lesson by pressing the key that matches the highlighted letter in the lesson's name, Works begins by describing what you'll learn in the lesson and approximately how long it will take to complete the lesson. See the screen at the top of the following page.

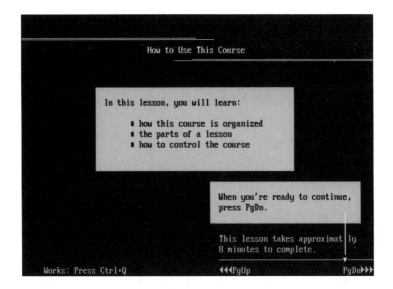

Each lesson begins with a list of the concepts it will cover, followed by an overview of the lesson. Next you'll read some descriptions of each concept and see an automated demonstration of the concept in action. Finally you'll be asked to perform the task yourself for practice.

Each lesson takes 10 or 15 minutes to complete. After you complete a lesson, an asterisk appears next to the lesson's name in the list for that section to remind you that you've completed that lesson.

If you haven't done the portion of the Works tutorial called Works Essentials, do it now. This section shows you how to use the keyboard and mouse, how to choose commands, how to work with files, and how to use the Help file as well as the Works tutorial itself.

After you finish the tutorial's Works Essentials section, quit the tutorial by pressing Ctrl-Q. You'll then return to Works.

The Help Function

Even if you complete all the lessons in the Works tutorial, you probably won't know everything about every Works command. The Help function helps fill the gaps in your knowledge by explaining every procedure in Works.

The Help function in Microsoft Works version 3 has been significantly expanded to provide specific instructions for performing basic Works tasks, as well as for commands and procedures for each tool. You can even get help about how to use the Help function itself.

For now, let's focus on the Help Table of Contents, which is where you find information about a specific procedure or command.

Choose Table of Contents (Alt-H-T) from the Help menu. Works displays the Table of Contents dialog box, as shown in Figure 1-3. Select the Basic Skills category.

In the Table of Contents dialog box, you can see different categories of information at the left. The list at the right contains the topics in each category, and it changes, depending on which category you select. To select a category and a topic, click the category whose topics you want to see, and then double-click the topic name to display help about that topic.

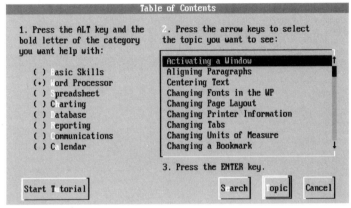

Figure 1-3.
The Help Table Of Contents.

KEYBOARD TIP: To select Help topics with the keyboard, hold down the Alt key and press the first letter of the category name you want. Press the Down arrow key to select the topic you want from the list, and then press the Enter key to display information about that topic. If you know the first word in a topic name, you can quickly scroll to that topic (or the group of topics that begins with the same letter) by typing the first letter of its name.

Let's choose a topic now to see how you can move through the Help file.

1. Display the Table of Contents dialog box, if it isn't already showing. Click the Basic Skills category, if it isn't already displayed.

2. Click the lower part of the scroll bar next to the list of topics until Microsoft Works displays the Moving Through a File topic, and then double-click that topic name. Works displays the topic, like this:

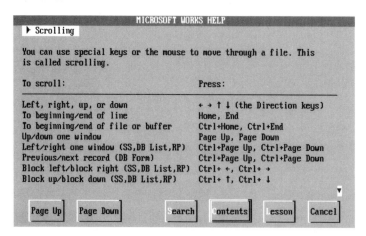

The topic name is shown at the top of the screen. You can see that this topic name is Scrolling, rather than Moving Through a File. Each topic can include several specific procedures, and the procedures themselves are named on the Help screens.

3. To see the second page of this topic, click Page Down or press the PgDn key.

Works stores all the Help screens in one big file, with each screen for each topic placed one after the other. When you reach the end of a topic, you can continue to click Page Down to see the next topic. In the same way, you can click Page Up to back up in the file and view the preceding topic.

Along with Page Up and Page Down, there are four other buttons at the bottom of each topic screen:

■ The Search button displays the Searching Help dialog box, where you can scroll through a list of more specific command or procedure names and then jump to the topic information about them. Click the Cancel button to return to the Works screen.

■ The Contents button returns you to the Help Table of Contents screen, where the same topic that you selected earlier remains selected.

- The Lesson button starts the Learning Works tutorial and opens a lesson that relates to the Help topic you've selected. You can press Ctrl-Q to return to the Help dialog box.

- The Cancel button returns you to the screen that Works displayed before you first chose the Table of Contents command from the Help menu.

Try choosing different categories and selecting different topics to see what kind of help is available.

USING ACCESSORIES

Three accessory programs are built into Microsoft Works, each of which is available from the Options menu. Let's look at them briefly.

The Calculator

The Calculator is an on-screen version of a pocket calculator, complete with buttons and a window to display results. You can use the Calculator to do quick calculations at any time while using Works. You can copy a number from any open document into the Calculator's window, and you can insert calculated results from the Calculator's window into an open document.

When you choose the Calculator command (Alt-O-C), Works displays the calculator on the screen, like this:

To enter numbers and arithmetic operators, click the buttons or press the number keys or the add (+), subtract (−), multiply (×), or divide (/) keys in the top row of your keyboard. Press Enter to execute the operation. As you enter values or operators, the current result appears in the Calculator window.

KEYBOARD TIP: If the Num Lock function is active on your keyboard, you can also use the numeric keypad keys to control the Calculator. If Num Lock is on, you'll see NL at the right side of the status line on the Works screen. To turn Num Lock on or off, press the Num Lock key on your keyboard.

Other than the number and operator keys, there are six special buttons on the Calculator:

- The CHS button changes the sign of the number currently displayed in the Calculator window.

- The CL button clears all numbers from the Calculator.

- The CE button clears the last number you entered; you must then press the = button to see the previous number.

- The Help button displays instructions for using the Calculator from Works' Help function.

- The Insert button inserts the number from the Calculator window into the place you indicate in an open Works document. (See the following discussion.)

- The Cancel button closes the Calculator.

To copy the displayed number from the Calculator to another Works document, you must first put the cursor or cell or field selection where you want the data to appear in an open Works document. Once you've done this, display the Calculator and click the Insert button. Works copies the number from the Calculator's display and inserts it at the current cursor position in the active document.

To copy a value from a Works document into the Calculator's window, select the value in the document, choose the Copy command from the Edit menu, and then open the Calculator. Works displays the number you copied in the Calculator window.

NOTE: *You can always display the Calculator from inside any open Works document by pressing Alt-O-C.*

The Alarm Clock

The Alarm Clock lets you instruct Works to display reminders on your screen. You can enter short reminder messages and set alarms to go off on any day or at any time in the future. You can choose to have an alarm go off only one time, or you can set it to go off at the same time every day, weekday, week, month, or year. Here's how to set an alarm:

1. Choose Alarm Clock from the Options menu (Alt-O-A). Works displays the Alarm Clock dialog box, like this:

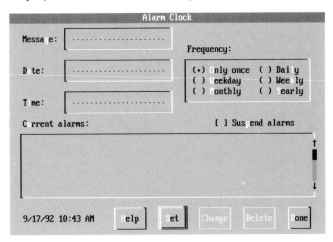

2. The cursor is blinking in the Message text box. Enter a message of up to 60 characters. When you finish, press the Tab key to select the Date box.

3. The lower-left corner of the Alarm Clock dialog box shows the current date and time, as supplied by your computer's internal clock/calendar. (If these times are wrong, reset them with the File Management command on the File menu. See "Managing Files," earlier in this chapter.) Enter the date on which you want the alarm to go off (using the MM/DD/YY format), and then press Tab to select the Time box. If you don't enter a date, Works assumes you want the alarm set for the current date.

4. Enter the time at which you want the alarm to go off. When entering the time, be sure to indicate AM or PM and use a colon, like this:

   4:00 PM

   If you don't specify AM or PM, Works assumes you mean AM.

5. Press Tab. The cursor moves to the Frequency options box.

6. Click a frequency option or press the highlighted letter key for the frequency option you want to select.

7. Click the Set button or press Enter to set the alarm. The Current Alarms box shows the alarm specifications and the message. You can then set another alarm, select an alarm in the Current Alarms list and change or delete it by clicking the Change or Delete button (Alt-C or Alt-T), or click the Done button (Alt-D) to exit the dialog box.

 KEYBOARD TIP: If you want to type information in several text boxes inside a dialog box, it's fastest to press the Tab key to move from one text box to the next.

If you want to temporarily turn off all the alarms you've set without deleting them from the list, click the Suspend Alarms check box.

When the date and time for the alarm arrive, Works beeps and displays a dialog box containing the alarm message, like this:

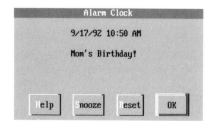

When an alarm message appears, you have four options:

- Click Help (Alt-H) to display Works Help screens about using the Alarm Clock.

- Click Snooze (Alt-S) to snooze an alarm, which tells Works to sound the alarm again in 10 minutes.

- Click Reset (Alt-R) to reset the alarm. Works displays the Alarm Clock dialog box again so that you can enter a new time or date for the alarm.

- Click OK (or press Enter) to shut off the alarm. When you shut off an alarm that you have set to go off only one time, Works deletes the alarm's setting from the Alarm Clock's list.

If the time and date for an alarm pass while you're not running Works or when your computer is turned off, the alarm will sound the next time you start Works. For more information about alarms, click the Help button in the Alarm Clock dialog box.

The Dial This Number Accessory

The Dial This Number accessory lets you use Works to dial telephone numbers for you if your computer is connected to a Hayes-compatible modem. (For information about Hayes-compatible modems and connecting them to your computer, see Chapter 11.)

 WORKS TIP: Do not choose the Dial This Number accessory unless you have a modem connected to your computer and turned on. It takes a minute or so for you to regain control of Works after you choose this accessory when there's no modem connected or turned on. You also might find that your mouse is disabled and, if so, you'll need to exit Works and restart your computer.

To prepare Works to use the dialer properly, you must set the appropriate Modem Port and Dial Type options in the Works Settings dialog box. (See "Customizing Microsoft Works Settings," later in this chapter.) After you set up Works properly, it's easy to dial a number.

1. Open the Works document that contains the telephone number you want to dial.

2. Select the telephone number in the document.

3. Choose the Dial This Number command from the Options menu (Alt-O-D). Works dials the number and then displays a message asking you to pick up the phone. (If you turn up the speaker on your modem, you can hear Works dialing.)

If you use Works in an office where you must dial an initial number to get an outside line, you must include that initial number in the telephone number you select. Works dials whatever numbers are selected in your Word Processor, Spreadsheet, or Database document at the time you choose this command.

USING THE CALENDAR

Unlike the other Microsoft Works accessories, the Calendar is a full-fledged tool that displays its own window, menus, and toolbar, exactly as the Word Processor, Spreadsheet, Database, and Communications tools do. We won't go into all the details of using the Calendar, but let's get an idea of what it can do.

To access the Calendar, you can either click the Open the Calendar button in the Works Quick Start dialog box or you can choose Calendar from the Options menu (Alt-O-E). You'll see a window, like this:

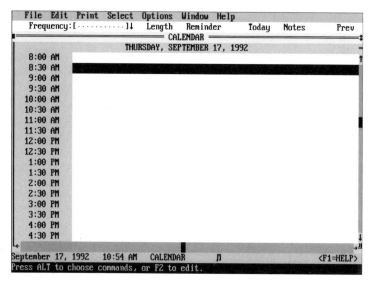

You can move, scroll, resize, or close this window just as you would any other Works document window. As you can see, Works displays the current date underneath the window title and lists time intervals down the left-hand side. The shaded bar at 8:30 AM is a selected appointment time, but there's no appointment scheduled there.

When you first display the Calendar on any given day, Works displays that day's schedule. If you've previously selected a different date with the Calendar during the current session with Works, Works will display that date when you next display the Calendar. (We'll see how to select different dates in "Changing Calendar Dates," later in this chapter.)

Entering Appointments

Let's schedule an appointment for 10:00 AM.

- Double-click the space next to 10:00 AM. The selection bar then moves there, and the cursor blinks at the beginning of the line.

- Type *Dentist, Dr. Brooks* and press the Enter key. Works displays the Appointment Length dialog box, like this:

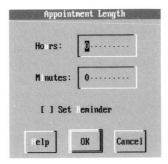

The cursor is blinking in the Hours box.

- Type *1* to tell Works the appointment will last an hour.

- Click OK or press Enter to close the dialog box. Works returns you to the Calendar window and draws a vertical line that indicates the appointment is for an hour, like this:

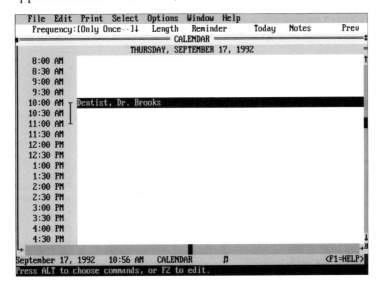

Now you can easily see that you have already scheduled this block of time. In fact, if you try to enter an appointment whose time overlaps this one (say, a one-hour appointment at 10:30 AM the same day), Works will warn you that there is a conflict.

To save this appointment and any others you've entered, click the Close box on the Calendar window. Works automatically saves your appointments.

Setting Recurring Appointments

To schedule regular staff meetings or other routine appointments in your calendar, you can enter an appointment on the current date and have Works automatically schedule it for every day, weekday, week, month, or year. Using the Appointment dialog box, follow these steps:

1. Click the time — not the space next to it — for which you want to set the appointment.

2. Choose the Appointment command from the Edit menu (Alt-E-A) to display the Appointment dialog box, like this:

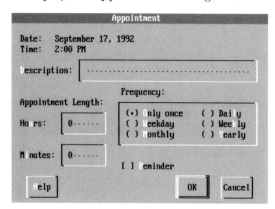

3. Type a description and length for the appointment, and then click one of the frequency options. Although you can specify an appointment of any length up to a full day, Works displays a line that rounds the appointment length up to the next half-hour.

4. Click the OK button.

MOUSE TIP: You can change an appointment's length, time, or reminder status by selecting it and clicking the appropriate tool in the toolbar. You can also display the Appointment dialog box by double-clicking the time for which you want the appointment.

For more on setting recurring appointments, click the Help button in the Appointment dialog box.

Setting Reminders

Both the Appointment Length and Appointment dialog boxes have a Reminders option. When you click this option to put an X in it, Works will display a reminder notice five minutes before the appointment time comes. You can also tell Works to display the reminder earlier by specifying a diffierent number of minutes in the Early Ring dialog box, which you access from the Options menu.

Moving and Changing Appointments

When you need to reschedule an appointment for a different time on the same day, select the appointment by clicking its time, choose the Move/Reschedule command from the Edit menu (Alt-E-M), or use the arrow keys to move to the new time where you want to move the appointment and then press Enter.

If you need to change the text of an appointment, click the appointment, drag the mouse across the text you want to change, type the new text, and then press Enter. To select the text of an appointment, click the text itself, and then edit the existing text or add new text.

Changing Calendar Dates

Naturally, not all of your appointments will be on the current date, so you need to change the Calendar to show other dates. It's easiest to change dates by clicking the mouse.

- Click the horizontal scroll bar on either side of the scroll box to move one week forward or backward from the current day.

- Drag the scroll box itself to move a week at a time.

- Click the right or left scroll arrows to scroll a day at a time.

As you change dates, the date at the top of the Calendar window shows you which day you're viewing. (The status line, however, always shows today's date and time.)

If you need to see standard monthly calendars in order to decide which date you need, choose the Go To command from the Select menu (Alt-S-G). Works displays two monthly calendars and highlights the day you're currently viewing, like this:

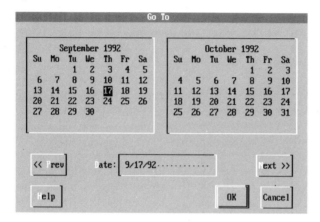

By clicking the Previous and Next buttons, you can display other months' calendars. When you find the month you want, simply double-click the date to display that date's appointments.

Click the Help button in the Go To dialog box for more information on its options.

MOUSE TIP: Click Today in the toolbar to return to the current date's appointments if you've been viewing the calendar for another date.

Entering Notes

You can make notes about any given calendar day by displaying the Notes window. To do this, choose the Show Notes command from the Options menu (Alt-O-N) or click Notes in the toolbar. Works displays a window, like this:

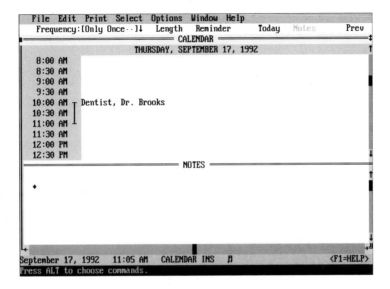

The cursor is already blinking in the Notes window, so you can then type notes about your day there. Each calendar date has its own Notes window, but the text you enter there isn't linked to any particular appointment — only to that particular day. To change a note, edit or delete the text in the Notes window. Moving or deleting any appointment has no effect on the note.

If the Notes window isn't large enough, you can make it bigger by dragging the split bar up or down. You can also scroll the Notes window up or down by using the scroll bar at the right.

 MOUSE TIP: Drag the split bar all the way to the top or bottom of the Calendar window to remove the Notes window, or click Notes in the toolbar to hide or display the Notes window.

Printing Appointments

To print appointment calendars for any day or range of days, choose the Print command from the Print menu. Works displays a dialog box like the one at the top of the next page.

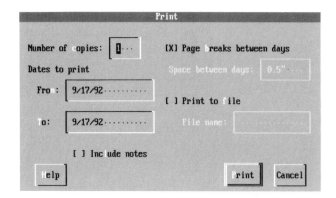

The default options here are to print one copy of the schedule for the current day. If you want different options, enter the number of copies you want and the range of dates you want printed, and then click the Print button or press Enter.

Notice that you can choose whether or not to print each day's notes along with the list of appointments. Simply click the Include Notes check box to print notes.

You can preview your work on the screen before printing by choosing the Preview command from the Print menu or by clicking Prev in the toolbar. For more on printing options, click the Help button in the Print dialog box.

Calendar Menus and Commands

We've only scratched the surface of what you can do with the Calendar. There are many options you can set by choosing commands from the Calendar's menus. You can see detailed information about any of the menu commands in the Calendar by choosing the command you want to know about and then pressing F1.

CUSTOMIZING MICROSOFT WORKS' SETTINGS

When you first select the various options to configure Works in the Setup program, the Microsoft Works program uses certain default settings. After Works is running, you can use a few specific commands to change some of these settings to better suit your hardware.

The Works Settings Command

The largest group of settings you can control from inside Works is located in the Works Settings dialog box, which appears when you choose the Works Settings command from the Options menu (Alt-O-W), like this:

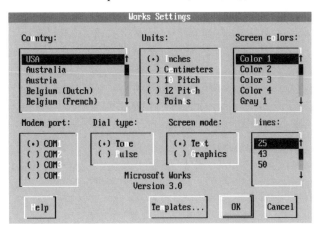

When you make changes to any of these settings, the changes take effect immediately. They apply to any document you open or create from then on, and Works keeps track of them between sessions. The way some of the options appear that are grouped under Country, Units, Screen Colors, and Lines in this dialog box depends on which video card you have in your computer, so your Works Settings dialog box might not exactly match the one shown above.

Here are the various settings and how they change Works:

- The Country options select a different page length and width, date and time format, and other preset options unique to the country represented.

- The Units options tell Works which unit of measurement to use when you specify measurements for margin sizes, page sizes, indents, tabs, and other format elements. Normally, Works assumes you mean inches when you specify format measurements. If you change the Units option, however, Works will assume that the numbers you type refer to that unit of measurement.

■ The Screen Colors options let you choose different colors or shades of gray to display on the screen. The effect of choosing each of these settings varies, depending on which video card you have installed. Try choosing different options to see which colors or shades are available with your video card.

■ The Modem Port option tells Works which of your serial communication ports to transmit data through when you use the Communications tool or the Dial This Number accessory.

■ The Dial Type option tells Works how to send telephone numbers to your modem when you use the Dial This Number accessory. Most telephone systems use the newer Tone dialing type, and that's the default option here. But if you have a rotary dial phone, you should select the Pulse option.

■ The Screen Mode option allows Works to display formatting elements on the screen in two different ways, providing your video card can handle them. In Text mode, for example, Works indicates any italic or underline formatting that you set by highlighting the characters on the screen (when you have a monochrome monitor) or by displaying them in different colors (when you have a color monitor). In Graphics mode, you would actually be able to see the italic type or underlining on the screen. Although the Graphics mode shows your formatting enhancements more faithfully, it also makes displaying text and scrolling a window a little slower.

■ The Lines option lets you select a new number of lines to be displayed on the screen. The normal PC-compatible character set will display a total of 25 lines on a Works screen, including the menu names, document name, and other elements of the interface. Depending on your video card, you might be able to display 43 or 50 lines, for example. When you change this setting, Works uses a smaller character to display more lines. It's useful to display more lines when you work with a large document, because you can see more of the document at one time without having to scroll the screen.

The Printer Setup Command

The Printer Setup command appears on the Print menu of every Works tool that has a Print menu. (The Communications tool doesn't have one.) Use this command to select a different printer brand, model, resolution, and port with which to print your documents. When you choose the Printer Setup command (Alt-P-S), Works displays a dialog box, like this:

```
┌─────────────────────────────────────────────────────────────┐
│                      Printer Setup                            │
│                                                               │
│  Current printer settings:                                    │
│                                                               │
│  Printer: Apple LaserWriter, LaserWriter Plus, NT/NTX         │
│  Option:  Internal & cartridge fonts                          │
│                                                               │
│  Graphics:        Paper source:      Page Feed:      Port:    │
│  ┌───────────┐↑   ┌───────────┐↑   ┌───────────┐↑   ┌──────┐↑ │
│  │ 300 dpi   │    │ Automatic │    │ Continuous│    │ LPT1 │  │
│  │           │    │ Manual bin│    │ Prompt each│   │ LPT2 │  │
│  │           │    │           │    │           │    │ LPT3 │  │
│  │           │    │           │    │           │    │ COM1 │  │
│  │           │↓   │           │↓   │           │↓   │ COM2 │↓ │
│  └───────────┘    └───────────┘    └───────────┘    └──────┘  │
│                                                               │
│  ┌─────┐     ┌──────────────────────┐   ┌────┐   ┌────────┐   │
│  │ Help│     │Change Printer & Option...│ │ OK │   │ Cancel │   │
│  └─────┘     └──────────────────────┘   └────┘   └────────┘   │
└─────────────────────────────────────────────────────────────┘
```

The specific printers and options you see under Current Printer Settings at the top of this dialog box depends on which printer drivers and options you installed with the Setup program when you first installed Works. If you didn't install any printer drivers, the Printer is listed as Teletype and the Option is Standard or TTY printer. This generic setting is always available, whether or not you install custom printer drivers; it tells Works to send plain, unformatted text to the printer port.

The Graphics options represent different print resolutions and reflect the capabilities of the installed printer shown at the top of the dialog box.

The Paper Source option lets you choose between manual feed and automatic feed paper-handling systems.

The Page Feed option is normally set to Continuous, which means either that you use continuous paper with a dot-matrix printer or that you use a laser printer with an automatic-feed bin. With the Continuous option set, Works doesn't stop printing between pages. If you want Works to prompt you to insert blank pages one at a time by hand, select the Prompt Each option.

Finally, the Port option lets you identify the printer port to which you've connected your printer. The default setting is LPT1, which is the first parallel printer port in your computer. If you're using a different port, you can specify it here. As you might remember, you set the printer port when you installed Works. (See Appendix A.) When you have finished specifying options, click OK or press Enter.

To change the current printer shown in the Printer Setup dialog box, click the Change Printer & Option button at the bottom. Works displays a dialog box, like the one at the top of the next page.

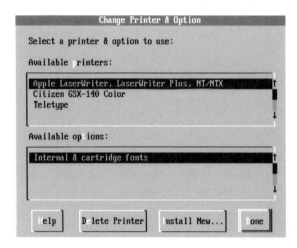

The printers you've already installed are shown in the Available Printers list, and after you select a printer there, you can select different options for it from the Available Options list, or delete it by clicking the Delete Printer button. After you select the printer and options you want, click the Done button.

If you don't see the printer you want in the Available Printers list, you can install a new printer driver from one of the Works installation disks. Simply click the Install New button and you'll be prompted to insert the appropriate Works installation disks, and then to select a new printer to install from there. When you have chosen your printer and options, click the Install button, insert the appropriate disks, and then click Done twice to return to the Printer Setup dialog box.

USING MACROS

Macros provide a powerful way in which to automate repetitive tasks. You can record any series of keystrokes, store the series as a macro under a single keystroke command, and then play the series back later by pressing the macro command. Simple macros play an ordered series of keystrokes when you type the macro command, but you can also create macros that repeat themselves until you tell them to stop, or macros that stop at a certain point and wait for you to type before they continue. You can even create macros that execute other macros.

Recording a Macro

The Microsoft Works macro facility is built into the program. To begin recording a macro, press Alt-/. Works displays the Macro Options dialog box, like this:

By selecting the appropriate option here, you can record a new macro, play an existing macro, temporarily skip a macro so that the macro's key doesn't activate it, delete a macro definition, change the key used to activate a macro, or turn the macro feature off. After you begin recording a macro, Works remembers every keystroke, so be sure before you begin recording that your document is exactly the way you want it and that the cursor is exactly where you want it. To begin recording a macro, do the following:

1. Press Alt-/. The Macro Options box appears, with the Record Macro option selected.

2. Press the Enter key. Works displays the Playback Key & Title dialog box, like this:

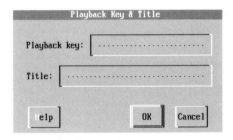

3. Press the key you want to use to activate the macro. Any key you press at this point except Tab, Esc, or Enter will be entered in the Playback Key text box, so be careful to press only the key you want. (You use Tab to move the cursor from the Playback Key box to the Title box. Pressing Esc cancels the operation and puts the dialog box away, and pressing Enter tells Works to start recording the macro.)

In choosing a playback key for a macro, you can press any single key, or you can press the Ctrl or Shift key in combination with another key. It's best to use the Ctrl or Shift key (but not the Alt key) in combination with another key to avoid running a macro when you don't mean to. For example, if you define a formatting macro as W, you'll run that macro every time you press the W key. If your macro keys are Alt-F, you might end up opening the File Menu instead. Using the Ctrl or Shift keys, though, you can come up with lots of playback key combinations that you'll probably never use in your daily work. Some key combinations, however, won't work as playback keys. (See Chapter 8 in the *Microsoft Works User's Guide* for a list of the keys you can use.)

4. Move to the Title box and type a title for the macro so that you can identify it in the macros list box later.

5. Click OK or press Enter to begin recording. If you selected a standard letter, symbol, or function key (like W, as described previously), Works displays a message asking if it's okay to redefine the key.

   At this point, Works begins recording the macro. The message RECORD appears at the right side of the message line. Every key you press is stored in the macro.

MOUSE TIP: Mouse movements are *not* recorded in macros. Works only records keystrokes, so you must perform all the operations you want to record by pressing key combinations.

When you want to stop recording the macro, do the following:

1. Press Alt-/. Works displays the Macro Options dialog box again, but because you're in the process of recording a macro, its options have changed, and the End Recording option is selected, like this:

2. Click OK or press Enter to select the End Recording option. Works then records the macro.

Correcting and Editing Macros

If you press the wrong key while recording a macro, you can cancel recording immediately and rerecord the macro from the beginning. Or you can forge ahead, pressing the keys you need to correct the mistake. The second of the alternatives is inefficient because each time the macro runs it repeats your mistake and the correction. But if you're recording a particularly long macro, it might be easier to make a correction than to start over from scratch.

Another option is to edit the macro. Works stores the macros you create in a file called MACROS.INI in the same directory as your Works program files. It stores the MACROS.INI file as a text file, and you can open that file as a Word Processor document. Works identifies each keystroke you make inside brackets in the document. In the macro file, for example, <*back*> is the Backspace key. Chapter 8 in the *Microsoft Works User's Guide* contains a guide to the key names that you'll find in the MACROS.INI file.

If you're adventurous, you can read the macro file, locate the keystrokes you made by mistake, and delete them from the file. In fact, you can write entire macros from scratch by entering them in the MACROS.INI file using the word processor.

For more information about editing macros, see Chapter 8 in the *Microsoft Works User's Guide*.

Playing a Macro

If you can remember the playback key under which you stored a macro, you can type that key and the macro will execute. As the macro plays, the word PLAY-BACK appears at the right edge of the message line. If you can't remember the playback key, you can select the Play Macro option in the Macro Options dialog box to display a list of the macros you've stored. You can then select the macro you want and press Enter to play it. If you begin playing a macro and want to stop it, press Alt-/ and then click Cancel.

Other Macro Options

As you gain experience with macros, you'll want to use some of the other macro options. Here are some brief descriptions:

- Skip Macro is the macro option you select when you've defined the playback key for a macro and then want to use that key temporarily for its original purpose. If you defined @ (Shift-2) as a macro and

43

find that you need to type the @ sign itself at some point, for example, you can display the Macro Options dialog box, choose the Skip Macro command, and then type the @ sign one time without running the macro.

■ Delete Macros displays a dialog box containing a list of the macros you've defined. To delete a macro, select its name and click Delete, and then click Done to close the dialog box.

■ The Change Key & Title option displays a dialog box that lists the macros you've defined. You can then select a macro name, click Change, and change the macro key or title. After you've made your changes, click Done to close the dialog box.

■ Turn Macros Off is the option to use when you have lots of macros defined, you don't want to execute any of those macros, and the work you're currently doing requires that you press a lot of pre-defined macro playback keys. If you've set up a lot of macros for a specific project, for example, you'll want the macros for that project to be turned on. But when you work on another project, you might want to turn off the macros so that you can use the keyboard normally, without activating any macros.

■ You can pause macros for either fixed or variable inputs so that the macro will pause for data entry from the keyboard. For example, you could have a macro that enters the text of a form letter up to the greeting line, pauses while you type the greeting, and then finishes entering the form letter. A fixed-input pause tells the macro to wait for a certain number of keystrokes before continuing. A variable-input pause tells the macro to wait until you press Enter before continuing so that you can enter as many characters as you want. When you finish typing, press Enter to play the rest of the macro.

■ You can create a repeating macro by pressing the macro's own playback key at the end of the macro definition, just before you stop recording.

■ You can pause a macro for a specific length of time, which is useful in a repeating macro that will continue until you tell it to stop. By inserting a pause at the end of the macro, you can gain some extra time to stop the macro between repetitions.

■ You can create nested macros, in which the definition for one macro contains the playback key for a second macro. To do so, you can create the second macro beforehand and then press its play-back key while you record the first macro.

Chapter 8 of the *Microsoft Works User's Guide* explains all these advanced options in detail.

This completes our overview of the basic Works techniques and procedures. You should be ready to begin exploring the individual Works tools. If you don't feel comfortable yet with the basics of Works, choose the Works Essentials section of the Learning Works tutorial from the Help menu, and work through the lessons.

2

Basic Word Processor Techniques

The Microsoft Works Word Processor lets you create many kinds of documents, from simple notes to fancy reports. It offers all the editing and formatting features common to most word processing programs, and it includes a built-in spelling checker and thesaurus. In this chapter, we'll run through some simple examples that show how Works handles basic text-entering, text-editing, format-ting, and printing operations.

THE WORD PROCESSOR SCREEN

To begin, start your Microsoft Works program if it isn't already running, and create a new Word Processor file:

1. Click Create a New File in the Works Quick Start dialog box, or choose the Create New File command from the File menu (Alt-F-N). The Word Processor file type and a Standard/Blank document are selected in the dialog box that appears.

2. Press Enter to choose this file and document type and to display a new Word Processor document, as in Figure 2-1 on the next page.

As with any other Works tool, the screen has a menu bar, a toolbar, and a title bar at the top and a status line and a message line at the bottom.

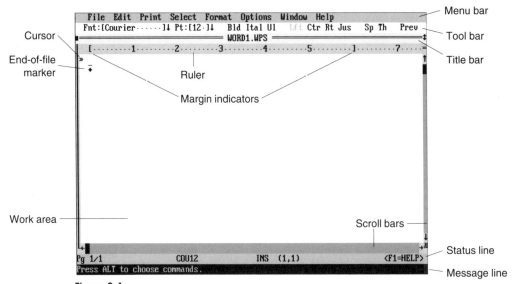

Figure 2-1.
The contents of the Word Processor screen.

The Toolbar

The *toolbar* lets you choose several Word Processor commands by pointing to an option and clicking the mouse button. From left to right, the Word Processor's toolbar has point-and-click options you can use to do the following:

- Change the font and point size
- Set bold, italic, or underline styles for text
- Set left, center, right, or justified alignment for paragraphs
- Activate the spelling program or thesaurus
- Preview the printed appearance of a document

The Status Line

Just above the *message line* at the bottom of the screen (which is the same in every Works tool), the *status line* in the Word Processor always shows the current state of the document. From left to right, it can show the following:

- The page you're on and the number of pages in the document
- Whether selected text has the boldface, italic, underline, or strike-through style, is superscript or subscript, or is a different color
- The font and point size

- Whether you're in Insert (INS) or Overtype (OVR) mode (See "Editing Text," later in this chapter.)

- The character and line number where the cursor currently is located

- Whether the Caps Lock or Num Lock feature is on

The indicators showing character styles, positions, and colors only appear in the status line when the cursor is on text that has a character style or color applied. (They're not showing in Figure 2-1, but we'll see how they look later in this chapter.)

The Title Bar, Scroll Bars, and Ruler

You'll also notice a *title bar* immediately below the toolbar, and *scroll bars* at the right edge of the screen and just above the status line across the bottom of the screen. These features appear on every Works screen. (See Chapter 1 for more details.)

The *ruler,* which is just below the toolbar, shows you the width of the text in your document. The brackets at the left edge of the ruler and at the 6-inch mark are the *margin indicators;* they define the default current line length.

The Work Area

The blank area between the ruler and the bottom scroll bar is the *work area,* which is where text appears when you type it. In a new document, the work area is blank except for the blinking underline character, called the *cursor,* and the diamond-shaped marker below it, which is the *end-of-file marker.* You can never delete the end-of-file marker or move the cursor beyond it. The cursor always indicates where text will appear when you begin typing. As you type, the cursor moves across the screen.

ENTERING TEXT

To start a document, you simply begin typing as you would on a typewriter. Type the following sentence:

> Sales have been simply stunning during the past quarter at Wonder Widgets, Inc.

Text starts at the left edge of the work area and extends across the screen as you type. When the text reaches the right margin (indicated by the right bracket in the ruler), it automatically wraps down to the next line — you don't have to press Enter to move to the next line. This feature is called *word wrapping.*

Finish this paragraph by adding a few more sentences. The blinking cursor should now be in the space after the period at the end of *Inc.* Press the spacebar one time and then type the following:

> Our Ypsilanti factory was flooded with orders for our new Vegi-Saver, and our established lines of kitchen and household hand appliances continued to sell well. Overall, sales were up 30% over the fall quarter of 1991. Here are the highlights for the fall, 1992 quarter.

To end this paragraph, press Enter. The cursor moves down to the next line. Each time you press Enter, you place an invisible paragraph marker in your document. (You can show the invisible paragraph markers, along with space markers and tab stops, by choosing the Show command from the Options menu and selecting Show All Characters in the Show dialog box.)

Press Enter again to insert one more blank line after this paragraph to separate it from the report's next section. Then type the following headline, press Enter twice, and type the next two paragraphs:

Fall Quarter Sales Update

> We had an exceptionally good quarter, better than we would normally have expected for the pre-Christmas selling season. The Voyager series of vacuum cleaners really cleaned up: HomeCo and Vacuum City both placed large orders.

> As for the Leaf Blaster, our improved muffler system strengthened demand for this unit in the Chicago suburbs, so the winds of public opinion have turned back in our favor after the spring passage of noise abatement ordinances in Elmhurst, Park Ridge, and Oak Park.

As you fill the screen with text, the text at the top of the screen scrolls up to make room for new text at the bottom of the screen. To return to the beginning of this document, you can scroll the window with the mouse or move the cursor. (See Chapter 1 for basic scrolling techniques.) When you scroll the window with the mouse, you move the text up or down on the screen without changing the cursor position. You can scroll to the top of the document, and the cursor still blinks at the bottom (or wherever you last entered text).

KEYBOARD TIP: If you scroll the window to view another part of a document and then want to return quickly to the cursor position, simply press any key — Microsoft Works automatically scrolls the window back to the cursor position and inserts the character that is on the key you pressed.

Moving the Cursor

Works has several cursor-movement key shortcuts to handle small and large cursor movements. Let's have a look at the complete list by using Works' built-in help function.

1. Choose Table of Contents from the Help menu (Alt-H-T).

2. Type a *W* to quickly scroll the list of topics to those that begin with *W*.

3. Double-click WP Movement and Selection Keys to display the list of cursor-movement shortcuts, like this:

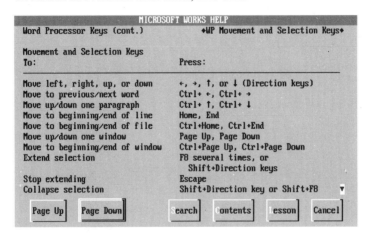

This screen shows all of Works' cursor-movement key shortcuts. To see other word processor keyboard shortcuts, click Page Up or Page Down.

4. Exit the Help function by clicking Cancel.

Try some of these shortcuts to move the cursor around in the text you've just entered. You'll also see some of these shortcuts mentioned throughout this book. To look up specific shortcuts when this Help topic isn't displayed on your screen, consult the Quick Reference page in the *Microsoft Works User's Guide.*

EDITING TEXT

Microsoft Works' editing features let you erase or edit individual characters or whole blocks of text. You can also move a block of text to a different place in a document and use special keys to delete individual characters.

Before you can delete, move, copy, or reformat a block of text, however, you must select it. You can select text by using either the mouse or the keyboard.

> **WORKS TIP:** If you want to replace text, you can choose Overtype from the Options menu (Alt-O-O). The code OVR replaces INS in the Status Line, and any text you type replaces the text at the cursor position, rather than being inserted in front of it.

Selecting Text

The fastest way to select text is with the mouse. Simply point to the text you want to select, hold down the mouse button, and drag across the characters, words, lines, or paragraphs you want to select. As you select text, it becomes highlighted on the screen, like this:

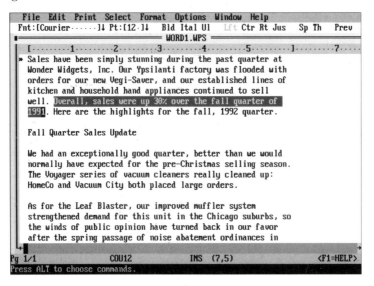

If you select more text than is visible on the screen, the contents of the Word Processor window scroll automatically.

Here are some shortcuts you can use to select blocks of text with the mouse:

- You can select one line of text by clicking next to the line at the left side of the window.

- You can select several lines of text by pointing to the left edge of the first line, holding down the mouse button, and dragging up or down to select other lines.

- You can extend a selection you've started with the mouse by *Shift-clicking*. Select the text at the beginning of the area you want to select, hold down Shift, and then click the end of the area where you want to extend the selection. Works automatically selects all the text in between.

- You can reduce a selection you've already made by Shift-clicking. Once you've selected text, hold down Shift, point to the place where you want the reduced selection to end, and click. Works automatically reduces the size of the selection.

You can deselect text that is already selected by clicking anywhere in the work area. To select text using the keyboard, press the Extend key, which is F8, or choose the Text command from the Select menu (Alt-S-E). When you press F8 or choose the Text command, you turn on Extend (EXT) mode, which lets you extend a selection by pressing the arrow or other cursor-movement keys.

When you turn on Extend mode, the code *EXT* appears in the status line to let you know it's on, like this:

```
Pg 1/1          COU12          INS (14,19)      EXT      <F1=HELP>
```

Now any cursor-movement key you press moves the cursor and selects text at the same time. For example, if you turn on Extend mode and then press PgUp, Works moves the cursor up one screen and selects all the text between the cursor's old position and its new one.

KEYBOARD TIP: You can use the Extend key (F8) by itself to select specific blocks of text. The following table shows the Extend key shortcuts:

Pressing the Extend Key	*Selects*
One time	EXT mode
Two times	Current word
Three times	Current sentence
Four times	Current paragraph
Five times	Entire document

To cancel a selection with the keyboard and return the cursor to its original position, press Esc to turn off Extend mode, and then move the cursor by pressing one of the arrow keys. If you press the Up or Down arrow key, the cursor moves to the beginning or end of the area that was selected.

Deleting and Replacing Text

After you select the text you want to work with, you can delete it, move it, copy it, or format it. Let's try deleting some text now.

1. Scroll to the top of the document.

2. Select the word *hand* in the fourth line on the screen by holding down the mouse button and dragging the pointer across it or by pressing the Extend key (F8) twice.

3. Press Delete to delete this word. (If you selected only the word and not the space after it, press Del again to delete the extra space.)

   You can also delete text by placing the cursor under a character and pressing Del or placing the cursor to the right of the text you want to delete and pressing Backspace.

MOUSE TIP: To quickly select a word and the space after it, point to the word and click the right mouse button. To select more than one word, hold down the right mouse button and drag across the words you want to select. This is easier than trying to drag exactly to the last character in a word.

Now let's edit another section of the document.

1. Select *simply stunning* in the first line of the document.

2. Press Del.

3. Type the word *excellent* with a space after it to replace the two words you just deleted.

KEYBOARD TIP: You can also press Alt-E-D to choose the Delete command from the Edit menu when you want to delete a selection, rather than pressing Del on your keyboard.

Finally, let's try using the Backspace key to change the percent symbol in *30%* to a word.

1. Move the cursor to the space at the right of the percent symbol in the first paragraph.

2. Press Backspace to delete the symbol.

3. Press the spacebar one time, and then type *percent.*

Moving and Copying Text

Moving and copying text are similar operations. In both cases, you must first select the text you want to work with, choose the Move or the Copy command from the Edit menu, and then indicate where you want Works to place the text (or a copy of the text). You can also press F3 to choose the Move command or press Shift-F3 to choose the Copy command.

When you move text, you delete it from one place and insert it in another. When you copy text, you insert a copy of the selected text at a second location. Let's move a sentence in our sample document now:

1. Select the last sentence in the first paragraph.

2. Choose the Move command from the Edit menu (Alt-E-M). The word MOVE appears in the status line, and the message line prompts you to position the cursor where you want to place the moved text.

3. Click at the beginning of the second paragraph (so the cursor is blinking under the *W* in *We*).

4. Press Enter. The selection moves to its new location. If you didn't select the space after the end of the sentence before you moved it, there's now no space between the period after *quarter* and the *We* that begins the sentence after it. If this is the case, click the *W* at the beginning of the second sentence and press the spacebar to insert a space before it.

WORKS TIP: You can avoid having to delete old text before typing the text that will replace it by choosing the Typing Replaces Selection command from the Options menu (Alt-O-Y). When this command is active, a dot appears next to its name on the menu, and anything you type replaces text you currently have selected. Choose this command again to disable it.

If you had chosen the Copy command instead of the Move command, the sentence would have remained in its original place, and a copy of it would have appeared at the cursor location.

Copying and Inserting Special Information

While the Move and Copy commands let you rearrange text, you can use other commands to insert other types of data. These commands are all on the Edit menu:

- The Copy Special command lets you copy character formats and paragraph formats from one section of text to another.

- The Insert Special Character command tells Works to insert end-of-line marks, non-breaking hyphens or spaces, or the current date or time. You can also have Works insert the page number, filename, date, or time in a document when Works prints it.

- The Insert Database Field command lets you select a field from an open Database file from which to merge data into your Word Processor document. You use this command to create form letters in Works.

- The Insert Spreadsheet Range command tells Works to insert a named range of cells from an open spreadsheet file into your document. The cells remain linked to the original spreadsheet from which they're taken, so changes in the spreadsheet are reflected in the cells inserted in the Word Processor document.

- The Insert Chart command lets you select a chart from a spreadsheet and then have Works print the chart in the Word Processor document when you print it. The chart doesn't show up in the document on the screen, however — Works simply places a marker for it.

- The Insert Picture command lets you insert clip art into a Word Processor document. As with spreadsheet charts, Works inserts a marker for the picture you choose, and it only includes the actual picture when you print the document.

 WORKS TIP: To view the spreadsheet range, chart, or picture in the document on the screen, select the Preview command from the Print menu or click Prev in the toolbar.

You'll see these commands in action in Chapter 4. (For more information now, choose one of these commands from the Edit menu and then click Help in the dialog box that appears.)

FORMATTING TEXT

You'll find three levels of formatting in the Microsoft Works Word Processor: character, paragraph, and page. Different groups of commands apply to each formatting level. The commands that affect character and paragraph formatting are on the Format menu, and there are some shortcuts in the toolbar. The commands that affect the entire page are on the Print menu.

Character and paragraph formats are so named because these commands can affect as little as one character or one paragraph. Therefore, you must select the characters or paragraphs you want to format before you choose a character or paragraph formatting command. (Actually, you can "select" a single paragraph for formatting by simply moving the cursor to any place in that paragraph. You need to select paragraphs by highlighting them only when you want to format more than one.) Page formats affect all the pages in a document so you don't have to select anything before changing these settings.

Viewing Character Styles

When you first begin typing in a new Word Processor document, the text appears in Plain Text style, which is much like the text you see in any MS-DOS program. But in Works, you can apply different styles to your text (such as boldface, italic, underlined, and strikethrough), and you can print text using different fonts, point sizes, and colors.

On the screen, text with different character formats shows up in various ways, depending on whether you have selected the Text or Graphics screen mode with the Works Settings command on the Options menu. (See Chapter 1.)

If you've set your screen to Graphics mode, text appears with the style and color you've chosen: Bold text looks bold, italic text looks italicized, and underlined text is underlined.

If you're using Text mode, text with boldface, italic, and underline formats appears in different colors or intensities to distinguish one format from another and from plain text. The colors and intensities depend on the type of display screen and display adapter you're using.

With both types of screen display, colored text with no other formatting has the color you set for it if you're using a color screen and display adapter.

Changing the Font and Size

Text with different fonts or font sizes always appears in the same font and size as plain text, but Works wraps words differently on lines to adjust for the different sizes. Let's see how this works:

1. If you've followed the other exercises up to now in this chapter, select the last paragraph of text in your sample document. Otherwise, type two lines of text, press Enter, type two more lines of text, and then select the last two lines on the screen.

2. Click the Down arrow to the right of the point box shown in the toolbar. Works displays the size menu, like this:

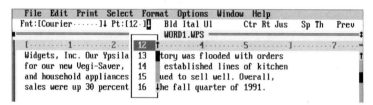

The sizes you see on this menu depend on the sizes available on your printer.

3. Scroll down the list with the size scroll box or arrows, if necessary, and then click a larger font size. Works reformats the selected paragraph so there are fewer words on a line, as in Figure 2-2.

4. Click underneath the last word in the paragraph to remove the selection highlighting, so the document appears as it does in Figure 2-2.

Your document might not look exactly like this, because you might have had different point sizes available on your size menu. If you chose a smaller point size for the selected paragraph, there will be more words on a line.

Regardless of what kind of display you're using or how you've set the display type in the Works Settings dialog box, however, you can always tell which font, size, and character style you have applied to text by moving the cursor to the text in question and glancing at the status line. As you can see in Figure 2-2, the status line shows *COU18* to indicate that the text at the cursor position is in 18-point Courier type. If you set this text to a different style or color, a letter would appear to the left of the font and size indicator to show the style, as shown in the table following Figure 2-2.

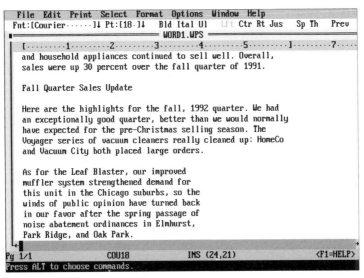

Figure 2-2.
When you change the point size of text, Works wraps words differently.

Style	Indicator
Plain text	No indicator
Bold	B
Italic	I
Underline	U
Strikethrough	S
Color (other than Black)	C
Superscript	+
Subscript	=

Before continuing, change the last paragraph in your sample document back to 12-point type, so it matches the other paragraphs.

Changing Character Styles

Works has two procedures for applying character formats. You can apply styles one at a time by choosing individual commands from the Format menu, clicking options in the toolbar, or typing keyboard commands; or you can apply several styles or font changes at one time using the Font & Style dialog box.

> **KEYBOARD TIP:** You can use keyboard shortcuts to apply styles. Instead of choosing the Bold command from the Format menu (Alt-T-B), for example, you can press Ctrl-B to apply that style to selected characters. For a complete list of all the keyboard shortcuts that are available for character formatting commands, choose the *Word Processor Keys* topic in the Word Processor category of the Table of Contents on the Help Menu.

Let's change some other character formats to see how this all works.

1. Select the text, *Fall Quarter Sales Update*.

2. Click *Bld* in the toolbar.

3. Click under one character in the text to remove the selection highlighting from the text. The text now appears in a different intensity or color on the screen (on nongraphics screens) or becomes boldface (on graphics screens), and the status line shows the B indicator, like this:

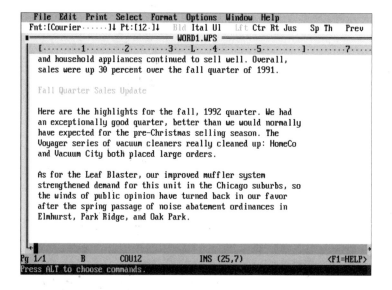

It's easy to apply individual character formats this way, or by pressing keyboard commands. When you want to apply more than one formatting change at a time, however, it's easier to use the Font & Style command. Let's try that now.

1. Point to *sales* in the last sentence of the first paragraph and click the right mouse button to select this word.

2. Hold down Shift, point to the right of the period at the end of the paragraph, and click the left mouse button. Works selects all the text between *sales* and the end of the paragraph.

3. Choose the Font & Style command from the Format menu (Alt-T-F). The Font & Style dialog box appears, like this:

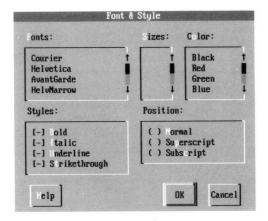

4. Click Bold and Underline in the Styles area, and then click OK or press Enter to confirm these choices.

5. Click under one character in the text to remove the highlight. The selected words in this sentence have changed to a different color or intensity (on nongraphics screens) or now appear bold and underlined (on graphics screens). Both style indicators appear in the status line.

In the Font & Style dialog box, you can set the color or position of text, and you'll also notice a list of available fonts and point sizes. As with the font and size menus in the toolbar, fonts and sizes listed here depend on which fonts are available for your printer.

Formatting Paragraphs

Paragraph formatting refers to the way text is placed on a page in terms of tabs, indents, line spacing, and alignment or justification. All these options affect the entire paragraph in which the cursor is located (or the paragraphs that are currently selected) at the time you select a formatting option. Each paragraph can have its own format settings, but Works assumes you want to continue with the current paragraph format settings when you begin a new paragraph. To see how this formatting works, we'll change some paragraph formats in our sample document.

As it is now, all the text in the document begins at the left edge of the screen and continues to the 6-inch mark, which is the default right margin. Let's set each paragraph so its first line is indented half an inch from the left.

1. Press F8 five times to select all the text in the document.

2. Choose the Indents & Spacing command from the Format menu (Alt-T-A). The Indents & Spacing dialog box appears, like this:

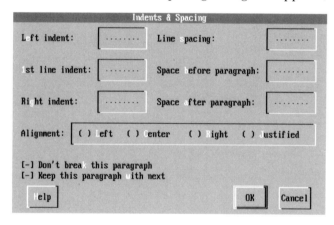

3. The cursor will be blinking in the Left Indent box. Press Tab once to move the cursor to the 1st Line Indent box.

4. Type *0.5* to indicate a 0.5-inch indent for the first line of each paragraph.

5. Press Enter to accept this new setting, and then click in a blank part of the document to remove the selection highlighting. The first line of each paragraph is now indented 0.5 inch from the left margin, like this:

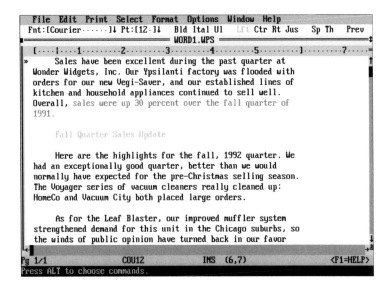

Notice that a new mark has appeared at the 0.5-inch mark in the ruler, to indicate the first line indent.

You can use the other settings in the Indents & Spacing dialog box to indent every line of a paragraph from the left or from the right, to set line spacing, to set spacing before or after each paragraph, or to indicate alignment.

WORKS TIP: To set a hanging first-line indent, so that the first line of a paragraph begins farther to the left than the other lines, set a Left Indent for the entire paragraph, and then enter a negative value for the 1st Line Indent. For example, set the Left Indent as 0.5 inch and the 1st Line Indent value as -0.5 inch. To have Works automatically set a 0.5-inch hanging indent, press Ctrl-H.

Now we'll use the Indents & Spacing dialog box again. The subheading above the second paragraph of our document shouldn't be indented, so we'll fix that and then center the same subheading for emphasis.

1. Click anywhere in the *Fall Quarter Sales Update* subheading.

2. Choose the Indents & Spacing command. The Indents & Spacing dialog box appears.

3. Press Tab once and type *0* in the 1st Line Indent box.

4. Click Center in the Alignment section or press Alt-C to select the Center option.

5. Press Enter or click OK to accept these settings. The subhead is now centered in the document.

Chapter 4 explores the line spacing, indent, and text alignment commands in more detail. For more information, choose the Indents & Spacing command from the Format menu, and then click Help in the dialog box that appears.

Setting Tabs

Before we move on to page formatting, let's take a look at how the tab settings work in the Word Processor. When you first open a new Word Processor document, tabs are set at every 0.5-inch mark on the ruler. See for yourself: Scroll to the end of the sample document and click in the blank line below the last paragraph. (Click at the end of the last paragraph and then press Enter to create a blank line if there isn't one.)

Press Tab three times, and the cursor moves under the 2-inch mark on the ruler (the 0.5-inch indent plus three 0.5-inch tabs).

The default tabs work fine in many situations, but they have two drawbacks. One is that you have to live with their 0.5-inch–mark settings. They also make it harder than necessary to move to a tab stop at the right side of the page. If you want to align text under the 5-inch mark on the ruler, for example, and you're using the default tabs in a document with no indents, you must press Tab 10 times to get there. By setting your own tab stops, you not only place them exactly where you want them, but you remove all the default 0.5-inch tab stops between the left margin and the tab you set, so you can tab directly to the position you choose.

Let's look at an example.

1. Press Home to move to the beginning of the line, type *Chicago,* and then press Tab once.

2. Type *Jones* and press Enter.

3. Type *Detroit* and press Tab once.

4. Type *Smith* and press Enter.

5. Type *Dayton* and press Tab once.

6. Type *Brown* and press Enter.

You now have two columns of data. Because our paragraphs were already indented 0.5-inch from the left, the first column lines up on the 0.5-inch mark, and because the text you typed extended beyond the 1-inch tab stops, the second column is aligned under the 1.5-inch tab stop.

Now we'll reset the tab stops so that the right-hand column is aligned under the 3.3-inch tab stop. Remember, because you pressed Enter at the end of every line, each of these lines is a separate paragraph, so you have to select all three lines to reset their tab stops.

1. Point to the left edge of the document in the line containing *Chicago.*

2. Hold down the mouse button, and drag down to select this line and the two below it.

3. Choose the Tabs command from the Format menu (Alt-T-T). The Tabs dialog box appears, like this:

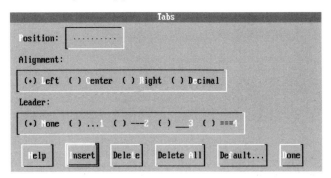

4. Type *3.3* in the Position box.

5. Press Enter or click Insert to insert the tab stop at the 3.3-inch position. An *L* appears at the 3.3-inch mark on the ruler to indicate that you've set a left-aligned tab stop there.

6. Click Done to return to the document screen, and then click in a blank part of the document to remove the selection highlight from the three lines of text.

The right-hand column is now left aligned at the 3.3-inch mark on the ruler, like this:

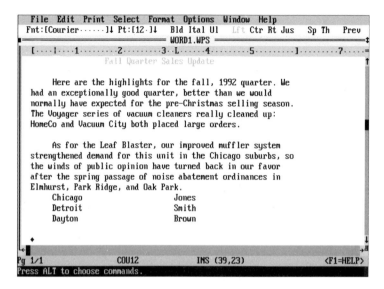

 WORKS TIP: Decimal tabs align a column of numbers on the decimal point, but if all the numbers in a column have the same number of decimal places (if they're all dollars and cents, for example), a right-aligned tab stop accomplishes the same thing.

Like indents, custom tab settings are set for individual paragraphs. If you delete the three lines of text for which we just set a custom tab stop, the tab will be deleted as well. For more information about the different types of tabs, choose the Tabs command from the Format menu and then click Help in the dialog box that appears.

Formatting Pages

The last level of formatting in Works is *page formatting*, which controls how your text will appear on the printed page. These options include margins, page size, page breaks, and headers and footers. Because all these options have to do with how your text will look when printed, their commands are located on the Print menu. You'll learn more about what these options are on the following pages.

One of the big differences between typing at a typewriter and writing using a word processor is that with a word processor you aren't typing directly on the paper. You see text on the screen as it will print on the paper, but you can't tell where that text will appear in relation to the edges of the paper. Using the margin commands lets you tell Works where to print text in relation to the edges of the paper.

Works needs to know the sizes of your top, bottom, left, and right page margins and the size of the paper to determine where to print your lines of text on paper. The margin and paper size commands are grouped together in the Page Setup & Margins dialog box.

The Word Processor window on your screen should be set to the default margin settings, so the text of your document appears on 6-inch lines. The right-margin marker in the ruler is at the 6-inch mark and the left-margin marker is at the 0-inch mark.

With these margin markers, you know that your lines of text will be 6 inches long and will print as you see them on the screen. But you can't tell by looking at the screen how large your left and right margins will be. To display the margin settings on the screen, choose the Page Setup & Margins command from the Print menu (Alt-P-M). A dialog box appears, like this:

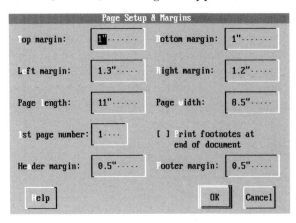

Using this box, you can enter settings for the top, bottom, left, and right margins. You can also use it to determine the page size, the starting page number, and the header and footer margins (the distance that headers and footers will print from the top and bottom of a page).

Let's change the left-margin and right-margin settings:

1. Be sure the Page Setup & Margins dialog box is displayed. (Press Alt-P-M if it isn't.) The cursor should be blinking in the Top Margin box.

2. Press Tab two times to move the cursor to the Left Margin box. (You can also press Alt-E or the Down arrow to move the cursor there.)

3. Type *1* to set the left margin to 1 inch instead of 1.3 inches.

4. Press Tab or the Right arrow one time to move to the Right Margin box.

5. Type *1* to set the right margin to 1 inch instead of 1.2 inches.

6. Press Enter to accept these settings and to return to the document screen.

Now the left and right margins are a total of 0.5 inch narrower than before, so the right-margin marker in the ruler now appears at the 6.5-inch mark, like this:

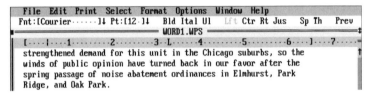

Because the right-margin marker has moved, your text lines are 0.5 inch longer and the text has been reformatted. This change occurs because Works calculates the length of text lines on the screen as the width of the paper (8.5) minus the total of the left and right margins (2). With the default left and right margins totaling 2.5 inches, the line length is 6 inches (8.5 − 2.5 = 6). But changing the left and right margins so that they total 2 inches creates an extra 0.5 inch of space on the line for text, so the line length increases to 6.5 inches.

Using Headers and Footers

Headers and *footers* are lines of text that appear in the same position on every page of a document. They usually contain identifying information such as the document title, section title, page number, date, author's name, and revision number. Headers and footers don't appear when you edit a document, but they do show up when you preview or print a document.

The Microsoft Works Word Processor lets you create two different kinds of headers and footers: standard headers and footers, which are limited to one line each, and header and footer paragraphs, which can contain as many lines as you like up to the length of the page. In any one document, you must choose whether to use standard headers and footers or header and footer paragraphs; you can't use a standard header with a footer paragraph, for example.

Headers appear at the top of the page above the text margin, and footers appear at the bottom of the page below the text margin, as in Figure 2-3.

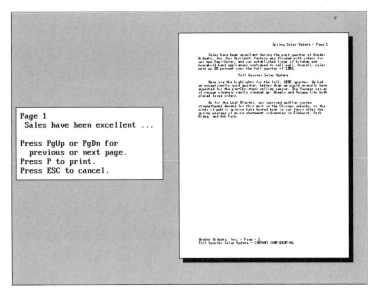

Figure 2-3.
A single-line header (top) and a two-line footer paragraph (bottom).

Standard headers can only be one line high, and they require that you use special formatting commands to align your text at the left or right margin instead of in the center or to insert the page number, filename, time, or date. Let's create a standard header to see how this works. Suppose you want your header to contain the following text, aligned at the left margin:

This is a header - Page <the current page number>

Here's what to do to create this header:

1. Choose the Headers & Footers command from the Print menu (Alt-P-H). A dialog box appears, like this:

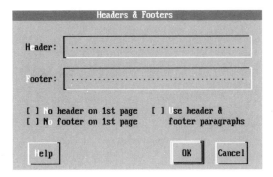

2. Type: *&LThis is a header - Page &P* in the header box.

3. Press Enter to store the header.

The header is stored with the document, but you won't see it until you print or preview the document. Because you used the format command, &L, at the beginning of your text, the text that follows it will be left aligned. And because you used the command to insert page numbers, &P, after the word *Page,* the page number will be printed on every page.

4. Click Prev in the toolbar to see the header you created. Press Esc to return to the document.

To create header and footer paragraphs, you put special marks in the document, and then type the text you want.

1. Choose the Headers & Footers command from the Print menu to display the Headers & Footers dialog box again.

2. Click the box next to Use Header & Footer Paragraphs, which makes the standard Header and Footer boxes unavailable, and then click OK.

3. Press Ctrl-Home to go to the top of the document. Works has put header and footer paragraph marks there, like this:

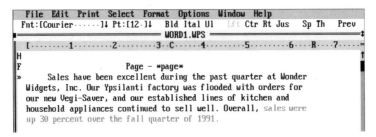

The two top lines of the document are spaces for header and footer paragraph text. Notice the *H* and *F* at the left edge of the document to identify each paragraph. As you can see, Works has automatically inserted *Page - *page** in the footer paragraph, and this text is centered on the page. (The page number marker and text won't remain centered if you add more text on this line.) The **page** text is a special marker that tells Works to insert the current page number on each page as it's printed.

To add or edit the header or footer text, simply click the appropriate line and type. To add a line to a header or footer paragraph, press Shift-Enter. (Works beeps if you press Enter alone while typing a header or footer paragraph.)

A header or footer paragraph can be as many lines tall as you like, as long as you set the header or footer margin large enough to accommodate it with the Page Setup & Margins command. After you enter the header or footer text, you can select it and format it with the character or paragraph formatting commands.

For more on headers and footers, see Chapter 3 or choose the Headers & Footers command from the Print menu, and then click Help in the dialog box that appears.

Setting Page Breaks

The last page-formatting option in the Word Processor is setting page breaks. To set a page break, click at the beginning or end of a line, and then choose the Insert Page Break command from the Print menu (Alt-P-I). Works inserts a dotted line across the document, right before the cursor, to indicate that it will begin printing a new page there. (If the cursor is in the middle of a line when you insert a page break, Works will split the line onto two pages.) Use page breaks when you want a section of a document to begin at the top of a new page. To remove a page break, place the cursor at the beginning of the line below the dotted break line and press Backspace, or place the cursor on the dotted line and press Del.

PREVIEWING AND PRINTING DOCUMENTS

When you're ready to print a document from the Word Processor, you can print it three different places: on the screen (previewing the document), into a file on disk, or on a printer. All these options are available from the Print menu.

To do this last exercise, use the document you have on your screen. If no text is showing, type some so that you'll have something to print.

1. Choose the Preview command from the Print menu (Alt-P-V) or click Prev in the toolbar. The Preview dialog box appears, like this:

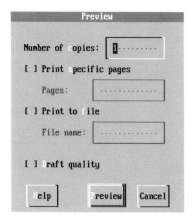

2. Press Enter or click Preview to preview the document on the screen. The page appears on the screen in a reduced size, with the exact headers, footers, margins, and paragraph formats (but not the character styles) that it will have when printed on paper. (See Figure 2-3, earlier in this chapter.) Press Esc to return to the document.

The Preview dialog box contains exactly the same options as does the Print dialog box in Microsoft Works. These options are available because you can print directly from the Preview screen that displays your document. You can enter the number of copies you want printed (but Works previews only one copy), a range of specific pages to print or preview, and the name of a file to create if you're printing the document to a file on disk. There's also a Draft Quality option you can use to quickly print a lower-resolution version of the document. For more information on the Print and Preview commands, choose either from the Print menu and then click Help in the dialog box that appears.

By now you should have a good idea of how to use the Microsoft Works Word Processor. You haven't yet covered many of the extra features, including searching for and replacing text; using footnotes; inserting pictures, charts, or spreadsheet data; correcting text using the spelling program; and using the thesaurus. We'll see many of these features at work in the projects covered in Chapters 4 and 12.

3

Making the Most of the Word Processor

The Microsoft Works Word Processor gives you a lot of flexibility in preparing documents, but some word processing approaches are faster or more efficient than others. In this chapter, we'll look at several strategies for making the most of the Works Word Processor. After considering a few general tips, we'll look at some of the Word Processor's limitations and how, if possible, to work around them.

Every user has his or her own way of getting along with a computer program, but if you're new to computing or new to Works, reading the tips in this section can help you develop some habits that will make you more productive. The tips are divided into functional groups that are based on the various aspects of word processing, such as entering and editing text or formatting.

ENTERING AND EDITING TEXT

Because most word processing involves entering and editing text, it's not surprising that most of the methods you can use to improve your word processing productivity fall into this category. Here are some techniques to consider as you work with your documents.

Use the Mouse to Select Text

It's much faster to select a word by pointing to it and clicking the right mouse button than it is to select a word by positioning the cursor with the arrow keys and then pressing F8.

Both the left and right mouse buttons can select blocks of text quickly, depending on where you point when you click each button. See the table at the top of the next page for text-selection shortcuts that you can use with the mouse buttons.

When You Use	To Click	You Select
The left button	A word	A character
The left button	The left margin	A line
The right button	A word	A word
The right button	The left margin	A paragraph

Use the Mouse to Work with Windows

Use the mouse to move or resize windows and use the scroll bar to scroll through a document. If you're moving only a screen or two up or down, the PgUp and PgDn keys work fine, but for larger jumps or for moving or resizing windows, the mouse is much faster.

Likewise, the arrow keys are a good choice when you're moving only a few characters in any direction, but the mouse is faster when you're moving farther than that. (Microsoft Works' Go To command is the fastest, most precise method of all, but you have to remember to use it. See "Use the Select Menu," later in this chapter.)

Use the Keyboard to Select an Entire Document

It's faster to type Alt-S-A to choose the All command from the Select menu or to press F8 five times than it is to drag the mouse pointer down through a whole document, especially if it's a long document.

Use the Keyboard to Select When the Cursor Is Already on the Selection

When the cursor is already at the beginning of the text you want to select, press the Extend (F8) key to select a word, a sentence, or a paragraph. (See "Selecting Text" in Chapter 2 to learn how to select blocks of text using F8.)

Use Keyboard and Mouse Shortcuts

Throughout this book and the *Microsoft Works User's Guide,* you'll find many suggestions for keyboard and mouse shortcuts. If you find yourself repeatedly choosing the same menu command, you may want to learn its keyboard shortcut and use that instead. If you normally make items boldface by choosing the Bold command from the Format menu, for example, learn to use Ctrl-B or to click Bld in the toolbar instead.

If you've memorized the Alt-key combinations, it might be easier to press a couple of keys than to choose commands with the mouse. If you don't remember the key combinations, however, it's often faster to select commands with the mouse than it is to press Alt and then use arrow keys to display the proper menu and select the right command with the Enter key.

For complete lists of keyboard shortcuts, choose the Keyboard Guide command from the Help menu, or choose the *Word Processor Keys* topic in the Word Processor category of the Help Table of Contents.

Use the Select Menu

The Select menu offers a powerful set of commands that you can use for several types of editing tasks. The Search and Go To commands let you move quickly to a certain place in a document. The Replace command lets you quickly make a series of changes to a document.

Using the Search command is faster than scrolling back and forth and manually scanning the document to find the spot for which you're looking. It's often easier to remember a subheading, proper name, or topic name in the area of the document to which you want to move. When you choose the Search command from the Select menu (Alt-S-S), Works displays a dialog box, like this:

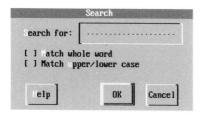

When you enter a string of text to search for, try to be as specific as possible, and use the Match Whole Word and Match Upper/Lower Case options to avoid finding unwanted occurrences of a text string. If you search for the word *Ban,* for example, and you don't use the Match Whole Word or Match Upper/Lower Case options, Works finds every occurrence of that text string, including *bank, abandon,* and *Banducci.* To continue searching for the same text string you last specified, press F7.

Along with text, you can type special characters in the Search For text box to search for tabs, spaces, or other special characters in a document. For a list of the special characters for which you can search, see the *Searching and Replacing in the WP* topic in the Word Processor category of the Help Table of Contents.

 WORKS TIP: Works searches from the cursor position forward, so press Ctrl-Home to move the cursor to the beginning of your document before starting a search.

When you choose the Go To command from the Select menu (Alt-S-G), Works displays a dialog box, like this:

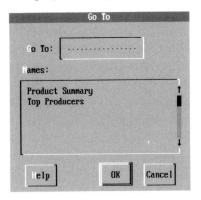

Using this dialog box, you can jump directly to a certain page by entering its number, or you can select a named location, called a *bookmark*, and jump to that.

To insert a bookmark, move the cursor to the place in the document where you want the bookmark to appear, and then choose the Bookmark Name command from the Edit menu (Alt-E-N). When you do, Works displays a dialog box, like this:

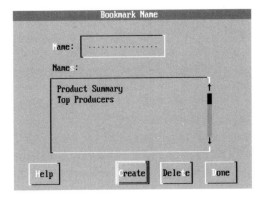

After you type a bookmark name in this dialog box and click Create, Works inserts an invisible, named bookmark at the cursor position and adds the bookmark name to the Go To dialog box. You can then jump to the bookmark position by using the Go To command, selecting the bookmark you want in the Names list, and clicking OK. If you have a question about some text you wrote, for example, leave a bookmark there and give the bookmark a descriptive name, no more than 15 characters long. Works lets you enter more characters than that, but only the first 15 characters appear in the Go To dialog box.

 KEYBOARD TIP: Press F5 to choose the Go To command. If you've already used Go To to locate a bookmark, press Shift-F5 to move to the next bookmark after that.

Finally, using the Replace command from the Select menu (Alt-S-R) is a good way to make global changes to your document. If you've left two spaces after the period at the end of each sentence and you decide you want only one, for example, you can use special characters to search for all periods followed by double spaces in a document and to replace each of them with a period and a single space. See the *Searching and Replacing in the WP* topic in the Word Processor category of the Help Table of Contents for more information about the Replace command.

Recycle Information

One of the best features of computers is their ability to store your work and to let you recall, change, and reuse it later. Writing projects are hard enough to complete without having to force yourself to redo them unnecessarily. You'll find many ways to reuse your work in the Word Processor. If you regularly produce a document such as a weekly report or a standard letter, save it as a template. That way, the original version of the file will remain intact for you to reuse later. It's much faster to open a template and make changes to it than it is to re-create the file from scratch.

Use Macros to Speed Text Entry

Works' macro feature can automate complex tasks that you perform repeatedly. Here are some examples:

- If you always begin your day with a look at your calendar and certain documents, such as a "to do" list, you can store a macro that automatically opens the Calendar and the documents for you.

- If you frequently use complex strings of text, such as your business's name or a copyright notice, store them as macros and then have Works type them automatically when you need them.

FORMATTING

This first formatting tip is a general one that applies to nearly any computer application. The tips that follow are more specific to the Microsoft Works Word Processor.

Edit First, Format Later

One time-honored rule in computing is to get the information into the computer first and then worry about how it looks. In word processing, it's important to enter your text as you think about it. Pausing to make a sentence or a paragraph look nice will only interrupt your train of thought and make writing harder.

Because some formatting can make the screen easier to read (and thus make it easier for you to write), you can set up most overall formatting in advance. If your eyes are more comfortable with double-spaced text or spacing between paragraphs, for example, you can use a template or macro to set this option automatically in each new document. After your train of thought is rolling along, however, don't complicate matters by playing with the character or paragraph formatting options.

Allow Enough Room for Headers and Footers

You can use header and footer paragraphs to create multiple-line headers and footers in your documents. When you select an option in the Headers & Footers dialog box, Works inserts header and footer paragraphs at the top and bottom, respectively, of your document. Type the text you want to appear in your header or footer in the appropriate text box. Each paragraph contains one line, but you can add lines to either paragraph by pressing Shift-Enter.

When you create multiple-line headers and footers, though, be sure that you have allowed enough room for them in your top and bottom page margins, or else they won't print completely. You must set the header and footer margins in the Page Setup & Margins dialog box to allow enough room. The default header and footer margins are set for 0.5 inch, which is enough space for a two-line header and a one-line footer. If your header and footer paragraphs have more lines than these margin settings allow, Works warns you that the headers and footers are too tall when you preview or print the document. If you continue without changing the appropriate margins, any additional lines will not print (because they would obscure text on the page if they did).

To accommodate taller headers and footers, you must increase the header and footer margins and enlarge the top and bottom page margins accordingly. If you're working with a three-line header with a 1-inch header margin, for example, you should set a page margin of at least 1.6 inches so that some space separates the header text and the text at the top of the page. Header and footer margins can't overlap text margins. As a result, the header and footer margins can never be larger than the top and bottom text margin.

Use Templates and Macros

If you like to use certain complex character or paragraph formats, you can record them as a macro when you select them the first time. Then you can apply them after that by using only one or two keystrokes.

 WORKS TIP: Record individual formatting choices as separate macros. Then you can combine several formatting choices into one macro by pressing the individual macro keys as you record the combination macro.

If you use the same document formats frequently, such as custom fonts or sizes, margins, alignment or line spacing, save a template document. For more on templates, see "Using Templates" in Chapter 1.

PRINTING

The following printing tips show you what happens when you print with Microsoft Works. Knowing this printing information in advance can help you anticipate potential printing problems.

Check Page Breaks Before You Print

Before you print, either preview the document with the Preview command or scroll through the document window and watch where the page breaks occur. You might want to adjust page breaks with the Insert Page Break command from the Print menu (Alt-P-I or Ctrl-Enter) so that subheadings or the first lines of new paragraphs begin at the top of a new page, rather than at the bottom of the previous one. If the automatic breaks don't suit you, you can set new page breaks manually.

Works uses two different markers for page breaks. The double-arrow marker in the left margin appears at all page breaks, both automatic and manual; the dotted line indicates manual page breaks, which you set yourself. Figure 3-1 on the next page shows both kinds of page breaks.

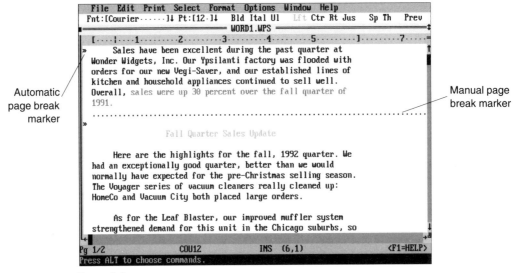

Figure 3-1.
Works inserts a dotted line to indicate a manual page break and a double arrow to indicate both automatic and manual page breaks.

Actual vs. Virtual Page Numbers

Works has two ways of tracking page numbers. The *status line* in the document window shows the total number of actual pages in the document and which actual page you are on at any time. But when you include page numbers in a header or footer or when you specify certain pages to be printed in the Print dialog box, Works uses the page numbering scheme that you set when you used the 1st Page Number option in the Page Setup & Margins dialog box.

Normally, Works starts numbering pages in a document with the number 1, so the default setting for the 1st page number in the Page Setup & Margins dialog box is *1*. But if you change a document's first page number, you must allow for that change when you specify which pages you want printed. For example, suppose you change the first page number in your document to *3* and you want to print the first and second pages of that document. To do so, specify in the Print dialog box's Print Specific Pages option that pages *3* and *4* are the pages to be printed.

WORKS TIP: It takes Works several seconds to repaginate a long document, so wait a minute or so before looking for page breaks to make sure they reflect the latest repagination.

> **WORKS TIP:** To specify a series of individual pages to print when you use the Print specific pages option in the Print dialog box, type each page number separated by a comma — such as 3, 7, 10. To specify a continuous range of pages, separate the beginning and ending page numbers with a colon, as in 3:10.

Use Microsoft Works to Specify Character Fonts, Sizes, and Styles

Some printers have controls that let you change the font, point size, or style. Works ignores these settings, however, and uses the settings you have selected in the document itself. For example, if you select the Courier font for a document using the Word Processor's format commands, and your printer is set to print with the Prestige font, Works overrides the Prestige setting and prints the document in Courier.

When you select a font in a document, Works shows only the fonts and point sizes your currently selected printer is capable of printing. You can use the Printer Setup command to select a different printer. When you use the Printer Setup command, Works displays every printer for which you have installed a printer driver. (For more information about installing printers in Works, see Chapter 1.)

WORKING AROUND THE WORD PROCESSOR'S LIMITATIONS

Although it's a capable tool, the Microsoft Works Word Processor lacks some of the features you'd find in stand-alone word processing programs. This part of the chapter looks at the possible ways to re-create the capabilities of each missing feature.

Outlining

An *outlining function* lets you build the structure of a document as an outline and then convert it to text. Microsoft Word, for example, lets you build an outline and then display the document in either outline or document mode so that you can quickly jump between a structural (outline) view and the actual text. Works doesn't have an outlining function. If your heart is set on using an outliner, buy a separate outlining program and then switch to it using the Run Other Programs command from the File menu.

Table of Contents

Table-of-contents generators use the headings in a program's built-in outliner as chapter and section names to create a table of contents. Because Works doesn't have an outliner, it won't create a table of contents. Instead, you can build a table of contents manually:

1. Open a new Word Processor document along with the document whose contents you want to gather. The new document will be the table of contents.

2. Select the first subheading in the text document that you want to appear in the table of contents (probably the document title).

3. Choose the Copy command from the Edit menu (Alt-E-C).

4. Select the table of contents document from the Window menu and click at the top of it. (You may find it helpful to choose the Arrange All command from the Window menu [Alt-W-A] to view the documents side by side.)

5. Press Enter to copy the subheading into the table of contents.

6. Repeat steps 2 through 5 for each subheading you want to put in the table of contents. If you want to collect subheadings from other documents, open them as well and follow the same procedure. After you've gathered all the headings and subheadings for the table of contents, scroll through your manuscript to determine the correct page numbers, and then add them to the document.

Glossary

A *glossary feature* is handy for storing complex names or other strings of text that you use repeatedly. If you're writing a report about the Athabasca Glacier, for example, you could easily get tired of typing that name over and over. Instead, you could store the name in a glossary and insert it when needed. Works doesn't have a glossary feature, but you can use its built-in macro capability to record any string of text as you type it and then reproduce that text string by pressing a key or two.

Line Numbering

Line numbers, which are printed in the margin next to each line, usually appear in legal paperwork. Line numbering is so specialized that most people don't miss it in Works. It can be useful, however, to know how many lines your document contains, especially when you're trying to create a specific number of lines to fill space in a flier or a newsletter. The status line always shows which line the cursor is on, like this:

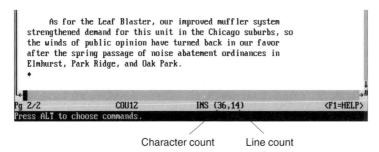

As for the Leaf Blaster, our improved muffler system strengthened demand for this unit in the Chicago suburbs, so the winds of public opinion have turned back in our favor after the spring passage of noise abatement ordinances in Elmhurst, Park Ridge, and Oak Park.

Pg 2/2   COU12   INS (36,14)   ⟨F1=HELP⟩
Press ALT to choose commands.

Character count   Line count

In this case, the cursor is on the 36th character from the left margin and in the 14th line of the document.

To find out how many lines are in any document, press Ctrl-End to move the cursor to the end of the document, and then check the line number in the status line. If your document has more than one page, add the number of lines on each page to determine the total number of lines in the document.

Columns

To display text in separate columns, set tab stops to create the columns, and then press Tab to fill in each column, one line at a time. (See "Setting Tabs" in Chapter 2.) Works offers no way to display and edit separate, newspaper-style columns. It is possible in Works, however, to print text in multiple, side-by-side columns if you're prepared to do a little juggling. Here's how you'd print two 3-inch-wide newspaper-style columns side by side on one page:

1. Enter all the text for the page.

2. In the Page Setup & Margins dialog box, set the left and right margins to 1 inch.

3. With the entire page selected, set a right indent of 3.5 inches. Because of the large right indent, Works formats the text in one 3-inch column on the left side of the page.

4. Use the Preview command to display the text on the screen.

5. Make a note of the contents of the last line on the first page.

6. Return to the editing screen, scroll to the double-arrow page break mark, and move the cursor to the beginning of the first line following the break mark.

7. Press Enter to move this line and all the lines below it into a new paragraph(s).

8. After selecting the remaining text, set the left indent to 3.5 inches, and set the right indent back to 0. Because of the large left indent, this move will produce a column of text 3 inches wide on the right side of the page.

9. Using the Print command, print only the first page of the document. Works prints the left-hand column of text.

10. Put the printed page back into the printer, and print only the second page of the document on the same side of the paper. Works prints the right-hand column of text on the same page so that both columns are now printed. Because of the left and right indents, each column is 3 inches wide, with a half-inch of gutter space between them.

This method is a little tedious and requires some trial and error if you're using a printer in which you feed paper with a platen or tractor mechanism. For high-volume production, this technique does not work well, but it's handy if you need to prepare multiple-column documents only occasionally.

On-Screen Fonts

Displaying different type fonts on the screen is a feature that's beyond the practical capabilities of standard MS-DOS–based systems; it requires the support of graphic screen environments such as Microsoft Windows.

Style Sheets

Style sheets provide a means to name and store complex paragraph or character formats so that you can apply them with ease elsewhere. If you create a paragraph of text to which you apply 10-point size Elite boldface font and a half-inch first-line indent, for example, you might give this group of formatting settings a name such as "Indent Style." Then you could apply all these settings at one time by specifying Indent Style. Works doesn't support style sheets, but there are three ways to work around this limitation:

- Copy character and paragraph formats from one part of a document to another by using the Copy Special command on the Edit menu (Alt-E-S).

- Save different character, paragraph, or document format commands as macros and then run a macro to apply a particular format.

■ Save a custom-formatted document as a template, and then create a new document with the template when you want a document with that format.

Facing Pages

Facing pages printing options let you alternate the positions of headers, footers, and of left and right margins so that they are laid out attractively when pages are printed on both sides and bound like a book. A single-sided document that was bound with a staple might have a right-aligned header and a wider left margin, for example. But if you printed that document on both sides of the paper and bound it like a book, the right-aligned header wouldn't look as good on the left-hand pages. Also, the wider margin on a book page should always be next to the spine of the book, so the wide margin would alternate between the left and right sides of the pages.

Works doesn't offer the option to alternate headers or margins for facing pages, but you can manually produce alternate page margins by creating two documents, one for the left-hand pages and one for the right-hand pages (each with different right and left margin settings), and then printing them separately. When you do this, however, you'll have to insert page numbers manually by placing them at the top or bottom of the body of each page, rather than in the header or footer. You'll have to insert even page numbers on the pages in one document and odd page numbers in the other document.

Changing Header or Footer Text

Changing the header or footer text in different parts of a document can be helpful when a document contains several sections or chapters. With each new section or chapter, the header or footer can show the name of that specific part of the document. For example, if you have several pages of front matter (such as a table of contents, an introduction, and a dedication), you might want to print those pages without a header, and then print the main text with a header containing page numbers. All headers and footers in Works remain the same for the entire document (except for the page numbers, which change with each page).

To use different headers, you can divide the document itself into separate Works files and then use a different header in each one. To print front matter without headers, copy the front matter into a separate document, delete the front matter from the document that contains the main text, and then print the new document with no headers. If you simply want to suppress the printing of a header or footer on the first page of the document, use the No Header On 1st Page option in the Headers & Footers dialog box.

File Chaining

File-chaining features let you print several documents in succession as if they were one. You could print several chapters of a book one after the other, for example, and have the page numbers continue in succession from one chapter to the next. Works doesn't have a file-chaining feature, but it's possible to approximate file chaining by noting the ending page number of each document and then setting the first page number of the following document so that it is consecutive. Here's the procedure:

1. Create a header or footer for the first document in the group, and use the Insert Special Character command on the Edit menu to include page numbers in the document.

2. Note the ending page number of the first document by checking the left edge of the status line. (If you have changed the 1st Page Number option in the Page Setup & Margins dialog box, the printed page number will be different from the actual page number. In this case, you may want to preview the document to check the last page number.)

3. Create a header for the second document in the group, and include a page numbering command.

4. In the Page Setup & Margins dialog box, change the second document's first page number so that it is one higher than the first document's ending page number. (If the first document ends at page 15, for example, the second document should begin at page 16.)

5. Repeat the preceding two steps for the other documents in the group.

After you set up consecutive page numbering, you can print all the files separately. When you finish, you can assemble the separate files into one consecutively numbered document.

These tips will help you work more productively with the Microsoft Works Word Processor. As you gain experience with Works, you will undoubtedly come up with more shortcuts and strategies of your own. If you're ready to try some typical business projects with the Word Processor, continue to Chapter 4.

4

Word Processing Projects

In this chapter, we'll look at the Microsoft Works word processor in action. We'll use it to create a letterhead template, a form letter, a mailing list and labels, and a monthly report template. While completing these projects, you'll learn how to use most of the Word Processor's features.

A LETTERHEAD

In this exercise, we'll use Microsoft Works' font selection and formatting commands to create a personalized letterhead and then save it as a template. You can open the saved Template file each time you write a letter and then save the document with a different name, thus preserving the letterhead template in its original state on the disk.

Inserting a Picture

To begin, we'll open a new Word Processor file and insert a picture for the logo.

1. Choose the Create New File command from the File menu (Alt-F-N). Works displays the Create New File dialog box. The Word Processor document type should be selected.

2. Double-click the Standard/Blank template in the Available Templates list. A new document appears on the screen.

3. To insert a picture as a logo for the letterhead, choose the Insert Picture command from the Edit menu (Alt-E-E). Works displays the Insert Picture dialog box, like the one at the top of the next page.

87

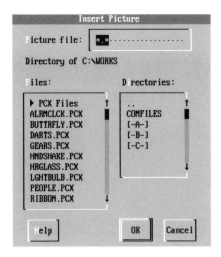

4. Because you'll want to use one of the clip art pictures that came with Works, you'll need to select the Works directory on your disk if it's not already selected. Scroll the Directories list and double-click the Works directory name, if necessary. You'll see a list of the Works clip art files at the left.

5. Double-click the file called DARTS.PCX. Works inserts a place-holder for the graphic in the Word Processor document, like this:

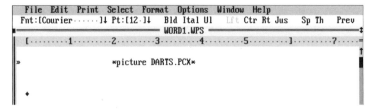

Adding the Letterhead Text

Now we'll add the company name, address, and phone number below this graphic logo. Type the following:

> Acme Toys - 123 Walden Pl., Ocean, CA 94515 - (408) 555-1111

When you finish typing, press Enter.

Formatting the Picture and Text

Now that we've entered the logo and text in the document, we'll apply some formatting to make it look more like a letterhead. First we'll realign the picture and resize it.

1. Click the picture placeholder with the right mouse button. Works selects the whole placeholder.

2. Choose the Picture command from the Format menu (Alt-T-E). (This command only appears on the Format menu when the cursor or selection is on a picture placeholder.) Works displays the Picture dialog box, like this:

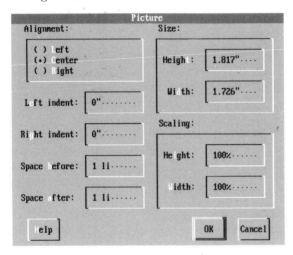

3. Click the Left option in the Alignment area to align the picture along the left margin.

NOTE: *You must set picture format options with the Format Picture command. Clicking the alignment options in the toolbar doesn't work when you're setting a picture format.*

WORKS TIP: Remember, you can always check the appearance of graphics with the Preview command to make sure you've sized them properly.

Notice the height and width measurements in the Size area. This picture is nearly 2 inches tall and 2 inches wide — far too large for a letterhead logo. So, we'll resize the picture proportionally by typing values in the Scaling area.

1. Click the Height box in the Scaling area and type *40%*.

2. Click the Width box in the Scaling area and type *40%*.

3. Click the Space After box to deselect the Width box. With the new scaling values, you can see that the height and width measurements in the Size area have changed considerably. Now the picture is a more appropriate size for a logo.

4. Click OK to accept these settings and return to the document window.

5. To reformat the letterhead text, click the margin to the left of the line of text. Works selects the entire line.

6. Press Ctrl-C or click Ctr in the toolbar to center the text on the page.

7. Next, to make all the letterhead text bold, press Ctrl-B or click Bld in the toolbar to set the Bold style. (The Bold style indicator, B, appears in the status line.)

Adding a Border

The text in the address line should still be selected. While it is, we'll place a border beneath it to separate the letterhead from the rest of the letter.

1. Select the address line if it isn't still selected.

2. Choose the Borders command from the Format menu (Alt-T-O). Works displays the Borders dialog box, like this:

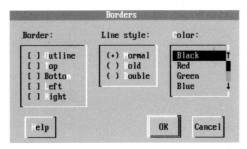

3. Click the Bottom option under Border (to create an underline).

4. Click the Bold line style for the border.

5. Click OK to confirm these settings and return to the document.

6. Click the border line to deselect the text and border.

Now the letterhead looks like this:

```
 File  Edit  Print  Select  Format  Options  Window  Help
Fnt:[Courier······]↓ Pt:[12·]↓   Bld  Ital Ul   Lft  Ctr Rt Jus   Sp Th   Prev
══════════════════════════ WORD1.WPS ══════════════════════════
[··········1·········2·········3·········4·········5·········]·······7·····
»                      *picture DARTS.PCX*

Acme Toys - 123 Walden Pl., Ocean, CA 94515 - (408) 555-1111

   ◆
```

KEYBOARD TIP: Because the Borders dialog box has no text-entry boxes, you can select any option in it simply by pressing the option's highlighted letter key — you don't have to press the Alt key at the same time. In this case, you can press M-B and then press Enter.

The letterhead text and the border both appear in highlighted characters, indicating that they will print in boldface type.

You could stop here with this letterhead project, but depending on the printer you're using, you might want to select a different font or size. For example, using Helvetica font with an 18-point size for the store name would make the letterhead look more attractive and make the name stand out a bit more.

Changing the Font

To set a different font or size for selected text, simply select the text you want to change, choose the Font & Style command from the Format menu (Alt-T-F), select the font and size (and style, if you like) that you want to apply to the selected text, and then press Enter to confirm the new choices. You can also click the font and size menus or the style tools in the toolbar to set font, size, and style options.

Remember, the Works screen won't show the text in the font and size you have selected. You can see an approximation of the font and size when you preview the document using the Preview command on the Print menu, but you really need to print the document to see exactly how it will look.

The fonts and sizes available depend on which printer you have selected, and the selection of printers available in the Printer Setup dialog box depends on which printer drivers you have installed with Works. (See Appendix A for more details about printer installation, and see Chapter 1 for more about the Printer Setup command.)

Changing the Top Margin

As it is now, the document has a top margin of 1 inch, which is probably too large because our logo and return address occupy another inch. To create more space on the page for letter text, we'll change the top margin.

1. Choose the Page Setup & Margins command from the Print menu (Alt-P-M).

2. Type *0.25* in the Top Margin box, and then press Enter to reset the margin.

Now the logo and address will print close to the top of the page as they should.

 WORKS TIP: You can insert graphics in header or footer paragraphs to make them appear on each page of a document, but be sure the header or footer margin is large enough to accommodate them.

Saving the File

Finally, save this letterhead as a template so you can use it each time you write a letter. To save the letterhead, do the following:

1. Choose the Save command from the File menu (Alt-F-S). The Save As dialog box appears.

2. Click the Save As Template option or press Alt-A, and then click OK. Works displays the Save As Template dialog box.

3. Type a descriptive name, like *Letterhead*, and then press Enter to save the template.

Now the letterhead file is on your disk. Each time you want to write a letter, you can open the LETTERHEAD template using the Create New File command, write a letter, and then save the file with a different name. The original letterhead template remains unchanged on your disk.

A FORM LETTER

Form letters are useful when you need to send the same information to several individuals. You might want to notify selected customers of a special sale, tell your friends about a new address, remind people of appointments they have made, or even issue invitations. You can use Microsoft Works' mail-merge features to create a form letter by merging data from a Database file with a letter you've created in the Word Processor.

Creating a Database File

To complete this project, you'll need a Database file from which to merge names and addresses. If you haven't created any Database files yet, you have two choices:

- Turn to Chapter 8, and then follow the instructions to create the ADDRESS.WDB Database file described there.

- Choose the WorksWizards command from the File menu (Alt-F-W), select the Address Book WorksWizard, and have Works create a Database file for you.

If you select the WorksWizard option, simply read the instructions on each screen and click the PgDn button to move through the file-building procedure.

1. Select the Personal type of address book on the second Works-Wizard screen, and then click the PgDn button. Works creates standard name and address fields on the screen.

2. Select No Thanks on the next screen and click the PgDn button.

3. Click the PgDn button to accept the standard title for the screen.

4. Click the PgDn button to see more options, and then click option number 7 and the PgDn button to move to the data entry screen.

5. Enter several addresses in your database, using the Tab and Shift-Tab keys to move from one field to another. Press Ctrl-PgDn to go to the next record. Press Enter when you've finished entering the last record.

6. Choose the Save command, and then save the file with the name ADDRESS. (Works will add the WDB suffix automatically.)

Whichever option you choose, you should end up with the ADDRESS.WDB file open on your screen. Now let's create the form letter document.

Opening the Letterhead File

Let's assume this is a business form letter, and that we want to use the form letter template we created in the first project in this chapter. (If you haven't done that project, you can create a new blank Word Processor document.)

1. Choose the Create New File command (Alt-F-N).

2. Scroll down to the LETTERHEAD document name in the Available Templates list and double-click it. Works opens this document.

3. Click the blank space above the end-of-file marker (below the border, under the letterhead address), and then press Enter three times to add three blank lines between the border and the first line of letter text, like this:

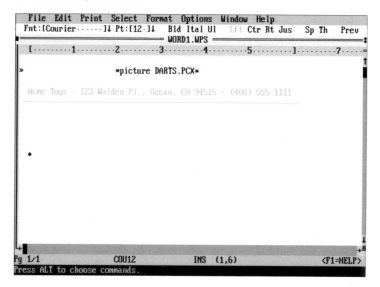

4. If you see a *B* in the status line of your letterhead document (indicating the Bold style), click Bld in the toolbar to remove this style before continuing.

Now we're ready to create the letter itself.

Inserting the Date

First we'll insert the date. We could type it, but let's use one of Works' special characters to insert it automatically. We'll use a special character that adds the print date (or the date when the document is printed). This way, the letter's date will be current if we decide not to print this file for several days.

1. Choose the Insert Special Character command from the Edit menu (Alt-E-P). Works displays the Insert Special Character dialog box.

2. Double-click the Print Date option. Works inserts a *date marker* at the cursor position.

3. Press Enter three times to create some more blank space in the letter.

 MOUSE TIP: Double-clicking an option inside a dialog box often selects the option and puts the dialog box away at the same time. Feel free to try this shortcut as you work in dialog boxes. If the feature isn't supported, double-clicking won't do any harm. Simply click OK as usual to close the dialog box.

Inserting Address Fields

Next we'll insert Database *field markers* to merge the database data into the address block. The fields from the ADDRESS.WDB Database file will merge into the address block, like this:

First Name Last Name

Address

City, State ZIP Code

These are the actual field names used in the ADDRESS.WDB file from Chapter 8, so you can refer to this example as you insert the field markers. Now insert the first field marker by following these steps:

1. Choose the Insert Database Field command from the Edit menu (Alt-E-A). The Insert Database Field dialog box appears, like this:

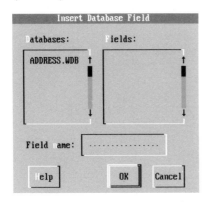

2. Click the ADDRESS.WDB Database filename in the list. Works displays the fields in that file in the Fields list.

3. Double-click the First Name field. Works places a field marker in the document, like this:

It helps to think of field markers as actual text when you place them in documents. If you merge the wrong field by mistake, simply delete the marker. You can also copy or move field markers.

Because we've just placed the first name from an address, your next step will be to insert a space after it and then insert the last name from the address.

1. Press the spacebar once.

2. Choose the Insert Database Field command again. The ADDRESS.WDB Database filename should still be selected in the dialog box, so you can double-click the Last Name field to insert the field marker in the document.

KEYBOARD TIP: When you want to insert several Database fields, it's faster to press Alt-E-A to choose the Insert Database Field command. Because the filename remains selected in the Insert Database Field dialog box after you merge the first field, you can press Alt-E-A, press the Right arrow key to move to the Fields list, press the Down arrow key as many times as necessary to select the field name, and press Enter to merge the field.

To merge the rest of the address information, press Enter to move down to each successive line, and then merge the field or fields on that line. Here's the general procedure if your cursor is now at the end of the Last Name field:

1. Press Enter to begin a new line.

2. Insert the Address field marker.

3. Press Enter.

4. Insert the City field marker.

5. Type a comma at the end of the City field marker, and then press the spacebar to leave a space.

6. Insert the State field marker.

7. Press the spacebar to leave a space between the state and zip code.

8. Insert the ZIP Code field marker.

After you insert all the field markers for the entire address block, the letter looks like this:

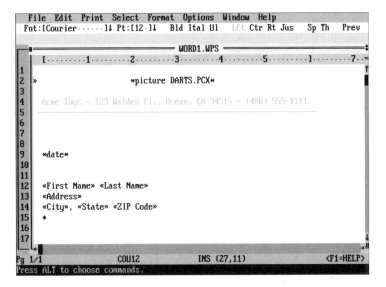

Entering the Greeting

The next step is to leave a couple of blank lines and then type the greeting. Because it's a form letter, you can use a merged field to create a personal greeting. The cursor should now be at the end of the ZIP Code field marker. If it isn't, move it there, and then follow the steps on the next page.

1. Press Enter three times to leave two blank lines below the address.

2. Type *Dear* and press the spacebar once.

3. Insert the First Name field marker from the ADDRESS.WDB database.

4. Type a colon (:) after the field marker to complete the greeting line.

5. Now press Enter two times to leave a blank line between the greeting line and the letter text, which you'll enter next.

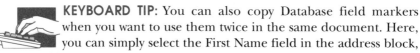

KEYBOARD TIP: You can also copy Database field markers when you want to use them twice in the same document. Here, you can simply select the First Name field in the address block, press Shift-F3 to copy the marker, move the cursor next to *Dear* on the greeting line, and press Enter.

Entering the Letter Text

Type the following text exactly as you see it here. Be sure to include the four blank lines between the words *Sincerely* and *Frank Acme* at the end of the letter. (Some mistakes are deliberately included in this text so that we can use Works' spelling commands to correct them later.) Here's the letter text:

As an Acme Toys prefferred customer, I'd like to give you an advance preview of some great new summer toys we'll be offering this year.

From 6:00 to 10:00 PM on Friday, May 7, our store will be closed to the public for a special invitation-only, adults-only preview. We'll have our full sales staff on hand to demonstrate toys and answer your questions, and we're offering special preseason prices on every item.

These toys will go on public sale at their regular prices on May 8, so take advantage of our prefferred customer preview night to beat the rush. I hope to see you there.

Sincerely,

Frank Acme

President, Acme Toys

After you enter the text, it's time to check the spelling.

Checking the Spelling

Works has a built-in spell-checking program that scans your document for spelling errors, matching each word against a dictionary that comes with the program. To check the document's spelling, do the following:

1. Press Ctrl-Home to move the cursor to the beginning of the document. (Works checks a document's spelling from the cursor position forward.)

2. Choose the Check Spelling command from the Options menu (Alt-O-S). Works begins checking the document's spelling. In a few seconds, the Check Spelling dialog box appears, like this:

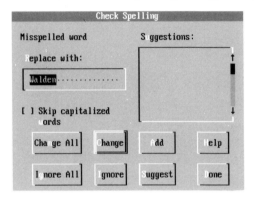

The Replace With box displays a suspect word (*Walden*) that Works could not find in its spelling dictionary. In this case, the word is a proper name that is part of the store's address. We could simply tell Works to ignore this word, but we might as well add the word to the spelling program's dictionary so that Works will consider it correct in the future.

3. Click Add to add the word to the Works dictionary. Works continues checking the document.

4. The next suspect word displayed in the dialog box is *Pl.*, the abbreviated form of "Place." This isn't a correct word, and it isn't a proper name, so tell Works to ignore this word and all future occurrences of the word by clicking Ignore All.

5. Works next displays *CA*, the abbreviation for California. Because you'll probably use this abbreviation a lot, add it to the dictionary by clicking Add.

6. The next suspect word that Works displays is *prefferred*, which is misspelled. But suppose that we're not sure if the word is misspelled or that we don't know the correct spelling. In this case, we can ask Works to suggest the correct spelling by clicking Suggest.

7. Works displays three words in the Suggestions list box, like this:

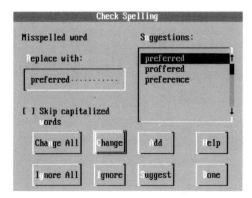

8. The first word in the list is selected, and it is the correct spelling. To replace all occurrences of the misspelled word with the correct version suggested by Works, click Change All. Works replaces *prefferred* with *preferred* throughout the document and continues the spelling check.

9. The next suspect word is *preseason,* which should be hyphenated. In this case, Works won't suggest hyphenating the word if you click Suggest, but you can edit the word in the Replace With box by clicking the first *s* in *preseason* in the Replace With box to move the cursor there.

10. Type a hyphen and then click Change. Works replaces the old spelling with the new one and continues the check.

At the end of the spelling check, Works displays a dialog box that announces the completion of the spelling check. Click OK to return to the document. (If you didn't start the spelling check with the cursor at the beginning of the document, Works now asks if you want to continue checking the spelling from the beginning of the document. Click OK to continue the spelling operation, or click Cancel.)

Printing the Form Letter

Our text is now letter-perfect, and this letter is now ready to print. When printing the letter, remember that we want to merge data from a database file into the places indicated by the field markers. To merge the data, we must choose a special printing command from the Print menu and indicate the Database file from which the Word Processor will pull data as it prints.

1. Choose the Print Form Letters command from the Print menu (Alt-P-F). Works displays a dialog box that lists all the Database files that are currently open, like this:

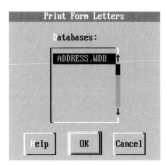

2. If the ADDRESS.WDB file is the only Database file open, it will be selected in the list. If more than one database file is open, select ADDRESS.WDB, if necessary.

3. Click OK to confirm the selection.

4. Works displays the Print dialog box. Press Enter, and Works prints the form letters, making one letter for each record currently displayed in the Database file. (For a tip on printing only one form letter or a small group of form letters from a Database file, see Chapter 9.)

You can try different formats for the letters you write by experimenting with the Indents & Spacing command and the other commands on the Format menu. Works lets you merge other database information into your form letters by inserting fields that contain other data such as amounts owed or prices or names of products. We'll see more examples of data-merging later in this chapter and in Chapter 12.

MAILING LABELS AND AN ADDRESS DIRECTORY

In this project, we'll create some mailing labels and an address directory that can serve as a desk reference. To complete this project, you'll need a Database file that contains names and addresses such as the ADDRESS.WDB file used in the form letter project. If you've already done the form letter project, use the same

Database file. Otherwise, read "Creating a Database File," earlier in this chapter to see how to create it. In any case, the ADDRESS.WDB file must be open before you continue with this project.

Using the Mailing Labels WorksWizard

To print mailing labels, you create a Word Processor document that contains merged names and addresses from a Database file. In the previous project, we inserted merged Database fields manually in a Word Processor document. This time, we'll use the Microsoft WorksWizard for creating mailing labels.

1. Choose the WorksWizards command from the File menu (Alt-F-W).

2. Click the Mailing Labels option and then click OK. Microsoft Works displays the introductory screen for creating Mailing Labels.

3. Click the PgDn button two times. Works lists all the currently open Database documents that contain the appropriate fields. The ADDRESS.WDB file should be one of the documents listed.

4. Click the ADDRESS.WDB document name and then click the PgDn button. Works shows the names of the fields that will print on the label, like this:

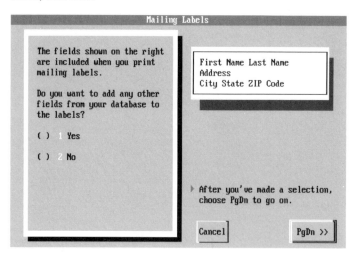

5. These fields are the only ones you want to include in the document, so select the No option and then click the PgDn button. Works then asks which type of labels you're using.

MOUSE TIP: If you don't have a Database file open when you begin using the Mailing Labels WorksWizard, click the PgDn button again. Works then searches the WORKS directory on your disk for Database files and lists the files it finds on the screen. Simply select the database file you want to use and click the PgDn button for the label document, and Works then opens the file.

6. Select option 1 (we'll assume you're printing sheet-fed labels), and then click the PgDn button twice.

7. Select the Yes option to tell Works you know the Avery label product number for the label stock you're printing on, and then click the PgDn button. (If you don't know the number, you can select the other option here and then enter the dimensions of the labels you're using.) Works displays a list of Avery label product numbers, like this:

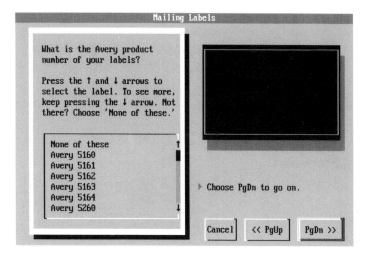

When you select any label number, a description of that label's size and the number of labels per sheet appears in the upper right corner of this dialog box.

8. Scroll down the list and click Avery 5660, and then click the PgDn button. Works asks if you want the labels printed in a certain order.

9. Select option 2 to have Works print the labels without sorting them, and then click the PgDn button. Works asks if you want to print all the addresses in the file, or just some of them.

10. Select option 1 to print all the addresses, and then click the PgDn button. Works creates the Word Processor document with the merged fields on it for the label you specified, and then it presents another dialog box that asks whether you want to test print one row of labels, print labels for all the records in your database file, or delay printing.

11. Select option 1 to test print one row of labels, or select option 2 to print all the Database records onto labels. When the printing is finished, Works asks you how the test or labels look. If you select Fine and click the PgDn button twice, you'll see the label document on the screen, like this:

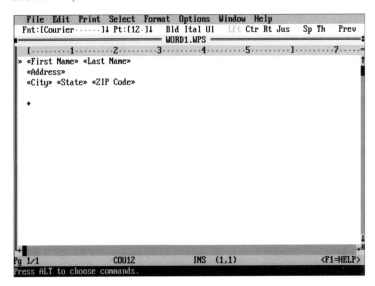

Saving the File

This new document will be our basic label document, so let's save it as a template called LABEL.

1. Choose the Save command from the File menu (Alt-F-S). The Save As dialog box appears.

2. Click the Save As Template option, and then click OK.

3. Type *Label* for the template name, and press Enter to save it.

Printing a Label Directory

You can also use this same mailing label document to print an address directory on plain paper. The only change we'll make is to set the document to print in two columns.

1. Choose the Print Labels command (Alt-P-L). The ADDRESS.WDB Database filename appears and is selected in the list box.

2. Click the Across Page box and type *2* to set Works for printing addresses in two columns.

3. Click the Down Page box and type *10* to print addresses in 10 rows.

4. Click OK. Works displays the Label Spacing dialog box, like this:

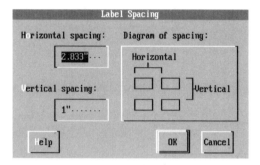

The dialog box should show the spacing values for printing three labels across a page. However, since we're printing only two columns on the page, we can increase the horizontal space between labels.

5. Type *3.5* in the Horizontal Spacing box, and then press Enter. Works displays the Page Size & Label Margins dialog box, like this:

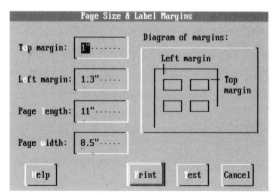

Because the addresses will be printed on a directory page, rather than on labels, let's change the top and left margins.

6. Type *1* in the Top Margin box, if necessary.

7. Click the Left Margin box, type *1,* and then press Enter to display the Print dialog box.

8. Click Print to print the addresses in two columns down the page.

Reusing a Label Document

You can use this basic LABEL template to create labels from any Database file as long as the Database file you select contains fields that have the same First Name, Last Name, Address, City, State, and ZIP Code field names as does ADDRESS.WDB.

To print on different sizes of labels, change the measurements in the Print Labels, Label Spacing, and Page Size & Label Margins dialog boxes to match the label sizes you're using.

If you want your mailing labels or directory to show names in a certain order, sort the ADDRESS.WDB database file before printing. See Chapters 8 and 10 for more information.

If you'd like to include page numbers or a date on your directory pages, add a descriptive header. Choose the Headers & Footers command from the Print menu, and enter the header or footer text you want.

A MONTHLY REPORT

In this project, we'll use some of Microsoft Works' other document formatting commands to create a standard report template. Many people in business create routine reports that are updated each month, or they create reports on different subjects that have essentially the same document structure. With this template, you'll be able to start any report with much of the document organization and formatting work already done.

Because of the way Works prints header and footer information, we'll have to break this project up into two documents: one to contain the title page and contents page (the *front matter* in the report) and the other to contain the text of the report. Let's create the front matter template first. Begin by choosing the Create New File command and double-clicking Standard/Blank template to open a new Word Processor document and display it on the screen.

Entering the Title Page Text

Now we're ready to enter the text for this document, which will consist of a title page and a table of contents page. The finished title page will look like this:

As you can see, the text is generic, so you can fill in the actual text each time you create the report. For now simply type the report title, byline, and author name without using any formatting. Leave one blank line between each line of the title and byline, and then press Enter six times to leave five blank lines between the title and the author information block. Finally type the text in the author information block.

Setting a Manual Page Break

The cursor should now be blinking at the end of the last line in the author information block. You've reached the end of the title page, so it's time to insert a page break.

1. Press Enter to move down one line below the author information block.

2. Press Ctrl-Enter to insert a page break. A dotted page break line appears, and the cursor moves to the line below the page break.

Entering the Table of Contents Text

Now we can enter the text for the table of contents page. The finished page looks like Figure 4-1.

We'll need to set a tab stop to separate the page numbers from the section names. As you can see, a tab leader character also fills the empty space between each section name and its page number. Enter the text as follows:

1. Type *Contents,* and press Enter three times to leave two blank lines.

2. Choose the Tabs command from the Format menu (Alt-T-T). Works displays the Tabs dialog box, like this:

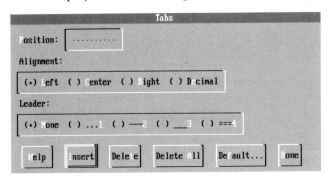

3. Type *5.5* in the Position box to set a tab stop at the 5.5-inch mark on the ruler.

4. Select the Right alignment option for this tab stop.

```
                            Table of Contents


        Section 1 . . . . . . . . . . . . . . . . . . . . . . . . . . . . . . . . . . X
        Section 2 . . . . . . . . . . . . . . . . . . . . . . . . . . . . . . . . . . X
```

Figure 4-1.
This template contains generic text that Works replaces when you write each version of the report.

5. Select option 1 in the Leader area to choose a dotted-line tab leader.

6. Click Insert to insert this tab stop. An *.R* appears at the 5.5-inch mark on the ruler.

7. Click Done to return to the document editing screen.

 KEYBOARD TIP: Press Tab to move to different sections of the Tabs dialog box, and then press the highlighted letter or number key to select an option in that section.

Now you can enter the section names and the page numbers as shown in Figure 4-1.

1. Type *Section 1* and press Tab.

2. Type *X* as the page number, and press Enter two times.

3. Repeat steps 1 and 2 for Section 2 as shown in Figure 4-1.

Formatting the Title Page

Returning to the first page of this two-page document, we'll now adjust the alignment of the text on the title page. Begin by centering the title and author information and by making the title bold.

1. Scroll to the top of the document, and select the title, byline, and author name by holding down the mouse button, pointing to the left margin, and dragging down through the top three lines of text in the document.

2. Click *Ctr* in the toolbar to center this text on the page.

3. Click the margin to the left of the top line of text to select only this line.

4. Click *Bld* in the toolbar to make the title bold.

Next align the author information block on the right margin.

1. Click the left margin to the left of the *Your Name* line, hold down the mouse button, and drag down three more lines to select the entire author information block.

2. Click *Rt* in the toolbar to right-align this block.

Previewing and Adjusting the Format

We left some blank spaces between the report title and the author information block, but we want to be sure the text is vertically aligned on the page. To really see this alignment, preview the title page.

1. Click *Prev* in the toolbar to preview the title page. Works displays the Preview dialog box.

2. Click Preview to accept the defaults. Works displays the title page on the screen, like this:

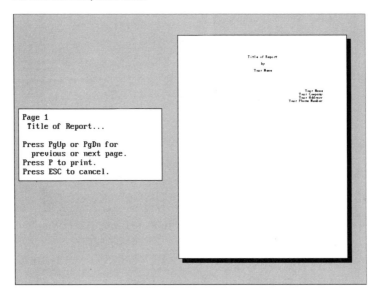

As you can see, the title and author information block are all at the top of the page. To move them down, insert some extra blank lines before the title and between the centered lines and the author information block.

3. Press Esc to cancel the preview and return to the document.

4. Click the beginning of the report title line.

5. Press Enter 20 times to insert 20 blank lines above the title.

6. Click the beginning of the line containing *Your Name* in the author information block.

7. Press Enter 15 times to insert 15 more blank lines between the centered lines and the author information block.

Now if you preview the document again, you'll see that the title is centered on the page and the author information block is located at the bottom of the page.

Formatting the Table of Contents

Finally, center the Contents line on the second page and make this text bold.

1. Click to the left of the Contents line on page 2.

2. Click *Ctr* in the toolbar to center the text.

3. Click *Bld* to make the text bold.

This document is finished, so we'll save it as a template.

1. Choose the Save command from the File menu. Works displays the Save As dialog box.

2. Select the Save As Template option. Click OK.

3. Type *Front* as the template name.

4. Press Enter to save the template.

Now we can always open the FRONT template as an untitled document when we begin a report. We can change the report title, author, and table of contents information and then use the Save As command to save the file as a standard Works Word Processor document. That way, our FRONT template remains untouched on the disk, ready for the next month's report.

Creating the Report Template

Like the front matter template, the report template contains generic text that serves merely as a placeholder for the text you'll enter as you create actual reports later. Along with the placeholder text, this template uses a footer paragraph that also contains text. Begin by opening a new file and creating the footer paragraph.

1. Choose the Create New File command, and then click OK to open a new Standard/Blank Word Processor document and to display it on the screen.

2. Choose the Headers and Footers command from the Print menu (Alt-P-H). Works displays the Headers & Footers dialog box, like this:

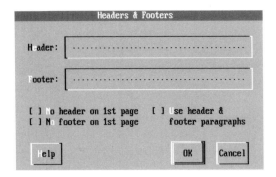

3. Select the Use Header & Footer Paragraphs option.

4. Select the No Footer On 1st Page option.

5. Click OK to return to the document. Works displays header and footer paragraph markers on the screen, like this:

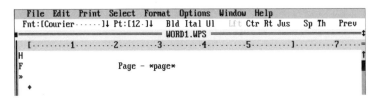

With header and footer paragraphs, Works lets you enter and format the header or footer text right on the screen. Next create a two-line footer that contains the report name and the page number on the first line and the author's name and the date on the second line. Here's how:

1. Click the left edge of the footer paragraph to move the cursor there.

 MOUSE TIP: If the footer paragraph line is selected when you click to the left of it, you're clicking too far to the left. Try to click just under the left-hand margin marker in the ruler, not to the left of it.

2. Type *Report Title* - followed by a blank space as a placeholder for the actual title of the report.

3. Click the *P* in *Page* on the same line.

4. Press Backspace once to move the *Page - *page** text so that it is one space to the right of the dash after the report title. The line should look like this:

   Report Title - Page - *page*

5. Delete the hyphen between *Page* and **page**.

6. Move the cursor to the space after **page**.

7. Press Shift-Enter to add a line to the footer paragraph and move the cursor down a line. (Works won't let you press Enter alone to add a line to a footer paragraph.)

8. Type *Your Name* - and add a blank space after the hyphen.

9. Choose the Insert Special Character command from the Edit menu (Alt-E-P).

10. Double-click the Print Date option in the Insert Special Character dialog box. Works adds the **date** marker to the footer.

Now the footer paragraph looks like this:

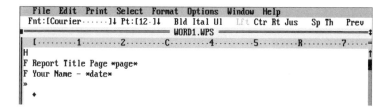

It's a two-line, left-aligned footer, and because it contains the **page** and **date** special characters, Works will print the current page number and the date when the document is printed. We haven't entered any text in the header paragraph, so it won't print at all.

Entering the Report Body Text

Now enter the rest of the text:

1. Click the first line of the document (the line below the second line of the footer) to move the cursor there.

2. Type *Report Title* and press Enter.

3. Type *Section 1* and press Enter.

4. Type *Section 1 text goes here.* and press Enter.

5. Type *Section 2* and press Enter.

6. Type *Section 2 text goes here.* and press Enter. Your document should now look like this:

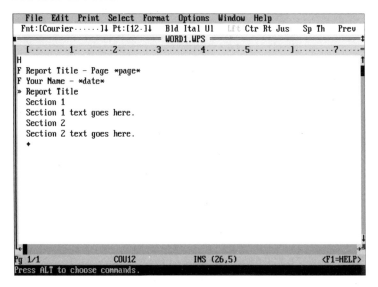

We'll work only as far as Section 2 in this project, but obviously you could add more sections to this document if your report were longer.

Setting Line Spacing

Now set the line spacing and paragraph indents for the paragraphs that will contain text rather than titles.

1. Click the beginning of the Report Title line in the body of the document (not in the footer) and drag down to the end-of-file marker to select all the text in the body of the document.

2. Press Ctrl-2 to set double spacing for the document.

KEYBOARD TIP: You can also press Ctrl-1 to set single spacing, rather than selecting an option using the Indents & Spacing command from the Format menu.

Setting First-Line Indents

Now reformat the paragraphs that will contain text so that they will have a first-line indent of 0.5 inch.

1. Click the beginning of the line that contains *Section 1 text goes here.*

2. Choose the Indents & Spacing command from the Format menu (Alt-T-A). Works displays a dialog box.

3. Click the 1st Line Indent box and type *0.5* to specify a 0.5-inch first-line indent.

4. Press Enter to confirm this setting.

Copying a Paragraph Format

With the left paragraph indent set on this first paragraph, we can simply copy the format to the text paragraph for Section 2.

1. Choose the Copy Special command from the Edit menu (Alt-E-S).

2. Click the line that contains *Section 2 text goes here.*

3. Press Enter. Works displays a dialog box that offers a choice of copying either the character or the paragraph format. The paragraph format is selected as the default.

4. Press Enter or click OK to copy the paragraph format. The text paragraph for Section 2 is now indented 0.5 inch.

Because the report title falls directly above the Section 1 title, the document will look better if the report title is centered and underlined.

1. Click the margin to the left of the report title line in the body of the document to select this line.

2. Press Ctrl-C or click Ctr in the toolbar to center the title.

3. Press Ctrl-U or click Ul in the toolbar to underline the title.

Setting a Page Break

Next we'll set page breaks so that each new section will begin at the top of a new page. The only page break we need to enter right now is the one for Section 2.

1. Click under the *S* in the Section 2 title.

2. Press Ctrl-Enter to insert a page break above this line.

Because we'll fill in this report later, it would also be nice to insert some bookmarks so that we can jump quickly to the beginning of any section. Insert a bookmark now so that we can jump to the beginning of Section 2.

1. The cursor should still be at the beginning of the Section 2 line. Choose the Bookmark Name command (Alt-E-N). The Bookmark Name dialog box appears, like this:

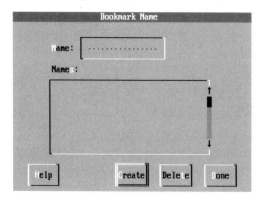

2. Type *Section 2* in the Name box, and click Create. Works inserts an invisible bookmark in this spot. When you want to jump to the beginning of Section 2, you can press F5 to choose the Go To command, select the Section 2 name from the list that appears, and click OK. Works will then scroll the document to the beginning of Section 2.

Aligning the Footer Paragraph

The finishing touch for this report will be to right-align the footer paragraph so that the text appears in the lower-right corner of each page:

1. Click the beginning of the first line of footer text, and drag down to select both lines of the footer.

2. Press Ctrl-R or click RT in the toolbar to indicate right alignment for this text. On screen, the finished template looks like this:

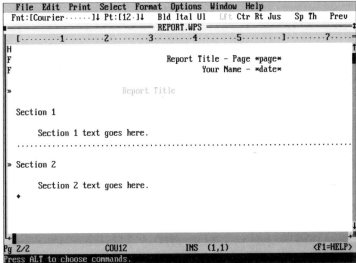

The report is finished for now, so you can save it as a template with the name REPORT.

Creating Monthly Reports

To use these templates the first month, open the FRONT or REPORT templates, replace the existing text with the text of your report, and then save the report as a standard Word Processor document. If there's a lot of boilerplate text in the first month's report that you want to reuse the following month, open the first month's report and edit the text, and then save the file with a different name so the first month's report remains unchanged. Whenever you want to create a new report text from scratch, start with the template files.

When you begin replacing the existing generic text in this template, first choose the Typing Replaces Selection command from the Options menu (Alt-O-Y). When this option is on, whatever you type replaces whatever you have selected instead of simply being inserted in front of it, which is Works' normal mode. Alternatively, you can simply type over the existing text without selecting it first by choosing the Overtype command from the Options menu (Alt-O-O). Using either of these approaches lets you avoid having to delete the old text before typing the new text.

As you fill in the text for each section, remember that Works carries the paragraph-format settings from the current paragraph into the next paragraph you create. Unless you deliberately select a paragraph and change its settings, all the text paragraphs will have a 0.5-inch first-line indent, and the whole document will be double-spaced.

If you need to add footnotes to your report, use the Footnote command from the Edit menu (Alt-E-T) to insert them. For more information on entering footnotes, press Alt-E-T and click Help.

These projects have shown you how to use most of the Word Processor's commands to work with text in a variety of ways. As you pursue your own projects, you'll develop additional techniques of your own. In Chapter 12, we'll create an expanded report that includes data copied from the Microsoft Works Spreadsheet and Database.

5

Basic Spreadsheet & Charting Techniques

In this chapter, we'll explore the basic features of the Microsoft Works Spreadsheet. If you're new to spreadsheets, this is a good place to begin learning about how they work and what they can do. By following some simple examples, you'll see how spreadsheets work in general and how the Works Spreadsheet handles fundamental spreadsheet operations.

THE SPREADSHEET CONCEPT

Computer spreadsheet programs are electronic versions of the paper ledgers that have been around for decades. A spreadsheet arranges numbers in a matrix of rows and columns. In a budget, for example, you can use the rows to track figures for income or expenses in several categories, and the columns can represent different periods of time. Because numbers are laid out in rows and columns, it's easy to see not only totals, but also the individual numbers that make up those totals and the relationships between the two. A common example of a spreadsheet is a budget like the one shown in Figure 5-1 on the next page.

The budget shown in Figure 5-1 contains rows for rent, utilities, telephone, equipment leases, and salary expenses, and columns that show the expenses in these categories for each month. The row at the bottom (the famous "bottom line") shows each month's total expenses. The column at the far right shows the total spent on each category for the entire quarter.

The totals in this spreadsheet are calculated by adding the numbers, or values, in each row or column. We could produce these same totals using a calculator, but seeing the values that contribute to the totals (as well as the totals themselves) shows us more. Looking only at the monthly totals, for example, we see only that expenses are rising from one month to the next. Because of

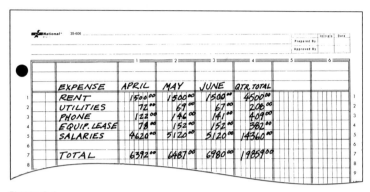

Figure 5-1.
A common type of spreadsheet is a budget.

the spreadsheet format, however, we can see that the equipment lease expenses
went up in May and that the salary expenses went up in June. In other words, we
know exactly where and when expenses went up.

Electronic spreadsheets are also composed of rows and columns, so they show
the relationships between numbers in the same way. But electronic spreadsheets
can also store formulas that calculate numbers automatically. You can change
the numbers contributing to a total, for example, and the total itself changes
automatically. If we were working on paper and we changed the rent value for
May in Figure 5-1, for example, we'd have to manually recalculate the rent total
for the quarter and the total expenses for May. In an electronic spreadsheet like the
one in Microsoft Works, the program makes these recalculations automatically.

Along with automatic recalculation, the Works Spreadsheet makes number
crunching easier in other ways. You can copy numbers or formulas, for example,
so that you don't have to reenter a formula over and over again in other areas
where essentially the same calculation is used. In Figure 5-1, for example, the
same basic addition formula is used to sum each month's expenses: In each
column, we want to sum the five values above. Formulas that perform calculations
can use arithmetic operators (+, −, *, or /), or they can use functions. The Works
Spreadsheet has dozens of predefined functions that perform various statistical
and financial calculations, from averaging a group of numbers to calculating the
rate of return on an investment.

By using formatting commands, you can set the Spreadsheet to display
values with dollar signs, commas, percent signs, or decimal points. You can also
draw attention to text or numbers by displaying them in boldface. In addition,
the Works Spreadsheet can quickly translate numbers into charts that clearly
show important relationships.

The features of the Works Spreadsheet can be divided into five groups according to function: entering and editing data, calculating, formatting, charting, and printing. We'll look at these features one group at a time, but first let's look at the elements of the Spreadsheet window.

THE SPREADSHEET WINDOW

To display the Spreadsheet window, we'll create a new Spreadsheet file.

1. Choose the Create New File command (Alt-F-N) from the File menu. Microsoft Works displays a dialog box in which you can choose the type of file you want to create.

2. Click the Spreadsheet file type and the Standard/Blank template, if it isn't already selected.

3. Click OK. Works displays a new Spreadsheet document on the screen, as in Figure 5-2.

The spreadsheet itself is divided into a matrix of *rows* (which are numbered consecutively from 1 through 16384) and *columns* (which are labeled alphabetically from A through Z, and then from AA to AZ, BB to BZ, and so on all the way to IV). The row and column labels frame the left and top side of the work area. Each intersection of a row and a column is called a *cell*, and each cell is

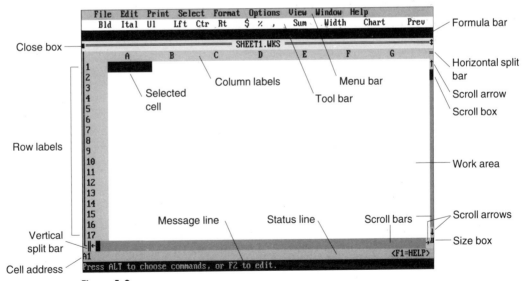

Figure 5-2.
The Works Spreadsheet screen.

identified with a *cell address* indicating the intersection it represents. For example, the first cell in the upper-left corner of the spreadsheet is cell A1 because it's at the intersection of column A and row 1. The cells make up the work area of the spreadsheet.

Because you often work with groups of cells in the spreadsheet, you can refer to a group of cells as a *range*. A range of cells is a rectangular block of adjacent cells that occupies one or more rows and one or more columns. Works identifies a range by the identifier for upper-left and lower-right cells of the block, separated by a colon. If you selected the cells A1, A2, B1, and B2, for example, that range would be designated as A1:B2.

The Toolbar

Below the *menu bar* at the top of the screen, the *toolbar* contains some tools you can click with the mouse to select common formatting commands, total a range, make a chart, or preview a document. Moving from left to right on the screen, the tools in the Spreadsheet's toolbar let you do the following:

- Set bold, italic, or underline styles for selected cells
- Set left, center, or right alignment for selected cells
- Set dollar, percent, or comma format for numbers
- Sum several cells in a column or row
- Set the width of one or more selected columns
- Make a chart from the selected series of values
- Preview the appearance of a document

To use any of these tools, you must first select the cell, row, column, or range of values you want the tool to affect. For example, to make the contents of cells A1 and A2 boldface, you would first select cells A1 and A2, and then click the Bld tool in the toolbar. We'll put some of these tools to work elsewhere in this chapter and in Chapter 7.

The Formula Bar, Scroll Bars, and Status Line

Below the toolbar, the *formula bar* displays the contents of any selected cell. As you enter text or numbers in a cell, what you've typed appears in the formula bar. At the right and along the bottom of the work area are *scroll bars*, which you can use to move quickly to other areas of the spreadsheet. In the *status line* immediately below the bottom scroll bar, the address of the currently selected cell or range always appears at the left. Depending on what you're doing at any given time, the status line might also have other indicators in it.

WORKS TIP: If you're trying to perform an operation, and Works displays a message saying you can't, check the status line and message line. You're probably in the middle of an operation like copying or moving data, and you can't do anything else until you complete the operation or cancel it by pressing Esc.

Selecting Cells

You must select a cell before you can enter text or data into it. At least one cell is always selected in the spreadsheet. When you open a new Spreadsheet file, cell A1 is selected, and when you press an arrow key or click a different cell, the cell selection moves.

To select one cell with the mouse, just click the cell. To select more than one cell, point to the first cell, hold down the mouse button, drag the pointer across all the cells you want to select, and then release the mouse button. The group of cells will remain selected until you select another cell or group of cells.

 MOUSE TIP: To select the entire spreadsheet, click the upper-left corner of the window, above the row numbers and to the left of the column designations, or press Alt-S-A. You can also extend a selection from the current cell to several adjacent cells by holding down Shift and clicking the lower-right cell in the group to which you want to extend the selection. For example, if the selected cell is A1 and you want to select all the cells from A1 to A5, hold down Shift and click cell A5, and the selection will extend from cell A1 to cell A5.

You can select individual cells with the keyboard by pressing the arrow keys to move the selection from cell A1 to the cell you want. Some special keys and key combinations let you select groups of cells or jump quickly to a filled group of cells.

For a complete list of movement and selection keys in the spreadsheet, choose the Table of Contents command from the Help menu (Alt-H-T), click the Spreadsheet category, if necessary, and then scroll down to and double-click the SS Movement and Selection Keys topic in the list of topics.

Try the movement key combinations to move the cell selection around the spreadsheet. The keys that move the selection from one block of data to another won't work correctly unless you've first entered data in the spreadsheet, so you might want to leave those commands for later.

If you don't want to use the mouse to select more than one cell at a time, you can use the Select Cells command (Alt-S-E), the Extend Selection key (F8), or Shift. Simply select the first cell in the group you want to select, press Alt-S-E, F8, or hold down Shift, and then use the arrow keys to extend the selection to other adjacent cells. To select cells A1, B1, and C1 in a new spreadsheet, for example, you could select cell A1, press Alt-S-E, F8, or hold down Shift, and then press the Right arrow key two times.

ENTERING AND EDITING DATA

Now let's create a simple budget spreadsheet based on the ledger shown in Figure 5-1 to see how to enter data in the Microsoft Works Spreadsheet.

1. Click cell A1 to select it, if it isn't already selected.

2. Type *Expenses*. Notice that as you type, the letters appear in the formula bar.

3. Press Enter to enter this text in cell A1. This cell remains selected. As you can see, Works places a quotation mark in front of the word *Expenses* in the formula bar. This mark identifies the data you've entered as a label, or text, rather than as a value, or number.

KEYBOARD TIP: To enter data in a cell and then move the selection to an adjacent cell at the same time (so you're ready to type the next label, value, or formula), press an arrow key or Tab. Pressing Tab moves the selection to the right, in the same way as pressing the Right arrow key does. Pressing Shift-Tab moves the selection to the left, in the same way as pressing the Left arrow key does.

The Works Spreadsheet considers data as one of three types: labels (text), values (numbers), or formulas. When you begin an entry with a letter, a blank space, a quotation mark, or certain other punctuation marks, Works assumes you are entering a label. When you begin an entry with a number or a period (decimal point), Works assumes you are entering a value. To let Works know you're entering a formula, you must begin the entry with an equal sign (=). After you enter a formula, Works displays the result of the formula's calculation rather than the formula itself. (See "Calculating," later in this chapter.) Works has a default alignment for each type of data: Labels are left-aligned in the cell; values and the results of formulas are right-aligned. (See "Formatting," later in this chapter.)

Editing a Cell's Contents

If you make a mistake while typing an entry and you haven't yet pressed Enter, simply press Backspace to back up and correct your mistake. If you discover a mistake after you've entered the data, however, you must first select the cell and then either replace or edit its contents.

To completely replace a cell's contents, simply select the cell, type the new data, and press Enter. But if you want to make only a small change to a cell's contents, you can edit the contents without completely replacing them. In cell A1, we entered the label *Expenses,* but we should have entered *Expense* instead. Let's edit this label.

1. Select cell A1, if it isn't already selected. The contents of the cell are displayed in the formula bar.

2. Click the formula bar to the right of the last *s* in *Expenses.* A blinking cursor appears there.

3. Press Backspace one time to delete the *s* at the end of *Expenses,* and then click cell A1 (or any other cell) or press Enter or Tab (or an arrow key) to confirm the change.

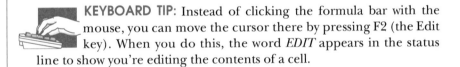 **KEYBOARD TIP:** Instead of clicking the formula bar with the mouse, you can move the cursor there by pressing F2 (the Edit key). When you do this, the word *EDIT* appears in the status line to show you're editing the contents of a cell.

Now let's enter the rest of the column titles in the top row of this spreadsheet. Cell A1 should still be selected — select it if it isn't.

1. Press the Right arrow key or Tab to select cell B1, and type *April.*

2. Press the Right arrow key again. Works displays the entry *April* in cell B1, and the cell selection moves to cell C1.

Repeat steps 1 and 2 to enter the labels for *May, June,* and *Qtr. Total* in cells C1, D1, and E1, respectively, as shown in Figure 5-1.

Because you can perform date and time calculations using the Works Spreadsheet, Works treats dates as values and formats them as such. You'll notice that the month labels are right-aligned rather than left-aligned as the other labels are. If you click a cell containing a month name, you'll also notice that Works has not added a quotation mark before the month name.

Widening a Column

Now enter the row labels in column A by doing the following:

1. Select cell A2.

2. Type *Rent* and then press the Down arrow key to confirm the entry and select cell A3.

3. Enter the labels *Utilities* and *Phone* in cells A3 and A4.

4. Select cell A5, and enter the label *Equip. Lease*.

5. Press Enter to confirm the entry.

You'll notice, however, that the label extends beyond the right edge of the cell selection, like this:

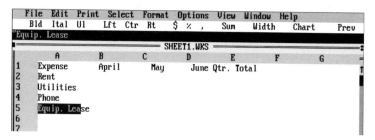

The label contains 12 characters, but the width of column A is the default 10 characters. When you enter more letters than will fit in a spreadsheet column, Works extends the entry into the adjacent cell in the next column, as long as that cell is empty. (If you enter more digits than will fit, Works either displays a series of hatch marks, displays the number in exponential notation, or rounds a number with a decimal.) In this case, Works has extended the last two letters of this label into column B. Because we want to use column B to store the expense numbers for April, we have to widen column A to accommodate the entire Equip. Lease label.

1. Click the Width tool in the toolbar. Works displays the Column Width dialog box, like this:

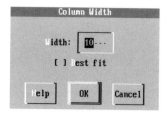

Column A is now 10 characters wide, but we need it to be at least 12 characters wide to contain the label. We could type 12 in the Width box, but let's have Works adjust the column width automatically to accommodate this label.

2. Click the Best Fit option, and then click OK. Works then widens column A to 13 characters so the label will fit.

Now finish entering the labels.

1. Enter the label *Salaries* in cell A6.

2. Enter the label *Total* in cell A8.

Entering Numbers

Entering numbers is exactly the same as entering labels, except that Works knows they're numbers and right-aligns them in their cells.

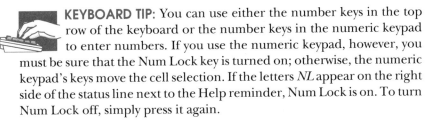

KEYBOARD TIP: You can use either the number keys in the top row of the keyboard or the number keys in the numeric keypad to enter numbers. If you use the numeric keypad, however, you must be sure that the Num Lock key is turned on; otherwise, the numeric keypad's keys move the cell selection. If the letters *NL* appear on the right side of the status line next to the Help reminder, Num Lock is on. To turn Num Lock off, simply press it again.

Next we'll enter the expense numbers (but not the totals) from the April column in Figure 5-1 in the appropriate cells in the sample spreadsheet.

1. Select cell B2.

2. Type *1500* and then press the Down arrow key to enter the number and select cell B3.

3. Enter the other values in cells B3, B4, B5, and B6 from Figure 5-1.

Copying Data into a Group of Cells

You can enter numbers in individual cells as you've just done, but you can also copy cell contents to enter repeated numbers or labels quickly. In Figure 5-1, you'll notice that the rent expense is the same for all three months. You could enter that number three times, but you could also use Works' Fill Right command to copy it quickly. Let's use Fill Right to enter the May and June Rent expenses.

1. Click cell B2, hold down the mouse button, and drag the pointer across to cell D2.

2. Choose the Fill Right command from the Edit menu (Alt-E-R). Works copies the value from cell B2 to cells C2 and D2, like this:

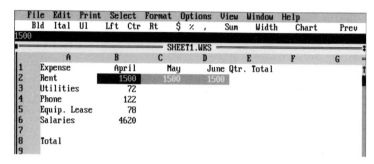

You can use the Fill Right command to copy any cell contents in the spreadsheet, whether they're labels, values, or formulas. The Fill Down command on the Edit menu (Alt-E-F) works in the same way, except that it copies down instead of to the right. The Edit menu also has commands to move data from one cell or group of cells to another and to copy a cell's contents. See *Moving Information* or *Copying Information* in the Spreadsheet category of the Help Table of Contents.

> **WORKS TIP:** You can use Fill Right or Fill Down to copy more than one column or row of data at a time. In our sample budget, for example, we could select cells B3:B4 and use the Fill Right command to copy the values in these cells to cells C3:D4.

For now, finish entering all the other values in rows 3, 4, 5, and 6, and in columns C and D. When you finish, we'll enter some formulas to calculate the totals in row 8 and column E.

CALCULATING

Whenever you want the Microsoft Works Spreadsheet to perform a calculation, you must enter a formula describing the type of calculation you want performed and indicating which cells or values you want calculated. Every formula starts with the equal sign (=). If a formula simply contains cell references or values, the equal sign must be followed by the cell references, numbers, and arithmetic operators that make up the calculation, like this:

$$= B1 + A2 - 3$$

If you use a function, such as the AVG function, in a formula, the formula must begin with an equal sign, which is followed by a function name and an argument enclosed in parentheses, like this:

$$= Function\ (Argument1, Argument2, ...)$$

Entering a Formula with the Keyboard

Let's enter a simple formula in cell B8 that calculates the total expenses for April, as follows:

1. Select cell B8.

2. Type an equal sign (=) to tell Works that you're beginning a formula.

3. Type *B2 + B3 + B4 + B5 + B6* to indicate which cell contents you want the formula to add.

4. Press Enter. The formula you typed still appears in the formula bar, and the result of this addition formula appears in cell B8, like this:

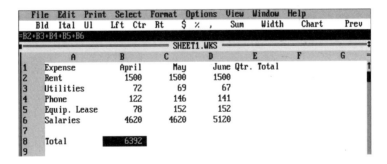

 KEYBOARD TIP: You can type cell references using lowercase letters, if you like; Works automatically converts them to uppercase when you enter the formula.

In this case, we told Works to add the contents of cells B2, B3, B4, B5, and B6, which contain the expense figures for April. We could have just as easily used the actual amounts inside those cells in the formula so that the formula would read

= 1500 + 72 + 122 + 78 + 4620

but by using the cell references instead we can now change the contents of any of those cells, and the formula will recalculate. Try it.

1. Select cell B3.

2. Type *82* and press Enter.

We have changed the contents of cell B3 from *72* to *82,* and the total amount shown in cell B8 now reads *6402* instead of *6392.* By using cell references in the formula, we have told Works to add the contents of those cells, so if we change the contents, the formula will recalculate the total. If we had used actual numbers in the formula, we would have had to edit the formula itself to produce a different total.

WORKS TIP: If you simply want Works to insert a value from one cell into another, you can type = followed by the cell reference, for example, = *A4.*

Specifying Cell References with the Mouse

Another way to specify cell references in a formula is to "point" to the cells you want to include. You can use the arrow keys to select a cell and then use the Shift or F8 key to extend the selection to select a whole range and include it in a formula, but it's easier to do it with the mouse. Let's total the expenses for May using this method.

1. Select cell C8.

2. Start the formula by typing =.

3. Click cell C2. The reference C2 appears in the formula bar, and you'll notice that the word *POINT* appears in the status line to show that you're pointing to cell references.

4. Press + and then click cell C3. Works adds the second cell reference to the formula.

5. Repeat step 4 for cells C4, C5, and C6, and then press Enter. The total amount appears in cell C8.

Using a Function to Add Adjacent Values

When you're adding many values from adjacent cells, it can be tedious to enter each cell reference individually, even if you're pointing to cells with the mouse. Fortunately, Works has functions that operate on ranges of cells. For example, the SUM function automatically adds up values in a continuous range of cells above or to the left of the currently selected cell. Let's use the SUM function now to total the June expenses.

1. Select cell D8.

2. Start the formula by typing *= Sum(*. The SUM function tells the Spreadsheet to add all the numbers in the argument, and the open parenthesis begins the argument itself.

   NOTE: *You can type function names in all lowercase letters, if you like; Works will automatically convert them to uppercase when you enter the formula.*

3. Type the range *D2:D6*.

4. End the argument with a closing parenthesis, and then press Enter to enter the formula. The total for June appears in cell D8.

Using the Autosum Feature

Works has dozens of functions for manipulating individual values or ranges of values in many different ways, but because adding values with the SUM function is such a common activity in spreadsheets, Works has an Autosum feature that makes using the SUM function even easier. To see how it works, let's sum the Rent expenses in the Qtr. Total column.

1. Select cell E2.

2. Click the Sum tool in the toolbar. Works automatically selects the three values to the left of this cell, and inserts them as the argument for a Sum formula in the formula bar, like this:

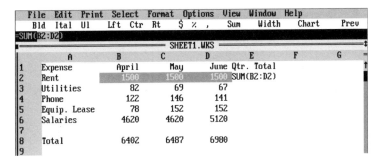

3. Press Enter to enter the formula. The total of all Rent expenses now appears in cell E2.

Copying a Formula into Several Adjacent Cells

This formula is essentially the same in all six places in which it appears (E2, E3, E4, E5, E6, and E8). The formula tells Works to add the contents of the three cells directly to the left. The Autosum feature is fast, but we can save even more time by using Works' Fill Down command to copy the formula from cell E2 to the cells directly below it.

1. Select the range of cells E2:E6 by holding down the mouse button and dragging the pointer over these cells.

2. Choose the Fill Down command from the Edit menu (Alt-E-F). Works copies the formula from cell E2 to cells E3, E4, E5, and E6.

Using Relative and Absolute Formulas

When Works copied this formula into the adjacent cells, it adjusted the formula to calculate the cells in the proper row. The range reference in the original Qtr. Total formula for the Rent row (in E2) was B2:D2. Try selecting cells E3, E4, E5, and E6 one at a time, and examine the formula bar for each cell. You'll see that the range reference changes to B3:D3, B4:D4, and so on.

Works adjusted the range references when it copied the original formula because the references in the formula were relative references. Spreadsheet formulas can use either relative or absolute references, so it's important to know the difference.

Relative references are the references used when you type a normal cell address in a formula argument or when you enter a reference in an argument by pointing to a cell. Relative references always change to reflect the position of the formula that contains them. In our previous example, for instance, the formula in E2 sums the contents of the three cells that are immediately to the left, so it sums cells B2:D2. Because the references are relative, formula is interpreted as "Sum the three cells immediately to the left." When we copy this formula into cells E3, E4, E5, and E6, Works sums the three cells to the left of the formula position and calculates the correct total in each location.

Absolute references are specified by entering a dollar sign ($) in front of the column or row designation in a cell reference. An absolute reference tells the spreadsheet to always use that specific column or row location no matter where the formula that contains it is moved or copied. See for yourself:

1. Select cell E2.

2. Click under the *B* in the B2 reference in the formula bar. The cursor begins blinking there.

3. Enter a dollar sign ($). The dollar sign appears to the left of the *B*.

4. Enter dollar signs to the left of the other three column and row references in the formula. When you finish, the reference should read *$B$2:$D$2*.

5. Press Enter to confirm the new formula. The formula argument now contains absolute references, like this:

```
 File  Edit  Print  Select  Format  Options  View  Window  Help
   Bld   Ital  Ul      Lft  Ctr  Rt    $  %  ,       Sum    Width    Chart      Preu
=SUM($B$2:$D$2)
                                          SHEET1.WKS
         A            B         C           D          E         F         G
1    Expense       April      May       June Qtr. Total
2    Rent          1500       1500       1500       4500
3    Utilities       82         69         67        218
4    Phone          122        146        141        409
5    Equip. Lease    78        152        152        382
6    Salaries      4620       4620       5120      14360
7
8    Total         6402       6487       6980
9
```

Because these references are absolute — meaning they always refer to the specific range of cells B2:D2 — Works always calculates the formula with the contents of those cells no matter where the formula is located. Let's copy the formula to check this out.

1. Select cell E2 if it isn't already selected.

2. Choose the Copy command from the Edit menu (Alt-E-C).

3. Select cell E9 as the copy destination.

4. Press Enter to complete the copy. The sum *4500* now appears in cell E9. As you can see, the formula in cell E9 is identical to the formula in cell E2. The cell references haven't changed to reflect the formula's new position because they are absolute references.

5. Select cell E9 if it isn't already selected, and choose the Clear command from the Edit menu (Alt-E-E) to clear the contents of this cell.

   NOTE: *You can also press Del to clear any selected cell, but if you have more than one cell selected, you must use the Clear command.*

Most of the time you will want to use relative cell references in formulas, but it's important to know how to create an absolute reference when you need one. Note that you can insert a dollar sign in front of only the column or only the row part of a reference so that Works treats only that part of the reference as absolute. We'll see some absolute references in Chapter 7.

Copying into a Nonadjacent Cell

The last formula we need to enter is the one located in cell E8. We could have copied the formula in E2 here by simply extending the selection down this far when we used the Fill Down command, but doing so would have placed an extra copy of the formula in the empty row at cell E7. Instead, we'll use the standard Copy command to copy the relative formula from cell E6 to cell E8.

1. Select cell E6.

2. Choose the Copy command (Alt-E-C or Shift-F3). Notice the word *COPY* appears in the status line to show that we're in the middle of a copy operation.

3. Select cell E8.

4. Press Enter to complete the copy.

Now we've entered all the labels, numbers, and formulas in this spreadsheet. Press the Down arrow. Your spreadsheet should look like the one in Figure 5-3.

```
 File  Edit  Print  Select  Format  Options  View  Window  Help
  Bld  Ital  Ul      Lft  Ctr  Rt    $  %  ,     Sum    Width     Chart      Prev

============================= SHEET1.WKS =============================
          A           B          C          D         E         F         G
 1   Expense       April       May       June Qtr. Total
 2   Rent           1500       1500       1500       4500
 3   Utilities        82         69         67        218
 4   Phone           122        146        141        409
 5   Equip. Lease     78        152        152        382
 6   Salaries       4620       4620       5120      14360
 7
 8   Total          6402       6487       6980      19869
 9
10
11
12
13
14
15
16
17
E9                                                              <F1=HELP>
Press ALT to choose commands, or F2 to edit.
```

Figure 5-3.
A completed budget spreadsheet containing labels, values, and formulas.

FORMATTING

Now let's use some of Microsoft Works' formatting features to make our spreadsheet look better.

Inserting a New Row

The first thing we notice about this spreadsheet is that it's a bit crowded. Works lets you insert or delete rows or columns to add or remove extra space between data in a spreadsheet. To see how this works, let's insert an extra row between the column labels in row 1 and the Rent expenses in row 2.

1. Select any cell in row 2.

2. Choose the Insert Row/Column command from the Edit menu (Alt-E-I). Works displays a dialog box where you can choose whether to insert a row or a column. The default selection is Row, so you don't have to change it.

3. Click OK or press Enter to accept the default selection and insert a row, as in Figure 5-4.

When you insert or delete a row or a column in the spreadsheet, Works renames any affected row or column, and the formulas you have entered adjust to their new locations. In our example, the Rent expenses row is renumbered to

```
 File  Edit  Print  Select  Format  Options  View  Window  Help
 Bld  Ital  Ul      Lft  Ctr  Rt   $  %  ,     Sum    Width    Chart     Prev

================================= SHEET1.WKS =================================
        A            B        C        D         E          F
1  Expense         April     May      June Qtr. Total
2
3  Rent            1500     1500     1500      4500
4  Utilities         82       69       67       218
5  Phone            122      146      141       409
6  Equip. Lease      78      152      152       382
7  Salaries        4620     4620     5120     14360
8
9  Total           6402     6487     6980     19869
10
```

Figure 5-4.
You can insert or delete rows or columns in any Works spreadsheet to create or remove extra space between data.

row 3, and the rows below it are renumbered accordingly. If you want to see how the formulas have adjusted, select cell E3 and look at the formula there: The old cell range $B$2:$D$2 is now $B$3:$D$3. (Even if you use absolute references, the row or column references change when you insert or delete a row or a column. The references remain the same only when you move or copy the specific cell containing that formula.)

Changing Cell Alignments

Next notice that in the spreadsheet shown in Figure 5-4, the Qtr. Total label in column E is butted up against the June label in column D. The problem is that the Qtr. Total label is aligned against the left edge of column E because Works recognizes it as a label, and the June label is aligned against the right edge of column D because Works recognizes it as a date.

To fix this problem, we'll change the alignment of the date labels so that they're centered in their columns, opening some space between the June and Qtr. Total labels.

1. Select cells B1, C1, and D1.

2. Click Ctr in the toolbar to change the alignment of these cells to centered.

Now that the month labels are centered, some space is displayed between the June label and the Qtr. Total label.

Changing a Number Format

The next formatting change we'll make is to display the values in this spreadsheet as dollars. The easiest way to do this is to select all the values in the spreadsheet and then change the number format for every cell at the same time.

1. Click cell B3.

2. Hold down the mouse button and drag the pointer across to column E and then down to row 9. Works then selects the entire block of cells.

3. Click the $ tool in the toolbar. Works automatically reformats the values as dollars with two decimal places, like this:

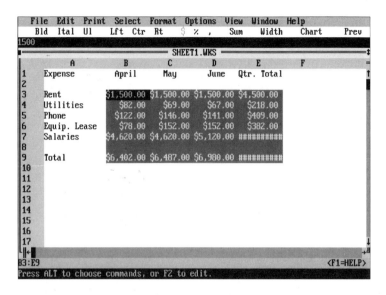

As you can see, Works displays hatch marks in cells E7 and E9 because there's not enough room in column E to display these numbers with two decimal places. We could widen column E to accommodate these two numbers, but because all these amounts are in even dollars, let's reset the number format instead so there are no decimal places. The block of cells is still selected, so we can go right to resetting the format.

1. Choose the Currency command from the Format menu (Alt-T-U). A dialog box appears where you can enter the number of decimal places you want to appear in the dollar amounts.

2. Type *0* as the number of decimal places.

3. Press Enter to return to the spreadsheet. The numbers are now formatted with no decimal places, and all the values fit in their columns.

Along with commands for setting the font or style of text and the width of columns, the Format menu offers 10 commands with a variety of options for displaying numbers, dates, times, and text in a spreadsheet. For more information about the different format commands, check out the *Formatting Numbers (SS)* and *Formatting Text in a SS* topics in the Spreadsheet category in the Help Table of Contents.

Changing a Text Style

Finally we'll set off the row and column labels in this spreadsheet by displaying them in boldface type. Doing so will also give us a chance to select entire columns and rows.

1. Click the *A* that designates column A. Works selects the entire column.

2. Click Bld in the toolbar. All the labels in column A are now displayed in boldface.

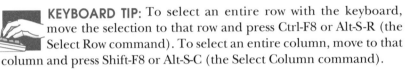

KEYBOARD TIP: To select an entire row with the keyboard, move the selection to that row and press Ctrl-F8 or Alt-S-R (the Select Row command). To select an entire column, move to that column and press Shift-F8 or Alt-S-C (the Select Column command).

Now we'll make row 1 bold to set off the column labels in the same way.

1. Click the *1* that designates row 1.

2. Click Bld twice. All the labels in Row 1 now appear in boldface. (You have to click the tool twice because the Expense label in cell A1 is already boldface; clicking Bld the first time makes the Expense label plain again, and clicking Bld the second time makes the whole row boldface.)

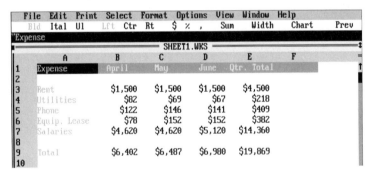

Our spreadsheet is now nicely formatted for presentation, so we're ready to look at Works' basic charting features.

CHARTING

Spreadsheet charts create a visual display of your data so that you can easily see relationships between different groups of numbers or data sets. With the Microsoft Works Spreadsheet, you can create different types of bar, line, and pie charts. Before we get into the mechanics of creating a chart, let's look at how the charting function works.

How Charting Works

With the Works Spreadsheet, you can create up to eight different charts for each Spreadsheet document. To create a chart, you must already have entered some data in your spreadsheet. You select the cells containing data you want to chart, and then tell Works to make a chart from that data. Works then displays the chart by itself on your screen.

After you view a chart and press Esc, you return to the Works Spreadsheet in Chart mode, as shown in Figure 5-5.

As you can see, the toolbar in Chart mode is different from the one in Spreadsheet mode, and you'll see a new Data menu in the menu bar. In addition, you'll also find that the Print, Format, Options, and View menus have

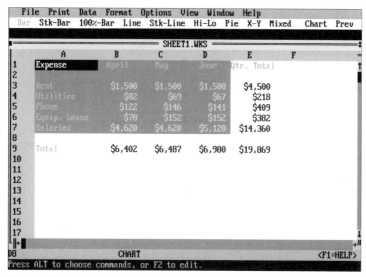

Figure 5-5.

The Spreadsheet's chart mode has a different toolbar, a new Data menu, and some new, chart-specific commands on the Print, Format, Options, and View menus.

chart-specific commands. Once you've drawn a chart, you can change its definition with these menu commands and tools. (See "Chart Mode Functions," later in this chapter.)

Each time you create a chart, Works names it "Chart1," "Chart2," "Chart3," and so on, up to "Chart8," and lists each chart's name at the bottom of the View menu. You can display any chart by choosing its name there. Charts don't have to be saved — they're automatically saved with the Spreadsheet file when you save it.

WORKS TIP: You can rename charts by choosing the Charts command from the View menu, selecting the chart you want to rename, typing a new name in the Name box, and clicking the Rename button.

After you've created a chart, any change in the spreadsheet data plotted in that chart causes the chart itself to change.

The Two Basic Chart Types

You can plot two basic types of charts with Works: time-series charts and pie charts. However, the Works Spreadsheet offers variations on these basic types: You choose from eight time-series chart types and one pie chart type.

A *time-series chart*, as shown in Figure 5-6, plots values along horizontal and vertical axes. The *vertical axis*, also called the *Y-axis*, is a vertical line that typically represents values. The *horizontal axis*, called the *X-axis*, is a horizontal line at the bottom of the screen that typically represents periods of time. (X-Y charts are an exception. See "X-Y Charts," later in this chapter.)

In a time-series chart, each group of values that you want to plot for one time period is called a *Y-series*. This group is a range of cells in a row or column of your spreadsheet. In Figure 5-6, each Y-series is a spreadsheet row representing a certain category of expenses. Works can plot up to six Y-series of data on a chart. You can also plot one *X-series* of data in an X-Y chart. (See "Microsoft Works Chart Types," later in this chapter.)

Other features of time-series charts, as shown in Figure 5-6, are titles, legends, and labels.

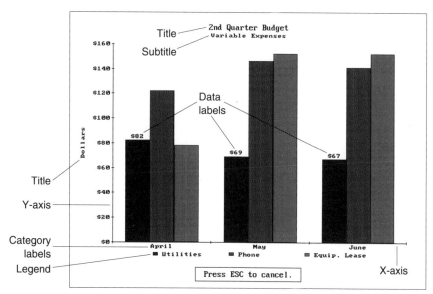

Figure 5-6.
A time-series bar chart.

- A *title* is identifying text that you can place at the top of a chart or on its axes. Figure 5-6 contains a chart title at the top, a subtitle, and a Y-axis title indicating Dollars. You can also add an X-axis title if you like.

- A *legend* describes each Y-series plotted on a time-series chart. Like the legend on a map, the legend on a time-series chart is a key that shows which of the bars or lines refers to which data series. Works differentiates each data series by displaying its bar, line, or points with a different color, pattern, or marker. The legend in Figure 5-6 shows which bar refers to which type of expense.

- *Labels* are extra text that you can add to identify categories of plotted data (*category labels*) or to identify the specific amounts each bar or line point represents on a chart (*data labels*). Category labels might be month names or dates, for example. Data labels can be used at the tops of bars or above points on a plotted line to show the actual value each bar or point represents so that each value stands out from the others. To create category or data labels, select the spreadsheet cells that contain the labels you want to use (usually the column labels in the spreadsheet), and choose the Data Labels command from the Data menu (Alt-D-D).

A *pie chart* plots values as slices of a pie. It shows just how much of the total amount (the total pie) each value represents. When you plot a pie chart, you must select values in only one time period (one Y-series), which means that you must select cells in only one spreadsheet row or column. Pie charts don't contain category labels because category labels are used on the X-axis, and pie charts don't have an X-axis. When you use data labels on a pie chart, they appear next to the pie slices they represent.

 WORKS TIP: To use the row labels in your spreadsheet as the data legends in a chart, simply select the labels along with the data when you select the cells to be plotted. If you want to add labels from spreadsheet cells to a chart later, use the Legends command on the Data menu (Alt-D-L).

MAKING A SIMPLE TIME-SERIES CHART

Now let's make a simple chart of our sample monthly expenses spreadsheet to see how the charting function works.

To create a chart, first select the data you want displayed. If you want to include data legends in the chart, you can also select the row and column labels that identify the data. So, to chart all the monthly expense amounts in our budget with legends, we'll need to select all the row and column labels and the expense amounts for each month.

1. Select cell A1.

2. Hold down the mouse button and drag across to cell D1 and then down to row 7.

3. Click the Chart tool in the toolbar. Microsoft Works displays a bar graph on the screen, like this:

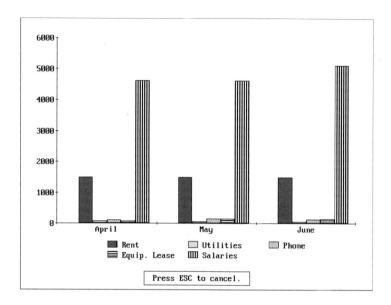

As you can see, this graph includes all the expense rows from our sample spreadsheet, rather than only the three rows shown in Figure 5-6. Because there's such a large difference between the Salaries and Rent amounts and the Utilities, Phone, and Equip. Lease amounts, the graph scale in this example must accommodate amounts from $0 to over $5,000, and small differences between the lesser amounts are hard to distinguish. (Chapter 6 offers some tips for accommodating wide ranges of values in charts.)

Bar charts or line charts are best for showing changes in data sets from one period to the next, but you can change the chart type to suit your data-representation needs. (See "Microsoft Works Chart Types," later in this chapter.)

Chart Mode Functions

To make adjustments to this chart, you must return to the spreadsheet. Press Esc. Works displays the spreadsheet again, but Works is now in Chart mode, as shown in Figure 5-5.

You know you're in Chart mode because the status line says *CHART,* and the menus and toolbar are different than they are when you're working with spreadsheet data.

When you're in Chart mode, you can change the chart type by choosing a different type from the Format menu or by clicking a tool for the new chart type in the toolbar. Each of the tools in the toolbar represents a different chart type, except for Chart and Prev, which let you draw a new chart and preview the document, respectively.

The Data, Format, and Options menus in Chart mode handle the following charting functions:

- The Data menu lets you select series of data to plot in a chart and to add titles, legends, and data labels to a chart.

- The Format menu lets you choose a different chart type, set a different default chart type, change the font used in chart titles and legends, and set the color or pattern of chart bars or pie slices. It also lets you designate markers for a line chart.

- The Options menu has commands that let you set minimum and maximum values for the Y-axis, specify the interval and unit of measure on the Y-axis, display grid lines, and assign data series to two Y-axes.

Any menu command that you choose when in Chart mode applies to the current chart, which is the chart you displayed on the screen before you pressed Esc to enter Chart mode. The current chart is indicated on the View menu with a bullet next to its name.

When you choose the Preview or Print commands from the Print menu in Chart mode, the chart, not the spreadsheet, will print. The Page Setup & Margins command in Chart mode lets you set the chart size and other options for the chart. To print or display a color chart in black and white, choose the Format For B&W command from the Print menu.

 WORKS TIP: The only way to change the options for a chart other than the current chart is by plotting the chart you want to change on the screen (by selecting it from the View menu) and then pressing Esc to move back to Chart mode.

Although you can edit cell contents, enter values in new cells, and scroll the spreadsheet in Chart mode, you can't copy cells, create range names, or change cell formats in this mode. To do this, you must return to Spreadsheet mode by choosing the Spreadsheet command from the View menu (Alt-V-S).

MICROSOFT WORKS CHART TYPES

You can plot nine types of charts with the Works Spreadsheet. Let's look at each type of chart and see how it presents data differently.

Bar Charts

Microsoft Works offers three bar chart types:

- A *bar chart* contains an X-axis and one or two Y-axes and plots individual values from a spreadsheet as bars. In each series of data, each value is plotted as a bar of a different color or pattern. If you plot three expense items for one month, for example, each expense item is plotted as a bar for a total of three bars. If you plot the three expense items for three months, three sets of three bars are included, with each set representing one month's expenses. Figure 5-6 contains a bar chart that shows three months' expenses.

- A *stacked bar chart* combines all the values for each series into one bar. Each value in the series represents a part of the bar equal to its proportion of the total amount in the whole series, like this:

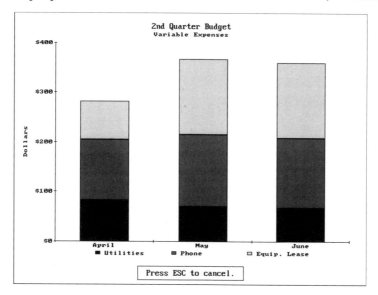

As you can see, each bar's height is determined by the sum of the values it represents, and each value is distinguished by a different color or pattern according to the part of the total it represents.

Also, the Y-axis scale changes to accommodate the higher amounts represented by each bar. Because all the values in a series are combined in one bar, there's only one bar per time period on the X-axis. Because the plot shows expenses for three months, three bars are included.

■ A *100% bar chart* is like a stacked bar chart, except that the X-axis scale is in percentages instead of in whole numbers, and the bars are always the same height, like this:

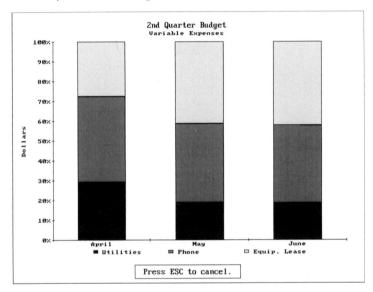

This chart plots the same data as does the preceding stacked bar chart, but you can see here that the bar for each data series is always 100 percent, and each value in the series is represented as a proportional amount of the total.

Line Charts

You can choose from two types of line charts in the Works Spreadsheet.

■ A *line chart* also shows changes in values over time, except that each line on such a chart represents one data series. In a way, a line chart is simply a bar chart in which Works has drawn lines that connect the tops of similar bars, like this:

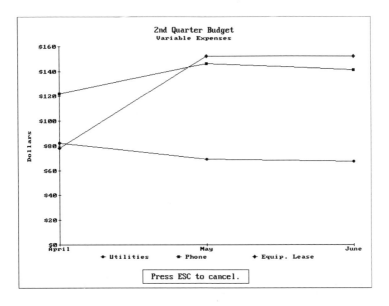

This line chart shows exactly the same expense data as the earlier bar charts. The advantage of a line chart is that you can easily see when one data series rises above or falls below another because the lines cross.

■ A *stacked line chart* also plots changes in data over time, except that the lines on the chart contribute to a total. Each line shows how the values it represents change in relation to the total over time:

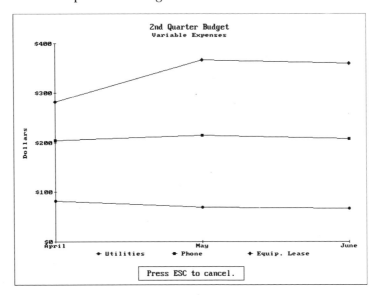

You could think of a stacked line chart as a stacked bar chart with lines that connect the tops of the bar segments.

Hi-Lo-Close Charts

A *Hi-Lo-Close chart* is also like a stacked bar chart, except that each bar is a vertical line and the bar segments are points plotted on that line, like this:

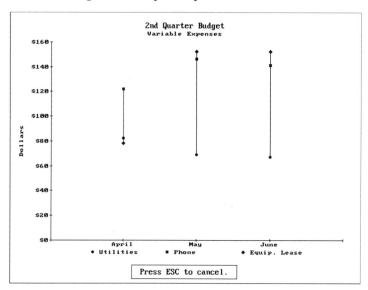

This chart is so named because it is frequently used to show high, low, and closing stock prices during a day.

Pie Charts

A *pie chart* is a plot of one data series, and each slice of the pie represents one value in that series, like this:

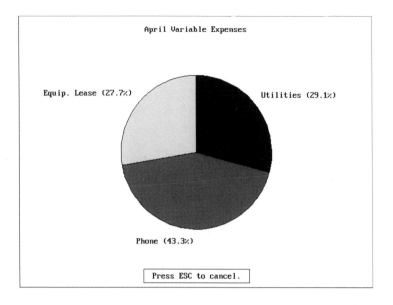

Because they show only one series, pie charts are useful only for showing relationships among values in that series. In a way, a pie chart is like one bar from a 100% bar chart, except that it's round instead of rectangular.

WORKS TIP: If you want to include data labels in a pie chart when you first define it, the data cells and label cells must be in adjacent columns. In Figure 5-5, for example, if you selected cells A3:B7, created a chart, and then switched to a Pie chart type, the labels in column A would be included.

To add labels to pie slices after you've created a pie chart, select the cells containing the labels, and choose the X-Series command from the Data menu (Alt-D-X). Works automatically calculates and displays percentages next to each of the labels.

If you want to draw attention to a particular category in a pie chart, you can explode that slice by using the Data Format command on the Format menu in Chart mode.

X-Y Charts

An *X-Y chart* plots the intersections of X-series and Y-series values. You can use these charts to plot the relative positions of different pairs of values so that you can see where each pair of measurement values stacks up against other pairs. When you define an X-Y chart, you first select an X-series of values, which defines the horizontal scale on the chart. Then you select one or more Y-series of values, which defines the range of the vertical scale and plots the sets of points above the X-axis, like this:

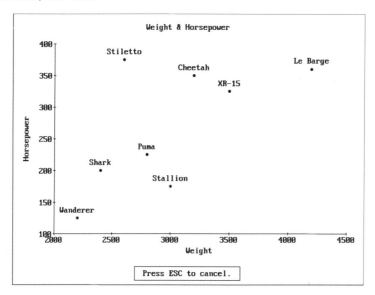

This example shows the horsepower and weight measurements of different cars. To look for the heaviest car with the most horsepower, we would look for the Y-value plot in the upper-right corner of the graph. In the original spreadsheet, the horsepower and weight figures were in two columns: The weight column was selected as the X-axis, and the horsepower column was selected as the first Y-series. The data labels were located in a third column and assigned to the first Y-series with the Data Labels command on the Data menu.

Mixed Charts

A *mixed chart* combines lines and bars in the same chart, like this:

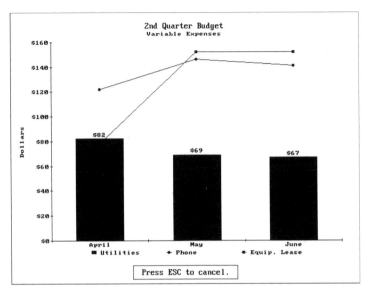

In this case, the Utilities expenses appear as bars, and the Phone and Equip. Lease expenses appear as lines.

> **NOTE:** *You can choose which data series is plotted as a bar or a line with the Mixed Line & Bar command on the Options menu.*

We've looked at the nine types of charts that you can create with the Works Spreadsheet. As you can see, each chart type reveals something a little different about the data being plotted.

For more information on charting, explore the topics in the Charting category of the Help Table of Contents.

PRINTING

Returning to the basic spreadsheet we created at the beginning of this chapter, suppose that we want to print it. Using commands on the Print menu, you can print a file on paper, print it into a disk file, or view its printed version on the screen. Let's preview the appearance of our spreadsheet on the screen.

1. If you are currently in Chart mode, choose the Spreadsheet command from the View menu (Alt-V-S) to return to the Spreadsheet.

2. Click Prev in the toolbar. The Preview dialog box appears.

3. Click the Preview button to preview the file on the screen. The page appears on the screen in a reduced size, with the layout it will have when printed on paper.

Microsoft Works displays the page on which the currently selected cell is located. Because spreadsheets can be both wider and longer than one printed page, Works Spreadsheet documents contain both horizontal and vertical page breaks, which are shown as dotted lines. (See "Use Page Breaks to Divide Data Logically" at the end of Chapter 6 for more information.)

To view preceding or following pages on the screen, press the PgUp key or PgDn key. If you like what you see, you can print directly from this screen by pressing the P key, or you can return to the spreadsheet itself by pressing Esc.

For more information about printing specific parts of a spreadsheet and about the options available in the Print and Preview dialog boxes, see the *Previewing Before Printing* and *Printing* topics in the Spreadsheet category of the Help Table of Contents.

In this chapter we learned about the basics of using the Microsoft Works Spreadsheet. You learned how to do a lot with numbers using this tool. If you're ready to learn more, turn to the spreadsheet and charting tips in Chapter 6, or the spreadsheet and charting projects in Chapter 7.

6

Making the Most of the Spreadsheet

The Microsoft Works Spreadsheet tool does just about everything you would want to do with a spreadsheet program. In this chapter, we'll look at some strategies for optimizing your productivity with the Spreadsheet tool.

Because the Spreadsheet's functions fall into several categories, we'll divide the tips the same way — into entering and editing data, calculating, formatting, charting, and printing.

ENTERING AND EDITING DATA

Most spreadsheets you create will grow beyond the boundaries of a single screen, and it's easy to get lost. The tips in this section will help you enter data more efficiently, move around in a spreadsheet faster, and bring your data into view more easily.

Plan First, Execute Later

Before you jump into a new Spreadsheet document and start entering labels, values, and formulas, it's a good idea to spend a few minutes thinking about the spreadsheet you want to build and planning how best to do it. If you're new to spreadsheets, you might want to draw a plan on paper, deciding how the rows and columns of data will be laid out. While drawing such a plan, you might discover that the first layout that occurs to you isn't the best one and that you can rearrange rows or columns to make the spreadsheet easier to read and use.

When you make a spreadsheet plan, think about the row and column titles, what kinds of formulas the spreadsheet will contain, and how you want the results to be displayed. In a budget spreadsheet, for example, you should have a good idea of what kinds of expense items you want to list and in what subcategories, if any, you want to place them. You might separate household expenses from installment credit expenses, for example, with a subtotal for each group of expenses.

 WORKS TIP: To get an idea of how some different types of spreadsheets are laid out, open the various spreadsheet templates that came with your copy of Microsoft Works.

Use the Keyboard to Choose Commands

Even if you begin by choosing commands from menus with the mouse, you'll probably find that it's often faster to type commands from the keyboard. Works lets you choose any command from a menu by typing a single letter, and you'll soon memorize the Alt-key combinations that open a particular menu and choose the command you want at the same time. To print a file, for example, you type Alt-P-P, and pressing these three keys is faster than using the mouse.

Use the Mouse for Dialog Boxes

Unless you're simply going to press Enter to accept the default choices in a dialog box, it's easier to use the mouse to select dialog box options. It's difficult to remember all the Alt-key combinations for selecting dialog box options, so it will be faster to point to the options you want and click the mouse button. You might memorize an option that you always select in a familiar dialog box, in which case using the Alt-key combination might be faster, but using the mouse is generally the best way to select options in dialog boxes.

Use the Mouse to Select Cells

To select cells using the mouse, hold down the left mouse button and drag across the cells you want to select. You can select an entire row or column by clicking its label. If you use the keyboard, you must hold down Shift or press F8 or Alt-S-E, and then use the arrow keys to extend the cell selection. The only time it makes sense to use the keyboard for selecting cells is when you're moving the selection from one cell to a cell immediately next to it as you enter data. In that case, it makes more sense to use an arrow key or Tab to move the selection than it does to take your hand off the keyboard to use the mouse.

WORKS TIP: To select all the cells in a spreadsheet quickly, press Alt-S-A or click in the upper left corner of the spreadsheet, above the row labels and to the left of the column labels.

Use the Sum Tool in the Toolbar

Instead of typing a formula to sum a column or row of numbers, click the Sum tool in the toolbar. Works automatically enters the SUM function and the range of cells directly above the current cell (if you're summing a column) or directly to the left (if you're summing a row). Press Enter to display the result of the formula in the cell.

> **NOTE:** *You can choose the Autosum command from the Edit menu (Alt-E-A) or press Ctrl-M to choose the Autosum feature.*

Point to Cells As You Build Formulas

When you specify cell references in formulas, it's faster and more accurate to point to the cells you want than it is to type cell references with the keyboard. After you type an equal sign (=) to let Works know you're beginning a formula (and after adding a function name and opening parenthesis to begin an argument, if necessary), you can enter any cell reference in that formula by simply selecting that cell, either by moving the selection to it using the arrow keys and then pressing Enter or by clicking it with the mouse.

When you point to cells, you eliminate the possibility of entering an incorrect reference in a formula because of a typing mistake. You can still point to the wrong cell, however, so be sure you point to the cell you really want to include in the formula.

Use Range Names to Speed Formula Entry

The Edit menu's Range Name command is a powerful feature that makes referring to groups of cells easy. After you define a group of cells — whether it's a budget total or subtotal or a column that contains expenses for April — you can define that group as a range by giving it a unique range name.

1. Select the group of cells you want to name as a range.

2. Choose the Range Name command from the Edit menu (Alt-E-N).
   Works displays a dialog box, as shown at the top of the next page.

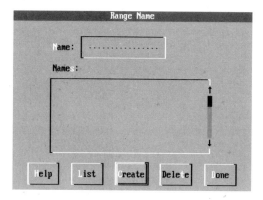

3. Type the name you want to give the range in the Name box. (If the upper left cell in the range you selected contains a label, Works suggests that label as the range name.)

4. Press Enter or click the Create button. Works creates the range name and returns you to the spreadsheet. The name now appears in the Names list in the Range Name and Go To dialog boxes.

Once you've created a range name, you can use it as a reference in a formula (to perform calculations on the group of cells in the range), or you can enter it in the Go To command dialog box when you want to move to and select the group quickly. (See the next section, "Use the Go To Command to Select Ranges.")

If you're new to using range names, you might not be sure when it's appropriate to use them. After all, you could name any rectangular group of cells as a range, but ranges are only useful if you'll need to refer to the group of cells as a whole group later. If you find yourself referring to a range of cells more than once as you create formulas, you should define a range name for those cells. When you've named a range, you'll know that you can accurately refer to a group of cells by specifying the range name, and you'll eliminate the possibility of entering the wrong cell range because of a typing or pointing error. Range names are also easier to remember than cell references when you need to use them in formulas.

Use the Go To Command to Select Ranges

In the *SS Movement and Selection Keys* topic in the Spreadsheet category of the Help Table of Contents, you'll find a list of the keyboard shortcuts that you can use to move around a spreadsheet. When you want to move to and select a specific range of cells, however, you can use the Go To command on the Select menu.

1. Choose the Go To command from the Select menu (Alt-S-G) or press F5. Works displays a dialog box, like this:

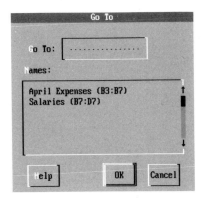

(This sample contains a couple of range names that were previously defined. If you haven't defined any ranges, the Names list on your screen will be empty.)

2. Click the range name you want to select, or type the cell reference or range in the Go To box.

3. Click OK. Works scrolls the spreadsheet to that cell or range and selects it.

NOTE: You can move from one named range to the next named range in the spreadsheet by pressing Shift-F5.

Use the Search Command to Select Individual Cells

When you want to select an individual cell, or you can't remember the cell reference or range name, you can use the Search command to find and select a single cell based on its contents. You might remember that a cell contains a certain value — for example, $150.00 — but not where that cell is located. In this case, you could use the Search command to have Works search for cells that contain the value $150.00.

1. Choose the Search command from the Select menu (Alt-S-S). Works displays a dialog box, like this:

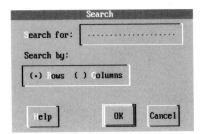

2. Type the exact text or number you're looking for in the Search For box. Works does not distinguish between partial and complete strings. So if you search, for example, for *12,* Works will find 12, 4120, $2.12, and 212 Elm Street.

3. Choose whether you want Works to search across rows and then down columns (the Rows option, which is the default) or down columns and then across rows (the Columns option).

4. Press Enter or click OK. Works locates the cell.

KEYBOARD TIP: If your spreadsheet contains more than one cell with the text or value you're searching for, press F7 to repeat the search and find other occurrences of the same text or value.

You can use the Search command to search the entire spreadsheet, or you can select a specific range of cells and have Works search only the cells in that range. Works searches from the selected cell forward, however, so press Ctrl-Home to move the selection to cell A1 if you want to search an entire spreadsheet beginning with the first cell. If you begin a search in the middle of a spreadsheet, Works will cycle back to A1 when it reaches the last cell.

If you can't remember the complete contents of the cell you're looking for, you can include either a question mark (?) or an asterisk (*) as a wildcard character in the search string you specify. Use the question mark character to replace any *single character* in a search entry, and use the asterisk character to replace any *group* of characters in a search entry.

If you're looking for a value and you can't remember whether it's 100, 120, or 150, for example, you could ask Works to search for *1?0.* Works does not distinguish between partial and complete strings, however, so with this search entry, Works would also find 4130 Shoremont Drive.

On the other hand, if you were looking for a four digit value that began with 46, you could ask Works to search for *46*.* Works would find each value that began with 46, and you could keep pressing F7 until you located the value you were looking for.

WORKS TIP: Works searches only displayed labels and values. If you want to search for an element of a formula, therefore, you must first choose the Show Formulas command from the Options menu (Alt-O-F) to display formulas (rather than the calculated results of those formulas) in the spreadsheet's cells. To display the results of formulas again, choose the Show Formulas command again.

Here are some considerations to keep in mind when using the Search command:

- Works does not search cells in hidden columns because the data in those columns is not displayed. (See "Use Zero Column Widths to Hide Columns," later in this chapter.)

- Works does not search for cell references or range names unless they are contained in a formula and you have chosen the Show Formulas command. You must specify as the search criterion the value, formula, or label that's contained in a single cell. If you know the cell reference or range name, use the Go To command.

- Works is quite literal in searching for text or values. If you're looking for a cell that contains $1,500 and you enter *$1500* (no comma), Works won't find what you're looking for.

- The Search command does not distinguish between upper- and lowercase letters. If you're looking for SUM, Works also finds Summer, summary, and assumption.

Use the Copy Shortcuts

When you copy the contents of a cell into a series of cells either immediately to the right of or immediately below the copied cell, use the Edit menu's Fill Right or Fill Down command to enter text or data in the whole series of cells in one operation. To copy the same expense amount from the January column through the December column in a budget, for example, it's much faster to select the range of cells from January through December and then choose the Fill Right command (Alt-E-R) than it is to copy the contents individually 11 times.

When you copy data from a cell into several nonadjacent cells, use the Repeat Copy command (Shift-F7) so that you don't have to select the original cell and copy from it repeatedly. When you use Repeat Copy, Works remembers the data you last copied and puts a copy of it in the selected cell. So you could copy data from cell A1 into A3 using the Copy command (or Shift-F3) and then select cell A5 and press Shift-F7 to place a copy of the same data in A5.

You can also combine the Fill Down or Fill Right command and the Repeat Copy command to speed up copying. Suppose, for example, that you want to copy data from cell A1 into A3 and then copy the same data into each cell in the range A5:A9.

1. Select cell A1 and press Shift-F3, or choose the Copy command (Alt-E-C) to copy the data.

2. Select cell A3 and press Enter to copy the data there.

3. Select cell A5 and press Shift-F7 to repeat the copy.

4. Select cells A5:A9 and press Alt-E-F to choose the Fill Down command.

Finally, the Fill Series command makes it much easier to enter a series of numbers or date labels in a range of cells in a row or a column. If you want to enter month labels for January through December in one row, for example, you do the following:

1. Enter the January label.

2. Select the January label and the 11 cells to its right.

3. Choose the Fill Series command (Alt-E-L) from the Edit menu. Works displays a dialog box, like this:

This dialog box lets you specify the number or time interval to use as a unit of measure, and then lets you indicate the Step By value, or the value by which you want each subsequent cell to increase.

4. Click the Month option (or press M). The Step By value default is 1, which is what we want, because we want each cell to contain the next month's label.

5. Click OK. Works fills the selected range with month labels.

This approach is much faster and more accurate than typing a whole series of labels or numbers by hand.

Use Viewing Options

Because spreadsheets can be so large, and your screen is relatively small, it can be hard to arrange your data so that you can see the data you want at all times. Fortunately, you can split a Spreadsheet window and freeze row or column titles on the screen.

You use the split bars at the lower-left and upper-right corners of the Spreadsheet window to divide the window in half vertically or horizontally. Simply drag the horizontal or vertical split bar to split the window in half. To split a window into top and bottom halves so that each half can vertically scroll independently of the other, for example, you do the following:

1. Click the split bar to the right of the Spreadsheet's column designations.

2. Hold down the mouse button and drag the split bar down to the row where you want the split to occur.

3. Release the mouse button. The spreadsheet window will be divided into two equal panes, each with its own vertical scroll bar, like this:

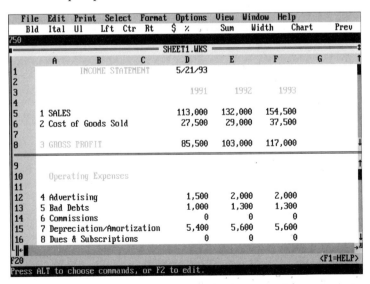

If you use both split bars at one time, you can divide the window into four scrolling panes. To move the selection from one pane to another, click the cell you want. To restore the window to a single pane, drag the split bars back to their original locations. For more information on splitting a Spreadsheet window, see the *Splitting a Window* topic in the Spreadsheet category of the Help Table of Contents.

 KEYBOARD TIP: You also can use the Split command on the Window menu (Alt-W-T) with the arrow keys to split the Spreadsheet window. Press F6 or Shift-F6 to toggle the selection back and forth between Spreadsheet panes.

Even if you split the Spreadsheet window, however, you might find that when you scroll to a distant row or column to enter, edit, or view data, the row and column titles scroll out of view, making it hard to tell which row or column is which. The Freeze Titles command locks row and column titles on the screen so that you can always see them. Simply select a cell directly beneath the row or to the right of the column whose titles you want to freeze, and then choose the Freeze Titles command from the Options menu (Alt-O-T) — the titles will remain on the screen when you scroll. To unfreeze titles, choose the Freeze Titles command again. For more information, see the *Freezing Titles* topic in the Spreadsheet category of the Help Table of Contents.

Turn Off Automatic Recalculation

The Works Spreadsheet is usually set to automatic recalculation, which means that it recalculates formulas whenever you enter or edit the contents of any cell. When you're first building a spreadsheet, however, your main goal is to enter a lot of data and labels as quickly as possible. As the spreadsheet grows and you add more formulas, it takes longer and longer for Works to recalculate each time you make a change. By choosing the Manual Calculation command from the Options menu (Alt-O-M), you can stop automatic recalculation while you enter a lot of data and formulas, thereby avoiding having to suspend data entry temporarily while Works recalculates.

Realistically, automatic recalculation isn't a problem until your spreadsheet has grown to several dozen rows and columns with several dozen formulas. At that point, you can eliminate recalculation delays by opting for manual recalculation. The only thing to remember is that after you choose the

Manual Calculation command, you must explicitly tell Works to recalculate formulas by choosing the Calculate Now command from the Options menu (Alt-O-N or F9). If you forget, your spreadsheet won't show the correct results. A good rule is to use manual calculation only when you know you'll be entering a lot of data. After you've finished, be sure to choose the Manual Calculation command again to turn it off and have Works recalculate after every change.

Use Templates

Early in this chapter we discussed the need for advance planning before you actually begin building a Works Spreadsheet document. If you save old spreadsheets as templates or use some of the predefined templates that come with Works, you can speed up the planning process by having some standard spreadsheet layouts on hand. Many budget spreadsheets look much the same, for example, so if you save a budget spreadsheet as a template, you can load that template file the next time you want to create a budget and change only the values and labels or add some new rows or columns to suit your new budgeting needs.

When you use templates to construct new spreadsheets, however, be careful to check all the formulas in the spreadsheet to be sure they make the right calculations. The references and formulas you used in the original spreadsheet might not be suitable for your new purpose.

NOTE: *Choose the Show Formulas command from the Options menu (Alt-O-F) to review all your formulas at one time.*

CALCULATING

Calculating shortcuts include not only easier ways to enter cell references in formulas but also ways to build formulas more quickly and efficiently.

Check All Formulas and Results

Even if you know a formula produced the correct result when you first entered it, you can't be sure that the result will always be accurate. After you enter a formula, you might sort, insert, or delete rows or columns in the ranges included in the formula and thereby change the results of the formula. Before printing a spreadsheet or presenting its calculated values as the truth, be sure you check each formula to verify that it refers to the cells you want to calculate and that the formula itself is making the calculation in the proper way. Again, you can use the Show Formulas command to see all the cell references in your formulas quickly and easily.

Use a Reference Area

It's a good idea to insert some notes at the top of the spreadsheet so that you and others can see what it is supposed to accomplish; what assumptions, if any, you're making; and where various parts of the spreadsheet are located. This *reference area* helps explain what's being done in the spreadsheet. You can also enter key values in the reference area at the top of the spreadsheet and then refer to them in the spreadsheet formulas. When you want to do "what if" calculations, it's easy to change the amounts in the reference area and have the change take place in every formula that refers to them.

Let's say you're making a sales forecast. In the reference area, you might type a line that reads *Assumed annual sales growth, 19%*. If you are careful to enter *19%* in its own cell to the right of the text, it becomes a value. You can then refer to that cell in calculating the growth rate for the forecast itself. If you want to see how sales will look if the growth rate is 22%, you can simply change the % value in the reference area to 22%, and the spreadsheet recalculates.

Reference areas are particularly useful when you have several values that you might want to change or several assumptions that you want to make known. In Chapter 7, we'll see a loan amortization template that contains a reference area.

Watch Out When Sorting Rows or Columns

Microsoft Works lets you sort rows in ascending or descending order based on the contents of up to three columns by using the Sort Rows command on the Select menu (Alt-S-O). (See "Sorting Groups of Rows" in Chapter 7 for more information.) You need to be careful when you sort rows that contain formulas or sort rows whose cells are referred to in formulas because sorting often changes the results of the formulas or moves the formulas to a different location. Let's look at two examples. Suppose that rows 1 and 2 of a spreadsheet contain values and that row 3 contains a formula that adds the values in rows 1 and 2, like this:

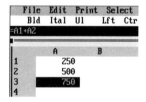

The formula in A3 is = A1 + A2, and the result it produces is *750*. If you select rows 1 through 3 and sort column A in descending order, however, Works rearranges the rows so that the contents of cell A3 are in cell A1, because 750 is the largest value of the three. When it moves the contents of cell A3, however,

Works actually moves the formula = A1 + A2, and it adjusts the cell references in the formula to reflect the formula's new location, like this:

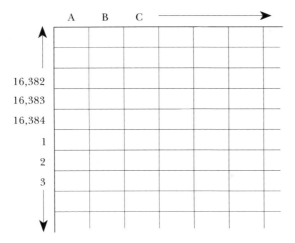

Now the formula in cell A1 adds the contents of the two cells above it, which are the two cells at the bottom of the spreadsheet, A16384 and A16383.

You can also run into problems when cells referred to in a formula (rather than the formula itself) move following a sort. Suppose you have a SUM formula that adds only the Utilities and Phone expenses in a budget, like the one in cell B11 here:

```
 File  Edit  Print  Select  Format  Options  View  Window  Help
   Bld  Ital  Ul     Lft  Ctr  Rt      $  %  ,     Sum    Width      Chart      Prev
=B4+B5
================================ SHEET1.WKS ======================================
        A              B          C          D          E          F
1   Expense        April      May        June      Qtr. Total
2
3   Rent           $1,500     $1,500     $1,500     $4,500
4   Utilities         $82        $69        $67       $218
5   Phone            $122       $146       $141       $409
6   Equip. Lease      $78       $152       $152       $382
7   Salaries       $4,620     $4,620     $5,120    $14,360
8
9   Total          $6,402     $6,487     $6,980    $19,869
10
11  Util/Phone       $204
12
```

The formula in cell B11 adds the contents of cells B4 and B5 to produce a total of $204. But if we sort rows 3 through 7 based on the contents of column A in ascending order, the locations of the expense values change, and the formula — which still adds the contents of cells B4 and B5 — produces a different result, as shown on the following page.

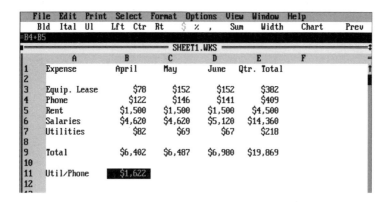

As you can see, it's a good idea to avoid sorting rows that contain formulas when those formulas refer to data in other rows. (Sorting a row using a formula that adds across cells in that same row wouldn't affect the formula.) If you sort rows whose cells are referred to in formulas, be sure to check the formulas carefully afterward to verify that Works is still calculating the values you want to calculate.

Tips on Using Dates and Times

The Works Spreadsheet treats dates and times differently from other numbers, and the results can be confusing in cells in which you've entered dates or times. Here are some ideas to keep in mind about dates and times in spreadsheets:

- When you enter a date, Works converts it to a value that equals the number of days between that date and January 1, 1900. If you enter *1/1/93*, for example, Works stores that date as 33970. (To view the actual date number, use the Show Formulas command on the Options menu.) Although Works might not display this sequential number as the contents of the cell, it will present the number when you refer to the cell in a formula. So if you enter the date *1/1/93* in cell A1 and then copy the contents of that cell into other cells or use the cell as a reference in a formula, Works copies the number 33970 into the other cells and uses that as the value of cell A1 in the formula.

KEYBOARD TIP: You can press Ctrl-; and then press Enter to enter the current date, and you can press Ctrl-: and then press Enter to enter the current time.

- You can enter times in the spreadsheet as hours and minutes, AM or PM, with or without seconds. However, Works stores times as fractions of the number 1, where 12:00 AM (midnight) is 0 and all other times are fractions of 1. For example, 12:00 PM (noon) is stored as 0.5.

- Works won't recognize dates earlier than 1/1/1900 or later than 6/3/2079. If you enter a date outside this range, Works treats it as text.

- You can use a formula that contains time or date functions to have the Spreadsheet calculate the value of the current date and time, extract the hour or day from a time or date, or perform other operations. See *Date and Time Functions* in Appendix A in the *Microsoft Works User's Guide* for more information.

 WORKS TIP: If you use a command to enter the current date or time and the information is wrong, choose the File Management command from the File menu, and then double-click the Set Date & Time command in the dialog box to set the correct date and time.

Use Macros to Speed Repetitive Operations

You can use the built-in macro feature in Works to handle operations that you perform repeatedly in the Works Spreadsheet. Works lets you record strings of commands or repetitive data-entry operations. Any time you need to execute a procedure that requires several commands — whether you're copying, formatting, moving, or inserting data — you can automate the procedure by using a macro. Be on the lookout for repetitive operations, and when you discover one, consider recording a macro to automate it in the future. For more general information about creating macros, see Chapter 1.

FORMATTING

Formatting is the last step before printing a spreadsheet. In Chapter 5, we explored some ways to insert rows and to align the contents of cells to make spreadsheets more readable. But Microsoft Works gives you other ways to arrange spreadsheet data to make it more useful or more easily comprehensible.

Consolidate Several Spreadsheets

The Works Spreadsheet doesn't allow you to link data between separate Spreadsheet files or to automatically consolidate or transfer data from several files to one master file. These features are often used for breaking one large spreadsheet into several smaller ones that are easier to work with. In a corporate budget, for example, you might have one file for the production budget, which you would give to the production manager, and another file for sales, which you would give to the sales manager.

Although Works doesn't support spreadsheet linking and consolidation (allowing values from separate spreadsheets to be copied onto a master spreadsheet), you can create separate spreadsheet areas in the same document. Using cell references, range names, and a little layout creativity, you can approximate linking and consolidation functions in Works.

Let's say you're making a corporate expense and income statement, and you want to divide it into separate areas that represent income and administrative, sales, and production expenses. Each area of the budget has several line items and a subtotal. The administrative area might look like this:

```
 File  Edit  Print  Select  Format  Options  View  Window  Help
  Bld  Ital  Ul     Lft  Ctr  Rt    $  %  ,    Sum   Width   Chart    Prev

═══════════════════════ ADMINBUD.WKS ═══════════════════════
          AC              AD        AE        AF        AG        AH
22  Administrative Budget
23                     January  February    March     April      May
24  Office Lease          2200      2200      2200      2200      2200
25  Office Utilities       120       121       118       130       132
26  Telephone              342       320       280       299       311
27  Liability Insurance    425       425       425       425       425
28  Workmen's Comp.        200       200       200       200       200
29  Health Insurance      1800      1800      1800      1800      1800
30  Salaries              9200      9200      9200      9200      9200
31  Office Supplies        125       140       132       200       110
32  Equipment Leases       350       350       350       350       350
33
34  Total Admin. Budget  14762     14756     14705     14804     14728
35
```

Along with the three budget areas, however, you want to create an overall budget *summary area* so that the top brass can see only the total income and total expense figures in each of the three areas.

First you would lay out each area on a diagonal to the others so that none of the rows and columns in one area would be used in any other area. Taking this approach, you could insert or delete rows or columns in one area as needed without affecting the data in other areas. This diagonal layout might look like the following:

168

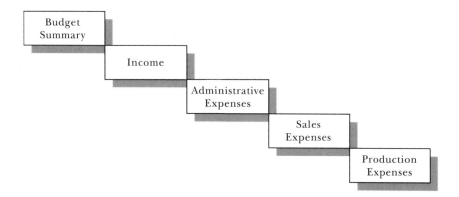

Notice that the budget summary is at the top of the spreadsheet because that's the area that top management would probably want to look at first. Following the budget summary — on the diagonal — are the income area and the three expense areas.

The summary area doesn't contain any values that you would enter manually. Instead, all its cells take their contents from other areas of the spreadsheet through cell references. When you first create the summary area, it might look like this:

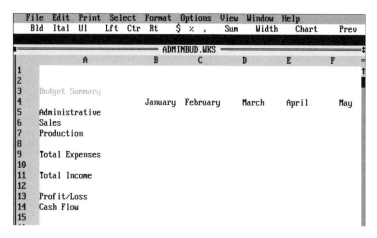

As you create the summary area, you can reference the Total rows in the income and expense areas. If the Income totals for the year are in cells P21:AB21 (starting below the lower-right corner of the summary area), you could enter the appropriate Income cell reference for each month in the Total Income row of the summary area. The January Total Income cell in the summary area (cell B11), for example, would contain the reference = P21. The February Total Income cell in the summary area (cell C11) would contain the reference = Q21, and so on. That way, as you entered and totaled the income amounts for each category in the Income area, Works would transfer the total amounts to the summary area.

The expense areas of the spreadsheet operate on the same principle; you would enter the references for the cells in the Total row of each area as the contents of rows 5 through 7 in the summary area.

To speed navigation from one area to another in this spreadsheet, you can select all the cells in each area and name them as a range. The cells in the income area could be given the range name Income, for example. With these range names, you could use the Go To command, and double-click the name of the range you want to view, and then Works would scroll the spreadsheet to that area immediately. In fact, if you include a reference area at the top of the spreadsheet, you could enter the range names in the same pattern and location that they occupy in the actual spreadsheet. (See the preceding section, "Calculating.") New users will know the location and range name of each section of the spreadsheet.

Another benefit of using range names is that you can select each area of the spreadsheet easily. When you use the Go To command, Works not only scrolls the spreadsheet to that area but also selects all the cells in the range. With all the cells selected in this way, it's easy to copy the entire area into a new spreadsheet file and then give that file to the manager responsible for filling in that budget area. After the manager fills in his or her budget area, you can open the manager's spreadsheet file, select the entire contents, choose the Copy command, and then select the entire budget area in the consolidated spreadsheet and press Enter. The manager's filled-in budget replaces the empty budget area in the master spreadsheet.

 WORKS TIP: When using a diagonal layout for separate sections of a budget, you can use the Insert Page Break command on the Print menu (Alt-P-I) to insert a page break at the upper-left corner of each area so that each area prints on a separate page.

As you can see, you can use several of the Works Spreadsheet features to create master, consolidated spreadsheets that are easy to use.

Use Zero Column Widths to Hide Columns

If you want to hide a spreadsheet column from view without deleting it, you can set the column width to 0. The spreadsheet then looks as if it skips the hidden column. If you hide column C, for example, the column labels at the top of the spreadsheet read A, B, D, E, and so on. It's useful to hide columns when you want to print the columns on either side of the one you hide.

If you hide a column, you need only widen it to reveal it again. Of course, after you hide a column, you can't select cells in it. And because you must select a column before you can specify a new column width value, you can't simply enter a new width for a hidden column. To reveal a hidden column, use the following procedure:

1. Select adjacent cells in the columns on either side of the hidden column. (If column C is hidden, select two adjacent cells in columns B and D, for example.)

2. Click the Width tool in the toolbar.

3. Click OK to confirm the current column width. Works then displays the hidden column again, with the same width as the two columns adjacent to it.

If you've hidden column A, however, this procedure won't work. To redisplay column A after you've hidden it, do the following:

1. Select the entire spreadsheet.

2. Click the Width tool in the toolbar, and then set a new width, or press Enter to accept the default width.

3. Click OK. Works then redisplays all columns, including column A, in the new width.

 WORKS TIP: Click the Width tool in the toolbar to choose the Column Width command quickly, and then click the Best Fit option to have Works automatically set column widths to accommodate the widest entries in those columns.

Format Spreadsheet Data in the Word Processor

Works restricts you to one font and one font size for an entire Spreadsheet document, but by copying spreadsheet data into a Word Processor document, you can gain the added formatting flexibility the Word Processor offers. Simply select the spreadsheet data you want to reformat, copy it into a new Word Processor document, select the specific labels or values that you want to reformat, and then change them using Format menu commands of the Works Word Processor.

In the Word Processor, you can select any label or value and change its font or font size, choose other options such as superscript or subscript, or place borders around groups of numbers. You might find that you need to adjust the spacing so that your numbers line up correctly.

CHARTING

Microsoft Works gives you a lot of flexibility in creating charts of spreadsheet data. It's easy to make a simple chart, and you can do a lot to dress up your data. Nevertheless, the array of options can be a little confusing. The techniques suggested in this section will help you make the most of Works' charting features.

Keep It Simple

The whole point of charting data is to use a visual method to show relationships between numbers quickly and dramatically. Works lets you create a combined line and bar chart, add a right-hand Y-axis, add data labels, and change a chart's colors, patterns, and markers. However, you must be careful not to sacrifice clarity by adding visual complexity. A chart should be no more complex than it needs to be to display the data relationships that you want to show.

Plot Values of the Same Magnitude to Avoid Using a Second Y-Axis

Try to select Y-series whose values are in the same numeric range. If some of the values in a chart are under 100 and others are over 10,000, the scale for that chart must be so broad that it will be difficult to see the difference between bars at either end of the scale. On a chart whose Y-axis scale runs from 0 to 10,000, for example, you won't be able to notice the difference between a bar that shows the value 120 and a bar that shows the value 150.

The purpose of a second (or right-hand) Y-axis is to present a second scale, which supposedly helps readers distinguish between widely diverse ranges of values from different Y-series in the same chart. Even when you use a second Y-axis, however, things often don't become much clearer. For example, the following chart has a right-hand Y-axis for the smaller Utilities, Phone, and Equip. Lease expenses:

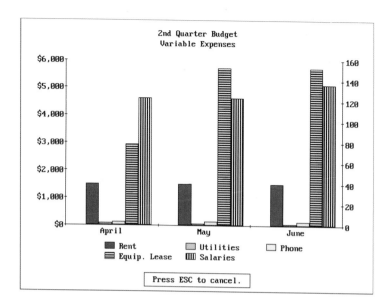

It's difficult to determine which expenses relate to which Y-axis. The best way to show the smaller Utilities, Phone, and Equip. Lease expenses is to plot them in a separate chart.

Don't Explode More Than One Slice of a Pie

You can explode a slice of a pie chart away from the rest for emphasis by using the Data Format command on the Format menu in Chart mode. However, when you explode more than one pie slice, you emphasize two or more data values equally and therefore do not give special emphasis to any of them.

Stick with the Default Colors and Patterns

Works does a good job of choosing different colors, patterns, and markers for displaying your data. When you change only one of the default colors, patterns, or markers, the chances are you'll choose a substitute that doesn't fit as well with the others in the chart. When this happens, you'll be tempted to change the color, pattern, or marker settings for other data series, and you'll end up spending a lot of time getting all the combinations right again.

Minimize Titles and Data Labels

Unless it isn't clear what measure you're using for an X-axis or a Y-axis scale, or unless it's critical to show the actual amount represented by a bar, line, point, or pie slice, avoid using extra titles and data labels. The more text you put on a chart, the more you divert the reader's attention from the graphic data relationship of the chart. When you must use titles, make them as short and clear as possible.

Duplicate Charts to Explore Options

If you're going to explore Works' charting options to embellish a chart, it's a good idea to first make a copy of the chart and modify the copy. That way, if you end up making the chart look unattractive and you can't remember how it got that way, you can easily return to the original, simple version. Use the Charts command on the View menu to copy and rename charts.

Check Chart Changes As You Make Them

Whenever you fiddle with a chart's definition, display the chart again to see how the change affects it. Press Shift-F10 or click the Chart tool in the toolbar to display a chart after you've changed its definition. By doing this after you make each change, it will be easier for you to undo the change if you don't like it. If you make a whole series of changes before displaying the chart, you'll have to remember which option controls which chart element.

Use Grid Lines to Aid Readability

Works' chart options don't include grid lines by default, but you might occasionally want to add them to your charts. To help readers match bar, line, or point positions with the values on the Y-axis, it helps to include a grid that extends from the Y-axis values across the chart, like this:

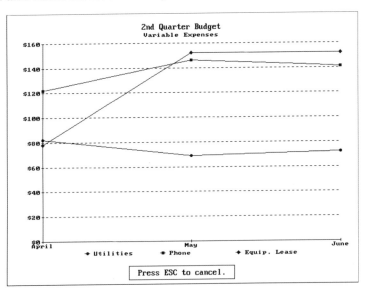

You can add a horizontal grid to the Y-axis by using the Y-Axis command on the Options menu (Alt-O-Y). If you're plotting an X-Y chart, it might also help to add vertical grid lines that extend up from the X-axis. Use the X-Axis command on the Options menu (Alt-O-X) to add an X-axis grid.

PRINTING

Spreadsheets can be difficult to print properly: Among other challenges, you often have more data than can fit on a single page. The following are some tips that make printing easy and that ensure the legibility of your spreadsheets. Also included are two tips on printing charts.

Use Efficient Column Labels and Cell Formatting to Maximize Horizontal Space on a Page

Typically, you end up with more columns in a spreadsheet than you can print across a page, so the challenge is to squeeze as many columns across the width of a page as possible. You can make the most of a page's width by keeping column labels short and by using efficient cell formats.

Whenever possible, a column label should be no wider than the numbers in the column itself. If your column contains five-digit numbers, try to use a five-character column label at the top. That way, you can reduce the column width to six characters to display the numbers without chopping off part of the column label.

Also, don't format cells for more decimal places than is necessary. If all your figures are in even dollars (no cents), for example, don't format the cells for dollars with two decimal places. By eliminating the decimal point and the two zeros from the end of each number, you can save three character spaces in the column width. Furthermore, if you use the Fixed cell format instead of the Currency cell format, you'll also save the extra character spaces used for dollar signs and commas in the Currency cell format.

Use Page Breaks to Divide Data Logically

Before printing a spreadsheet, use the Preview command on the Print menu or the Prev tool on the toolbar to check the page breaks to be sure that each page contains a logical grouping of data. If one of these breaks falls in the middle of a group of rows or columns, set a manual page break with the Insert Page Break command on the Print menu (Alt-P-I) so that the page doesn't end in the middle of a group. When you insert a page break, you will see a double arrow next to the row or column label that will begin the new page. On a budget spreadsheet, for example, you probably won't be able to print all 12 months on one page. Instead, try setting page breaks at each quarter, or after six months, so that the data is more logically grouped on each page.

NOTE: *To delete a page break, use the Delete Page Break command on the Print menu (Alt-P-D).*

Print Extra Information to Aid Other Spreadsheet Readers

If you're printing a spreadsheet for others, it might be a good idea to use the Print Row and Column Labels option in the Print dialog box. Selecting this option tells Microsoft Works to include the row and column labels on the printed spreadsheet, which make it easy to refer to specific cells. If you're in a meeting, for example, it's easier to say "cell B23" than it is to say "the fourth cell below the Income totals, in the second column."

Print Only Selected Parts of a Spreadsheet

If you need a printout of some numbers, they'll be easier to read if you don't also print a lot of numbers that you don't need. Works normally prints whole pages from a spreadsheet, but you can use the Set Print Area command on the Print menu to print only a selected part of a spreadsheet. Simply select the group of cells you want to print, choose the Set Print Area command (Alt-P-A), and click OK or press Enter to confirm the selection. When you print the page, Works prints only the cells you selected.

Make Sample Printouts of Charts

What you see on your screen isn't necessarily what you'll get from your printer — and this is more often the case with charts than it is with text-only documents. You might start with a nice pie chart on the screen, only to discover that your printer turns the round pie into an oval when it prints. Or you might find that a pattern that looked good on the screen looks awful on paper. These problems often crop up when you resize charts or change their default colors, patterns, or markers. Always print your charts on paper to make sure that they look the way you want before you consider the job done.

Display Charts in Black and White to Match Monochrome Printing

If your screen is set to display in color and you've selected color printing options using the Data Format command in the Format menu or you've had Works automatically assign colors (which is the default chart display mode), your chart will appear in color when you view it on the screen. If your printer prints in black and white, however, it would be better to view the chart in black and white so that you can see how Works substitutes different patterns for colors. To view a chart in black and white, choose the Format For B&W command from the Print menu (Alt-P-F).

These are some ideas you can use to get more out of the Microsoft Works Spreadsheet. As you gain experience using this tool, you'll discover other shortcuts and techniques that will make Works work harder and faster for you.

7

Spreadsheet & Charting Projects

In this chapter, we'll see Microsoft Works' Spreadsheet and Charting tools in action as we create a budget and cash flow spreadsheet, produce an advertising tracking and analysis spreadsheet, and use the loan amortization template. By completing these spreadsheet projects, you'll learn some practical uses for the Works Spreadsheet's features.

A BUDGET AND CASH FLOW SPREADSHEET

The column-and-row structure of a spreadsheet is ideally suited for tracking various expenses or income sources over a designated period to create a budget. Nearly everyone can benefit from a budget and cash flow spreadsheet because such a tool can show exactly what the cash position is each month and help to predict future financial needs.

We built a simple budget spreadsheet in Chapter 5. The Microsoft Works program also comes with a Personal Budget template that tracks actual expenses and income versus budgeted amounts for one month. In this project, we'll build another variation on this theme that shows month-to-month cash flow. The finished budget and cash flow spreadsheet is shown in Figure 7-1 on the next two pages.

To complete this spreadsheet, we'll fill in sample expense and income categories and sample dollar amounts. We'll save the spreadsheet as a template so that you can open it later as a new document and then fill in your actual

```
                                    Budget - 5/5/93 - Page 1

                 A          B        C       D      E      F     G
       1                  January February March April  May  June
       2    Home Expenses
       3
       4    Food            300      300     300    300   300   300
       5    Garbage          12       12      12     12    12    12
       6    Insurance       150      150     150    150   150   150
       7    Medical          25       25      25     25    25    25
       8    Phone            50       50      50     50    50    50
       9    Rent            750      750     750    750   750   750
      10    Utilities        75       75      75     75    75    75
      11    Water            10       10      10     10    10    10
      12
      13    Subtotal Home  1372     1372    1372   1372  1372  1372
      14
      15    Auto Expenses
      16
      17    Auto Exp.        50       50      50     50    50    50
      18    Auto Ins.        65       65      65     65    65    65
      19    Auto Loan       145      145     145    145   145   145
      20
      21    Subtotal Auto   260      260     260    260   260   260
      22
      23    Total Expenses 1632     1632    1632   1632  1632  1632
      24
      25    Income
      26
      27    Wages          2300     2300    2300   2300  2300  2300
      28    Interest          5        5       5      5     5     5
      29    Other           100      100     100    100   100   100
      30
      31    Total Income   2405     2405    2405   2405  2405  2405
      32    Total Expenses 1632     1632    1632   1632  1632  1632
      33    Cash Flow       773     1546    2319   3092  3865  4638
```

Figure 7-1.   *(continued)*
This spreadsheet helps track expenses and income so that you can project future financial needs.

expense and income categories and amounts. The spreadsheet's structure suits it for both business and personal use.

WORKS TIP: We printed the spreadsheet in Figure 7-1 using the Print row and column labels option so it would be easier to identify specific cells.

Figure 7-1. *continued*

```
                                    Budget - 5/5/93 - Page 2

                H       I        J         K          L          M        N
        1     July   August  September  October  November  December  Total
        2
        3
        4      300     300      300       300       300       300     3600
        5       12      12       12        12        12        12      144
        6      150     150      150       150       150       150     1800
        7       25      25       25        25        25        25      300
        8       50      50       50        50        50        50      600
        9      750     750      750       750       750       750     9000
       10       75      75       75        75        75        75      900
       11       10      10       10        10        10        10      120
       12
       13     1372    1372     1372      1372      1372      1372    16464
       14
       15
       16
       17       50      50       50        50        50        50      600
       18       65      65       65        65        65        65      780
       19      145     145      145       145       145       145     1740
       20
       21      260     260      260       260       260       260     3120
       22
       23     1632    1632     1632      1632      1632      1632    19584
       24
       25
       26
       27     2300    2300     2300      2300      2300      2300    27600
       28        5       5        5         5         5         5       60
       29      100     100      100       100       100       100     1200
       30
       31     2405    2405     2405      2405      2405      2405    28860
       32     1632    1632     1632      1632      1632      1632    19584
       33     5411    6184     6957      7730      8503      9276
```

Entering the Spreadsheet Labels

To begin this project, we'll open a new spreadsheet file and enter all the row and column labels.

1. Choose the Create New File command from the File menu (Alt-F-N).

2. Click the Spreadsheet document type.

3. Double-click the Standard/Blank template name. Works opens a new Spreadsheet file.

Most of the column labels are months of the year, so we can use Works' Fill Series command to enter them quickly.

1. Click cell B1.

2. Type *Jan* and press Enter. Works recognizes Jan as the abbreviation for a month name, converts it to *January,* and enters the label.

3. Click cell B1, and drag the pointer to cell M1 to select this group of 12 cells.

4. Choose the Fill Series command from the Edit menu (Alt-E-L). Works displays the Fill Series dialog box, like this:

In the Fill Series dialog box, you can specify a series of values or labels to be entered in a selected range of cells.

1. Click the Month units option. The Step By value is set at the default of 1, which tells Works to enter a series of month labels, moving from one month to the next. We want column labels for every month, so this setting is correct.

2. Click OK to confirm the selection. Works fills the selected cells with month labels from February through December in cells C1 through M1.

The final column label will show total amounts in each expense and income category.

1. Click cell N1.

2. Type *Total* and then press Enter.

Now we'll enter the expense and income category labels in column A. Before we do, however, we'll widen column A so it will have enough room for the labels we're about to enter.

1. Press Home to select cell A1.

2. Click the Width tool in the toolbar. Works displays the Column Width dialog box.

3. Type *15* and press Enter. Works widens column A.

When you create a new spreadsheet, you don't always enter labels in exactly the order in which you want them to appear. For this exercise, we'll deliberately enter the labels out of order so that we can use Works' sorting and editing features to fix them.

1. Select cell A2.

2. Type *Expenses* and then click cell A4. Works enters the label in cell A2.

3. Type *Rent* and press the Down arrow key.

4. Repeat step 3, entering the rest of the expense and income labels shown in Figure 7-2 on the next page.

 MOUSE TIP: If you're only typing labels or values, clicking another cell always tells Works to complete the entry in the current cell. However, if you're entering a formula, clicking another cell adds that cell's reference to the formula.

Inserting Extra Rows

The expenses rows might be easier to work with later if we could divide them up into household and auto groups and if they were alphabetically sorted within each of those groups. Let's add some subcategory and subtotal labels and move the expense labels around to make this change.

1. Click to the left of cell A12 to select all of row 12. Choose the Insert Row/Column command from the Edit menu (Alt-E-I). Works inserts a blank row. The Auto Ins. label and the labels below it all move down, and a blank row appears.

2. Repeat step 1 four more times so that five blank rows separate the Medical and Auto Ins. labels. You could also select rows 12 through 16 (row 12 plus four rows below it), and choose the Insert Row/Column command to insert these five blank rows.

3. Select cell A13, type *Subtotal Home,* and press Enter.

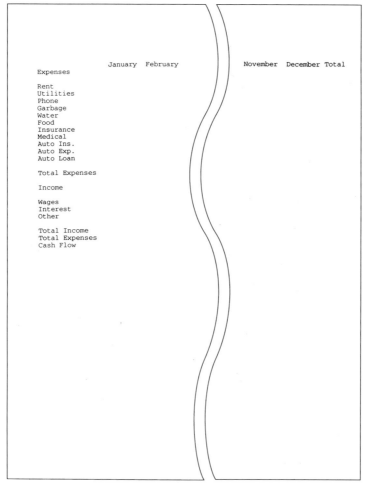

```
                         January  February            November  December Total
        Expenses

        Rent
        Utilities
        Phone
        Garbage
        Water
        Food
        Insurance
        Medical
        Auto Ins.
        Auto Exp.
        Auto Loan

        Total Expenses

        Income

        Wages
        Interest
        Other

        Total Income
        Total Expenses
        Cash Flow
```

Figure 7-2.
These spreadsheet labels must be sorted before they'll be in the same order as the labels in Figure 7-1.

WORKS TIP: If you select a single cell and choose the Insert Row/ Column command, Works presents a dialog box where you must choose whether to insert a row or a column. If you select an entire row or column first, however, Works automatically inserts a new row or column, depending on which you have selected.

4. Select cell A15, type *Auto Expenses,* and press Enter.

5. Select row 20 and insert two more rows between the Auto Loan and Total Expenses labels.

6. Select cell A21, type *Subtotal Auto,* and press Enter.

7. Select cell A2 (where the Expenses label is now located), and type *Home Expenses.* Then press Enter to change the label.

KEYBOARD TIP: When you're repeating the same menu command several times, as in step 2, it's faster to use the keyboard command (Alt-E-I in this case) and then press Enter to confirm the selection in the dialog box, if necessary.

Sorting Groups of Rows

With the number of rows and the labels now correct, let's sort each group of expense labels. We can't simply select all the labels in column A because Works would sort the category titles and subtotal rows together in one list. Instead, we have to select the labels within each category.

1. Select cell A4, hold down the mouse button, and drag the pointer down to cell A11.

2. Choose the Sort Rows command from the Select menu (Alt-S-O). Works displays the Sort Rows dialog box, like this:

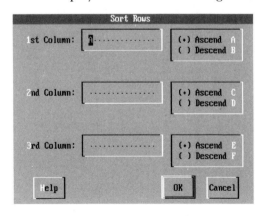

Works lets you sort on up to three columns at one time, but in this case we want to sort based on only the labels in column A. We want them to be in ascending alphabetic order. These options are already selected as the defaults, so do the following:

3. Click OK to confirm the default sort settings. Works arranges rows 4 through 11 so that the labels are in ascending alphabetic order.

4. Sort the Auto Expenses category labels in rows 17 through 19 in the same way.

Now our labels are arranged in the way that we want them.

Entering the Spreadsheet Values

Next we'll enter the initial spreadsheet values. In this type of budget spreadsheet, we would first enter our best estimates of our expenses and income and then adjust those values to actual values as each month passes. Here we'll enter some projected amounts, using Works' Fill Right command to help.

1. Select cell B4.

2. Type *300* and press Enter.

3. Select the range B4:M4 by holding down the mouse button and dragging the pointer over it.

4. Choose the Fill Right command from the Edit menu (Alt-E-R). Works fills the Food expense cells for every month with the value 300.

As you can see in Figure 7-1, each of the expense and income category amounts in this spreadsheet is the same for every month. You can use the Fill Right command to enter all the like amounts more quickly. In fact, where several adjacent rows have like amounts — as in rows 5 through 11, 17 through 19, and 27 through 29 here — you can select all the rows at the same time and use the Fill Right command to fill them. Here's how:

1. Select cell B5, and type all the values in cells B5:B11, as shown in Figure 7-1.

2. Select cell B5, hold down the mouse button, and drag the pointer down to cell B11 and then across to column M to select the block of cells in the range B5:M11.

3. Choose the Fill Right command. Works then fills all the rows, each with the value it contained in column B.

Enter the other expense and income amounts for January in column B from Figure 7-1 in rows 17 through 19 and 27 through 29. Then use the Fill Right command to insert the values in columns C through M. When you finish, the values should match those in Figure 7-1. Don't enter values in the Total or Subtotal cells — we'll fill these cells by entering formulas in them.

 WORKS TIP: Check the left edge of the status line if you're not sure that you've selected the correct range. The current selection always appears there.

Using Autosum to Sum Rows and Columns

Now we'll use Works' Autosum feature to quickly calculate some subtotals and totals in this spreadsheet. First we'll do the monthly subtotals for each expense and income category.

1. Select cell B13, which is the Home Expenses subtotal for January. We want to total all the January home expenses in cells B4 through B11, and the fastest way to do this is to use Works' Autosum feature.

2. Click the Sum tool in the toolbar. Works creates a formula to sum the cells above cell B13, like this:

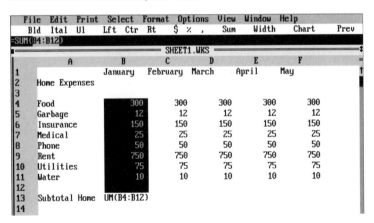

When you use Autosum, Works always sums all the cells above or to the left of the current cell, as long as they don't contain text. In this case, Works begins the range at the first cell that contains a value (B4) and extends it down to the cell directly above the selected cell (B12), even though row 12 is blank. We could leave the formula the way it is, but let's edit it to make it more accurate. The cursor is already blinking in the formula bar, so the edit will be easy.

1. Click cell B4, and drag the pointer down to cell B11. Works inserts this range inside the formula's parentheses.

2. Press Enter to complete the formula. Works calculates the formula, and the total of the home expenses for January appears in cell B13.

Next use the same basic procedure to create a subtotal of the auto expenses in cell B21 and the total income in cell B31:

1. Click cell B21, click the Sum tool, edit the formula to contain the proper cell references (B17:B19), and press Enter.

2. Click cell B31, click the Sum tool, edit the formula to contain the reference B27:B29, and press Enter.

Finally we can use the Autosum feature to create formulas for the yearly totals in column N. This time there are no blank columns in the range Autosum will create, so we don't have to edit the formula at all.

1. Press F5 and type *N4* in the Go To dialog box to go to and select cell N4. Click the Sum tool. Works creates a Sum formula with the range B4:M4, which is the range we want.

2. Press Enter to enter the formula. Works calculates the year's total for food expenses.

3. Repeat steps 1 and 2 in cells N17 and N27.

Copying Formulas

Because these row and column formulas are the same for every month-total cell in row 13 and every year-total cell in column N, we can copy them using the Fill Right and Fill Down commands, in the same way as we copied the values earlier.

1. Go to and select cell B13, hold down the mouse button, and drag the pointer across to cell M13.

2. Choose the Fill Right command (Alt-E-R). Works fills all the subtotal cells in row 13 with copies of the formula in cell B13 and calculates the totals. Because we used relative cell references in the formula, each copy of the formula Works made with the Fill Right command contains the correct cell references. (See Chapter 5 for more information about relative cell references.)

3. Select the range of cells B21:M21, and choose the Fill Right command to fill in the Subtotal Auto row.

4. Select the range of cells B31:M31, and choose the Fill Right command to fill in the Total Income row.

5. Go to and select the range of cells N4:N11, and choose the Fill Down command (Alt-E-F) to copy the total formula into these cells.

6. Select the range of cells N17:N19, and choose the Fill Down command to copy the total formula into these cells.

7. Select the range of cells N27:N29, and choose the Fill down command to copy the total formula into these cells.

8. Finally, use the Sum tool in the toolbar to enter the missing formulas in cells N13, N21, and N31 to complete this part of the spreadsheet.

Entering and Copying Simple Addition Formulas

Next we'll enter the formulas to calculate each month's total expenses in row 23.

1. Go to and select cell B23, and then type = to begin a formula. For this formula, we will add together individual cells that aren't located in a contiguous range, so we won't use the SUM function.

2. Select cell B13, which is the cell that contains the subtotal of home expenses for January. Works adds this cell reference to the formula.

3. Type +. Works adds the + sign to the formula after the B13 cell reference and returns the cell selection to cell B23.

4. Select cell B21. Works adds it to the formula, like this:

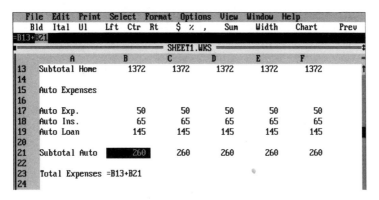

5. Press Enter to end the formula entry. Works calculates the sum of ceils B13 and B21 and displays the total in cell B23.

This formula also uses relative cell references, so use the Fill Right command to copy it into the Total Expenses cells for February through December and the Total column in the range C23:N23.

Creating the Cash Flow Formulas

The summary area at the bottom of the spreadsheet compares total expenses with total income and shows the monthly cash flow. The total expenses in row 32 are the same as the values in row 23, so we can tell Works to enter the contents of cell B23 in cell B32.

1. Select cell B32.

2. Type = to start a formula.

3. Select cell B23. This cell reference appears in the formula bar.

4. Press Enter to enter this formula.

The formula in cell B32 now reads = B23, which tells Works to copy the value from cell B23. Because this is a relative reference, we can now use the Fill Right command to copy the formula in cell B32 to the range C32:N32.

To calculate the cash flow in column B, we subtract the total expenses in cell B32 from the total income in cell B31, as follows:

1. Select cell B33, and type = to start a formula.

2. Select cell B31. This reference is added to the formula.

3. Type − to indicate subtraction, and then select cell B32.

4. Press Enter to enter the formula. Works subtracts the amount in cell B32 from the amount in cell B31 and displays the result in cell B33.

WORKS TIP: In a real budget, a cash flow will probably carry over from the previous month (December). To figure January's cash flow accurately, the carryover amount would have to be included in the total income figure represented by cell B31. The simplest way to handle this is to put the carryover amount in the Other row (cell B29) for that month.

Because we're calculating cash flow in row 33, we'll want the February cash flow to show any remaining cash in January, plus February's income minus February's expenses. To enter this formula, do the following:

1. Select cell C33, and type =(to begin the formula.

2. Select cell B33 (January's cash flow), and then type +.

3. Select cell C31 (February's total income), and then type).

4. Type − and then select cell C32 (February's total expenses). The formula now looks like this:

```
 File  Edit  Print  Select  Format  Options  View  Window  Help
  Bld  Ital  Ul     Lft  Ctr  Rt    $  %  ,    Sum   Width   Chart      Prev
=(B33+C31)-C32
                              SHEET1.WKS
          A            B        C        D        E        F
21  Subtotal Auto     260      260      260      260      260
22
23  Total Expenses   1632     1632     1632     1632     1632
24
25  Income
26
27  Wages            2300     2300     2300     2300     2300
28  Interest            5        5        5        5        5
29  Other             100      100      100      100      100
30
31  Total Income     2405     2405     2405     2405     2405
32  Total Expenses   1632     1632     1632     1632     1632
33  Cash Flow          773 3+C31)-C32
34
```

5. Press Enter. Works calculates the formula and displays the result in cell C33.

Now you can copy this formula in cell C33 into the Cash Flow cells for March through December (D33:M33) using the Fill Right command. There is no formula needed in cell N33 because this row shows month-to-month cash flow, and a yearly total of all months would be meaningless here.

Formatting the Labels

Now let's make the spreadsheet a little more readable, both on the screen and on paper. First we'll make all the column labels bold.

1. Press Ctrl-Home to return to cell A1, and click to the left of row 1 to select the entire row.

2. Click Bld in the toolbar to make these labels bold.

3. Click Rt in the toolbar to specify right alignment for these labels.

Now add emphasis to some other labels on your own. Select the Home Expenses, Subtotal Home, Auto Expenses, Subtotal Auto, Total Expenses (both of them), Income, Total Income, and Cash Flow labels, and make them bold. Because most of these labels are separated only by blank lines, you can select the labels as a group (A13:A15, A21:A25, A31:A33) and make them all bold at the same time. However, if you later enter text in the intervening blank cells, it will appear in bold.

NOTE: *You can also press Ctrl-B to make a cell's contents bold.*

Adjusting the Format for Printing

The next formatting step concerns preparing the spreadsheet for printing. As it is, this spreadsheet will require three sheets of paper to print. Each page will contain all the rows, but more columns are included than will fit across one page. So, using the current layout, the first page will print from the January through the April expenses, the second page will print from the May through the October expenses, and the third page will print the remaining months and the Total column.

We can't squeeze all these columns across only one sheet of paper, but we can make the columns narrower so that a little space remains between each column, and the whole spreadsheet fits across two pages.

1. Choose the All command from the Select menu (Alt-S-A) to select the entire spreadsheet, or click the space just above and to the left of the row and column labels.

NOTE: *You can also press Ctrl-Shift-F8 to select an entire spreadsheet.*

2. Click the Width tool in the toolbar to display the Column Width dialog box.

3. Click the Best Fit box, and then click OK. Works adjusts each column so it is just wide enough to accommodate its widest entry.

Finally, because this is a two-page spreadsheet, we'll add a header that contains the spreadsheet name and the page number.

1. Choose the Headers & Footers command from the Print menu (Alt-P-H). Works then displays the Headers & Footers dialog box, like this:

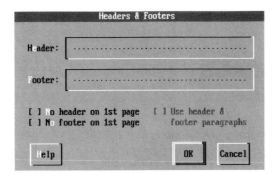

2. Type *&RBudget - &D - Page &P* and click OK.

3. Click Prev in the toolbar and then click the Preview button to see the spreadsheet's two pages and header.

 WORKS TIP: In the Spreadsheet, the Use Header & Footer Paragraphs option is unavailable. You can have only one-line headers and footers in the Works Spreadsheet.

As you can see in the printout in Figure 7-1, the header commands insert the current date and page number when you print or preview the file. The &R, &D, and &P are special header formatting codes that tell Works to right-align the header (&R), insert the current date (&D), and insert the current page number (&P). For more information about header formatting commands, choose the Headers & Footers command from the Print menu, and then click the Help button in the dialog box that appears.

Saving and Using the Template

To reuse this budget spreadsheet for your own finances, you can save it and then use it later as a template.

1. Choose the Save As command (Alt-F-A). Works displays the Save As dialog box.

2. Click the Save As Template option, and then click OK.

3. Type the filename *Budgtemp*.

4. Press Enter to save the file.

Now this file will appear in the Templates list when you choose the Create New File command and choose Spreadsheet documents. You can open this file as an untitled spreadsheet, make the changes you need, and then save the changed file with a different name. The template will remain unchanged on the disk.

For your own purposes, you'll probably want to make some modifications to this spreadsheet such as adding or changing expense or income categories. Here are some tips for doing so:

- Edit the existing category names to change them to the names you want, rather than deleting rows.

- If you must insert additional rows, insert them in alphabetic order to maintain the alphabetic sort of the expense and income categories. Do not sort this spreadsheet again because sorting could make the formulas that refer to the sorted rows inaccurate.

- Check all formulas when you're finished to be sure that they still refer to the cells you want to calculate. Use the Show Formulas command on the Options menu (Alt-O-F) to display all your formulas at once.

Now let's move on to an analytical task that puts Works' charting features to use.

AN ADVERTISING ANALYSIS

In this project, we'll see how Microsoft Works' charting features can reveal different bits of information about our data. In this spreadsheet, a mail-order business is tracking the responses it has received from various advertisements. The ads are running in the June, July, and August issues of four monthly magazines, and the spreadsheet shows the number of responses for each month. By plotting those response results in different ways, we can reveal different trends.

Entering Spreadsheet Labels and Values

To begin this project, we'll need to create a spreadsheet from which to chart the data. The spreadsheet we'll use is shown in Figure 7-3.

After we enter the labels and values, we'll add formulas to calculate the totals in row 8 and column E.

1. Open a new Works spreadsheet with a Standard/Blank template. Choose the Save As command (Alt-F-A), type the name *Advanal*, and then press Enter to save the file as ADVANAL.WKS.

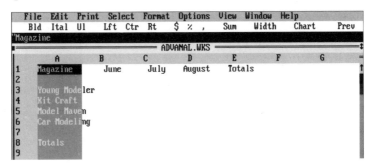

```
 File  Edit  Print  Select  Format  Options  View  Window  Help
  Bld  Ital  Ul      Lft  Ctr  Rt    $  %  ,     Sum    Width      Chart       Prev

                         ADUANAL.WKS
        A           B        C        D        E        F
1 Magazine        June     July    August   Totals
2
3 Young Modeler     11        8        9       28
4 Kit Craft         17       14       15       46
5 Model Maven       13       28       19       60
6 Car Modeling      25       35       45      105
7
8 Totals            66       85       88      239
9
10
11
12
13
14
15
16
17
A10                                                        <F1=HELP>
Press ALT to choose commands, or F2 to edit.
```

Figure 7-3.
This spreadsheet tracks responses to advertisements in various magazines.

2. Cell A1 is selected. Type *Magazine,* and press Tab to select cell B1.

3. Type *June* and press Tab.

4. Repeat step 3, and enter labels in row 1 based on Figure 7-3.

5. Select cell A3 and type *Young Modeler.*

6. Select cell A4 and type *Kit Craft.*

7. Enter the other labels in column A, and then click on the column label above the *Magazine* label to select the entire column. The spreadsheet looks like this:

```
 File  Edit  Print  Select  Format  Options  View  Window  Help
  Bld  Ital  Ul      Lft  Ctr  Rt    $  %  ,     Sum    Width      Chart       Prev
Magazine
                         ADUANAL.WKS
        A           B        C        D        E        F        G
1 Magazine        June     July    August   Totals
2
3 Young Modeler
4 Kit Craft
5 Model Maven
6 Car Modeling
7
8 Totals
9
```

As you can see, column A is currently too narrow to accommodate three of the magazine titles, so they've spilled over into column B. We need to use column B for numbers, so let's use the Best Fit feature to have Works widen column A.

1. Click the Width tool in the toolbar. Works displays the Column Width dialog box.

2. Click the Best Fit box, and then click OK. Works widens column A to accommodate all the magazine titles.

Now enter the values as shown in Figure 7-3, except for the total amounts. Notice that the Totals label in cell E1 is right-aligned; you can align the label this way by selecting cell E1 and clicking the Rt tool in the toolbar.

Entering and Copying Formulas

The totals in column E and row 8 are all produced by SUM formulas. We can enter one formula in cell B8 and copy it to the right, and we can enter one formula in cell E3 and copy it down.

1. Select cell B8 and click the Sum tool in the toolbar.

2. Select cell B3, hold down the mouse button, and drag the pointer down to cell B6. Works enters the range B3:B6 in the formula.

3. Press Enter to finish the formula.

4. Select cells B8 through E8.

5. Choose the Fill Right command from the Edit menu (Alt-E-R). Works copies the formula across the spreadsheet. Notice there's a 0 in cell E8 at this point, because there are no values in the cells above it yet.

6. Select cell E3, and then click the Sum tool in the toolbar. Works automatically creates the formula SUM(B3:D3).

7. Press Enter to enter this formula.

8. Select the range of cells E3 through E6, and choose the Fill Down command from the Edit menu (Alt-E-F).

Works now displays all the totals in this spreadsheet, just as in Figure 7-3.

Saving the File

Now let's save this spreadsheet again by choosing the Save command from the File menu (Alt-F-S).

> **WORKS TIP:** Works only displays the Save As dialog box when you choose the Save command and you haven't yet saved a new file. Once you've saved the file, choosing the Save command saves the file with the same name at the same location, and Works doesn't present a dialog box.

With the completed spreadsheet safely on disk, we're ready to begin charting our data.

Creating a Bar Chart

The spreadsheet shows monthly response figures for each of four magazines, but displaying this data in charts will help us spot some key relationships and facts. Let's suppose we want to plot a chart that shows which magazines did the best each month. To begin charting, we must first select the data we want to chart. Because we want to compare the monthly response figures for each magazine each month, we'll select all three months' data from all four magazines.

1. Select cell A1, hold down the mouse button, and drag the pointer down to cell A6 and then across to cell D6. The entire block of response figures, magazine labels, and month labels is selected. We've selected the month labels in row 1 and the magazine names in column A so that Works will use them in the chart as the X-axis labels and the data legends, respectively.

2. Click the Chart tool in the toolbar. Works displays a bar chart on the screen, as shown on the following page.

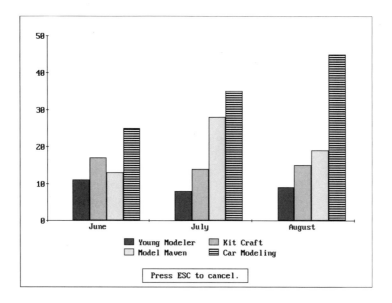

This chart makes it clear that *Car Modeling* magazine is the response leader every month, with *Model Maven* coming in second. Thus, if we could afford to advertise in only two magazines each month, this chart would make it easy to identify the two best-selling magazines each month.

 WORKS TIP: If you're using a color monitor, your chart will be in color instead of black and white, as it is here. To make your chart look like this one, choose the Format For B&W command from the Print menu (Alt-P-F) after you return to the Chart mode screen (discussed below).

Changing the Chart Type

Let's change the chart format to a stacked bar chart so that we can get a better idea of exactly how much of the total response volume each magazine represents every month.

1. Press Esc to display the Chart mode screen.

2. Click the Stk-Bar tool in the toolbar.

3. Click the Chart tool to display the chart again, like this:

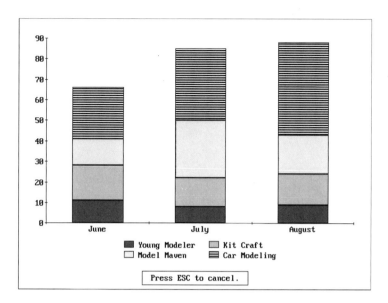

Now we can easily see that *Car Modeling* magazine represents from one-third to one-half of the total response volume every month — it's obviously a good advertising vehicle for us. The chart also shows that although *Kit Craft* and *Young Modeler* were fairly consistent from month to month, *Model Maven* had a big month in July and continued pulling in the second most responses in August. Finally, we can easily see that the largest number of responses came in during July and August, so if we could afford advertisements during only two months, these two would be the best choices.

Making a Pie Chart

Now let's suppose that we want to see how each magazine contributed to the total number of responses for the entire period so that we can determine, for example, whether the most expensive magazine is delivering the most orders. To see how each magazine contributes to total response volume for the three-month period, we'll make a pie chart, as follows:

1. Press Esc, and then select cells E3 through E6.

2. Choose the New Chart command from the View menu (Alt-V-N). Works displays a new bar chart based on this data selection. Works always defaults to the bar chart type, so we'll have to change this chart type by selecting a different one in Chart mode.

3. Press Esc to display the Chart mode screen.

4. Click the Pie tool to choose this chart type, and then click the Chart command to display the chart again as a pie, like this:

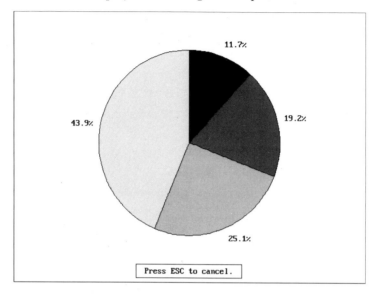

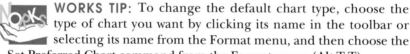

This chart clearly shows that *Car Modeling* magazine's share of the total responses is 43.9%, but it would be nice if the name of each magazine were listed next to each pie slice.

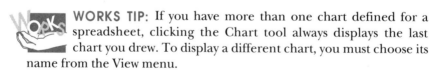 **WORKS TIP:** To change the default chart type, choose the type of chart you want by clicking its name in the toolbar or selecting its name from the Format menu, and then choose the Set Preferred Chart command from the Format menu (Alt-T-T).

WORKS TIP: If you have more than one chart defined for a spreadsheet, clicking the Chart tool always displays the last chart you drew. To display a different chart, you must choose its name from the View menu.

Adding Category Labels to a Pie Chart

To show a magazine name along with each percentage in the pie chart, we must add category labels to the chart. Unlike the chart title, X-axis or Y-axis titles, or subtitles — all of which can be created from scratch — category labels must be the contents of cells that you select in the spreadsheet. We want to use the magazine names in column A as the labels for our pie slices, so do the following:

1. Press Esc to return to the Chart mode screen.

2. Select the magazine labels in the range of cells A3:A6.

3. Choose the X-series command from the Data menu (Alt-D-X). Doing so tells Works to use that range of cells (the magazine names) as the labels for the X-series data. In a pie chart, each slice is one value in the X-series — pie charts have no Y-series — so the labels will be applied to the chart slices.

4. Click the Chart tool to view the chart again. It now has labels on the pie slices, like this:

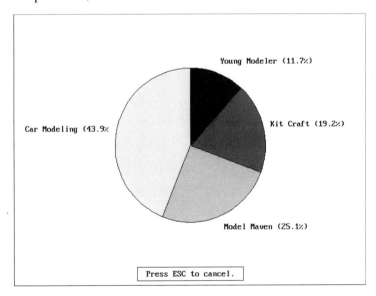

To finish this chart, let's add a title and subtitle.

1. Press Esc to return to the Chart mode screen.

2. Choose the Titles command from the Data menu (Alt-D-T). Works displays the Titles dialog box, as shown at the top of the next page.

3. The cursor is already blinking in the Chart title text box, so type *Summer Ad Campaign.*

4. Click the Subtitle box.

5. Type *Share of Total Responses,* and then click OK or press Enter to confirm these titles.

6. Click the Chart tool to display the pie chart again. Now it contains the title and subtitle. Press Esc to return to Chart mode.

KEYBOARD TIP: You can press the Up and Down arrow keys or Shift-Tab and Tab to move from one entry box to another in dialog boxes.

These few examples have shown how different kinds of charts can reveal different facts about collections of data. For more information about charting, see Chapter 3 in the *Microsoft Works User's Guide.*

THE LOAN AMORTIZATION TEMPLATE

Instead of building a spreadsheet from scratch in this project, we'll take a close look at the Loan Amortization template that comes with Microsoft Works. This template uses a number of functions and other Works Spreadsheet features we haven't used so far.

1. Choose the Create New File command from the File menu (Alt-F-N).

2. Click the Spreadsheet document type, and then double-click the Loan Amortization template at the right. Works opens a document that looks like this:

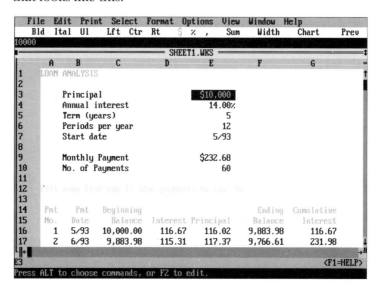

This spreadsheet has three distinct areas: the Loan Analysis area in rows 1 through 10, the instructions in row 12, and the Loan Activity area whose labels begin in row 14.

The Loan Analysis Area

In the Loan Analysis area, the labels in column B identify values in column E. Let's look at these values now.

In cell E3, you enter the principal, or the initial amount being loaned. In the Loan Amortization template shown above, the amount is $10,000, but you could enter any value here to calculate the payment on different loan amounts. This cell is set to the Currency format with no decimal places.

In cell E4, the interest rate is shown as 14.00%. This cell is set to the Percent format with two decimal places. However, when you click this cell and look in the formula bar, you can see that the value is entered as *0.14*, as shown at the top of the next page.

```
 File  Edit  Print  Select  Format  Options  View  Window  Help
  Bld  Ital  Ul      Lft  Ctr  Rt    $   %   ,    Sum    Width   Chart      Prev
0.14
                               SHEET1.WKS
       A      B       C         D        E         F          G
 1  LOAN ANALYSIS
 2
 3          Principal                $10,000
 4          Annual interest             14.00%
 5          Term (years)                    5
 6          Periods per year               12
 7          Start date                   5/93
 8
```

This is because 0.14 is 14%. If you entered *14* in cell E4, it would show 1400%. You must remember to enter interest rates as decimal fractions.

The term in cell E5 is expressed in years because that's the way most loan terms are quoted. Cell E6 shows that there are 12 periods per year, so the payments and interest on this loan are calculated monthly. By changing the value here, you could calculate payments bimonthly, quarterly, or semiannually if you wanted.

Finally the start date is 5/93. Works automatically understands this as a date because it's entered in Month/Year format. (However, if you entered = 5/93 in this cell, Works would divide 5 by 93.)

At the bottom of the Loan Activity area, cells E9 and E10 contain the monthly payment and the number of payments. The number of payments specifies the number of periods in the loan. (The value is 60 here because there are 12 periods per year for 5 years.) Works calculates the monthly payment with a formula using the PMT function.

The Payment Formula

The heart of this whole spreadsheet is cell E9, which contains the formula that calculates the monthly payment on this loan. Click cell E9, and look in the formula bar. You'll see the formula there, like this:

```
 File  Edit  Print  Select  Format  Options  View  Window  Help
  Bld  Ital  Ul      Lft  Ctr  Rt    $   %   ,    Sum    Width   Chart      Prev
=PMT(prncpl,'rate'/period,pmts)
                               SHEET1.WKS
       A      B       C         D        E         F          G
 1  LOAN ANALYSIS
 2
 3          Principal                $10,000
 4          Annual interest             14.00%
 5          Term (years)                    5
 6          Periods per year               12
 7          Start date                   5/93
 8
 9          Monthly Payment            $232.68
10          No. of Payments                60
11
```

204

The PMT is a financial function that calculates payments based on a loan's principal (the amount in cell E3), interest rate (the amount in cell E4), and the number of payments (in cell E10). If you look in Appendix A of the *Microsoft Works User's Guide,* you'll see that the PMT formula is always structured like this:

= PMT(*Principal, Rate, Term*)

The principal, rate, and term values in the formula are often expressed as cell references, so that specific loan amount, interest rate, or loan term values in those cells can be changed and the formula will recalculate to show the new payment. However, this formula contains no cell references. Instead, the cells that contain the principal, interest rate, and term values have range names, and the formula refers to those range names.

To see all the range names in this spreadsheet, choose the Range Name command from the Edit menu (Alt-E-N). Works displays the range names, like this:

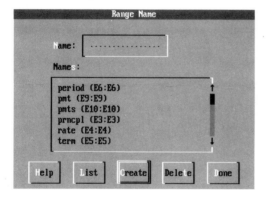

Here you see that cells E3, E4, E5, E6, E9, and E10 have each been given range names that identify their contents. It's much easier to remember a range name that explains what the cell represents (the principal, the interest rate, or the term, for example) than it is to remember cell coordinates, so range names make it easier to refer to these cells in formulas.

To make a range name, do the following:

1. Select the cell or range of cells you want to name.

2. Choose the Range Name command from the Edit menu (Alt-E-N). Works displays the Range Name dialog box as shown earlier.

3. Type a name for the range, and click Create.

We'll see range names used in many places in this spreadsheet.

WORKS TIP: To list all of a spreadsheet's named ranges in the spreadsheet itself where you can easily refer to them, select a cell in an area of the spreadsheet where there are several blank cells below and at least one blank column to the right, choose the Range Name command, and then click List in the Range Name dialog box. Works pastes all the range names and the ranges they represent into your spreadsheet. This information might be useful to include in your spreadsheet reference area.

For now, let's see how the formula in cell E9 works. The range names correspond to cell coordinates, and the cells at those coordinates contain values. This formula would calculate the same payment in either of the two following formats:

= PMT(E3, (E4/E6),E10)

or

= PMT(10000,(.14/12),60)

Obviously, though, the advantage to using range names or cell references instead of specific values is that you can calculate new payments by changing the values in the cells referred to by the formula. In the last formula example given here, however, you would have to edit the formula itself to calculate a different loan payment.

Another issue in the PMT formula is the second portion of the argument, 'rate'/ period. You might wonder why the interest rate is divided by the period. The reason is that we are calculating a monthly payment, but the interest rate is specified as a yearly one. In order to calculate a monthly payment, we must derive a monthly interest rate, so we divide the yearly rate (14.00%) by the number of periods per year (12).

One final point about the PMT formula in cell E9: You'll notice that the range name *rate* has single quotation marks around it. This is because RATE is itself the name of a function in the Works Spreadsheet. If we entered *rate* without single quotation marks around it, Works would think we were adding another function to the formula and would display an error message. By placing the word inside single quote marks, we can use it as the name of a range. In general, however, it's best to avoid using function names as range names.

The Instructions

This spreadsheet contains a line of instructions in row 12. If you're designing a spreadsheet for others to use, it often helps to include one or more lines of instructions about how to use the spreadsheet.

In this case, the instructions tell us to fill the spreadsheet down from row 17 to row 75. If you scroll the spreadsheet down right now, you'll see that the Loan Activity area only contains two rows, enough to show the activity for two months of payments. Because the loan we're currently calculating contains 60 months of payments, the instructions tell us to fill in formulas in rows 17 through 75, so every month of the loan's activity will be shown.

Even in a simple row of instructions, however, this spreadsheet uses a formula to produce information automatically. Click cell A12. Works displays the contents of that cell in the formula bar, like this:

```
 File  Edit  Print  Select  Format  Options  View  Window  Help
   Bld  Ital  Ul    Lft  Ctr  Rt    $  %  ,    Sum    Width    Chart      Prev
"Fill down from row 17 (2nd payment) to row:
================================ SHEET1.WKS ================================
        A      B      C         D         E          F          G
1   LOAN ANALYSIS
2
3         Principal               $10,000
4         Annual interest          14.00%
5         Term (years)                  5
6         Periods per year             12
7         Start date                 5/93
8
9         Monthly Payment         $232.68
10        No. of Payments              60
11
12  Fill  down from row 17 (2nd payment) to row 76
13
```

Notice that the cell contains everything in the instruction line except the value 75. That's because that value is calculated by a formula in a separate cell (cell F12), and the value shown depends on the length of the loan, as specified in cell E10. See for yourself. Click on cell F12. Works displays the formula:

= pmts + 15

Because the Loan Activity area begins in row 15, Works simply adds 15 to the number of payments shown in cell E10 (which has the range name *pmts*).

By using this formula, the instructions line always calculates the correct number of rows needed to fill out the Loan Activity area. Let's follow these instructions now:

1. Select cells A17 through G17, hold down the mouse button, and drag the pointer down to cell G75. Drag the pointer down one additional row to cell G76 so you can see the results.

2. Release the mouse button, and choose the Fill Down command from the Edit menu (Alt-E-F). Works fills in rows 17 through 76 in the Loan Activity area, as shown on the following page.

```
 File  Edit  Print  Select  Format  Options  View  Window  Help
  Bld  Ital  Ul    Lft Ctr  Rt   $  %  ,    Sum   Width   Chart    Prev
=A17+1
                              SHEET1.WKS
      A     B      C          D        E          F           G
61    46   2/97   3,184.94   37.16    195.52    2,989.41    3,692.81
62    47   3/97   2,989.41   34.88    197.81    2,791.60    3,727.68
63    48   4/97   2,791.60   32.57    200.11    2,591.49    3,760.25
64    49   5/97   2,591.49   30.23    202.45    2,389.04    3,790.49
65    50   6/97   2,389.04   27.87    204.81    2,184.23    3,818.36
66    51   7/97   2,184.23   25.48    207.20    1,977.03    3,843.84
67    52   8/97   1,977.03   23.07    209.62    1,767.42    3,866.91
68    53   9/97   1,767.42   20.62    212.06    1,555.35    3,887.53
69    54  10/97   1,555.35   18.15    214.54    1,340.82    3,905.67
70    55  11/97   1,340.82   15.64    217.04    1,123.78    3,921.31
71    56  12/97   1,123.78   13.11    219.57      904.20    3,934.42
72    57   1/98     904.20   10.55    222.13      682.07    3,944.97
73    58   2/98     682.07    7.96    224.73      457.35    3,952.93
74    59   3/98     457.35    5.34    227.35      230.00    3,958.27
75    60   4/98     230.00    2.68    230.00        0.00    3,960.95
76    61   5/98       0.00    0.00     N/A         N/A      3,960.95
77
A18:G76                                                      <F1=HELP>
Press ALT to choose commands, or F2 to edit.
```

Notice that in row 76, the month after the loan is paid off, the beginning balance and interest are 0, the principal and ending balance read *N/A,* (we'll discuss that later), and the cumulative interest amount hasn't increased from the previous month, because no new interest has been paid.

Now let's look at how Works calculates all this activity.

The Loan Activity Area

The Loan Activity area of this spreadsheet shows exactly how each month's loan payment is divided between reducing the principal and paying the interest. In this area, you can also see how much of the principal remains to be paid off on the loan at any given time and how much interest has been paid up to that point.

Scroll up to the beginning of the Loan Activity area. Rows 14 and 15 simply contain stacked labels. The labels are stacked in two rows because otherwise each column would have to be so wide to accommodate them that the spreadsheet would require two pages to print its full width, instead of one. Notice also that the column widths vary from 5 characters (column A) to 12 characters (columns C, F, and G) to maximize the horizontal space on the screen (or on paper) without crowding the data too much.

To see all the different formulas in the Loan Activity area, we can examine the first two months of the loan (rows 16 and 17). Let's work across row 16 first. Click each cell in your copy of the Loan Amortization spreadsheet to see the formulas as we go through them.

Calculating the First Month's Loan Activity

In cell A16, the payment number is simply entered as the value 1. In cell B16, the payment date is the date of the first payment, which is the same as the Start Date shown in cell E7. So, cell B16 contains the reference = E7. Cell B16 is set to the Month, Year date format, so the day number isn't shown.

Cell C16 contains the beginning loan balance, which is the same as the loan's principal shown in cell E3. Cell E3 is the range named *prncpl,* and that range name is what's entered in cell C16.

Cell D16 calculates the interest on the loan principal in cell C16. Remember, we want each row to calculate one month's loan activity, so this cell must calculate one month's interest on the balance of the loan shown in cell C16. Therefore, the formula here looks like this:

```
 File  Edit  Print  Select  Format  Options  View  Window  Help
  Bld  Ital  Ul    Lft  Ctr  Rt    $  %  ,    Sum    Width    Chart    Prev
=$'rate'/$period*C16
============================ SHEET1.WKS ============================
     A       B       C         D        E        F         G
1  LOAN ANALYSIS
2
3          Principal              $10,000
4          Annual interest         14.00%
5          Term (years)              5
6          Periods per year         12
7          Start date              5/93
8
9          Monthly Payment        $232.68
10         No. of Payments          60
11
12
13
14  Pmt    Pmt    Beginning                    Ending   Cumulative
15  No.    Date   Balance   Interest Principal  Balance   Interest
16   1     5/93  10,000.00   116.67   116.02   9,883.98   116.67
17   2     6/93   9,883.98   115.31   117.37   9,766.61   231.98
```

This formula uses the range names *'rate'* (referring to the contents of cell E4) and *period* (referring to the contents of cell E6), so given the current contents of cells E4 and E6, the formula actually calculates *(14.00%/12)*10,000.*

WORKS TIP: Because you copy the formula in cell D16 down to fill out the Loan Activity area, the range names have absolute value marks ($) in front of them. This way, Works always refers to the same rate and period cells (E4 and E6) when the formula is copied to other locations. See "Using Relative and Absolute Formulas" in Chapter 5 for more information.

Because we calculated the amount of interest this month in cell D16 and we know the total monthly payment (we calculated it in cell E9), cell E16 simply subtracts the month's interest from the total payment to arrive at the difference, which is the principal paid that month. In its simplest form, this formula would simply subtract the interest from the payment amount, so it might read *'pmt'-D16*. However, when we click cell E16 and view its contents in the formula bar, the formula is a bit more complicated, as shown here:

```
 File  Edit  Print  Select  Format  Options  View  Window  Help
  Bld  Ital  Ul     Lft  Ctr  Rt    $  %  ,    Sum   Width    Chart      Prev
=IF(C16>0.1,$'pmt'-D16,NA())
========================= SHEET1.WKS =========================
     A      B      C         D        E          F          G
 1  LOAN ANALYSIS
 2
 3         Principal                $10,000
 4         Annual interest           14.00%
 5         Term (years)                  5
 6         Periods per year             12
 7         Start date                 5/93
 8
 9         Monthly Payment         $232.68
10         No. of Payments             60
11
12
13
14  Pmt    Pmt    Beginning                   Ending  Cumulative
15  No.    Date   Balance  Interest Principal  Balance  Interest
16   1     5/93   10,000.00  116.67   116.02   9,883.98   116.67
17   2     6/93    9,883.98  115.31   117.37   9,766.61   231.98
```

In this case, there's a logical formula that tells Works to display two different results, depending on the contents of cell C16 (the remaining loan balance in this month). The formula states, "If cell C16's value is greater than 0.1 (10 cents), then subtract the contents of cell D16 (the month's interest) from the payment amount; and if cell C16's value is not greater than 0.1, enter the value *N/A* in the cell."

As with the formula in cell D16, this one includes an absolute value marker in front of the *'pmt'* range name so the formula will always refer to cell E9 no matter where it is copied.

Another point about this formula is the NA function at the end. This function tells Works to insert the value *N/A* in this cell. Using the NA function is the only way to have Works place N/A in a cell as the result of a numeric calculation. If we had simply typed the text *N/A* without the parentheses, Works would display an error message when you tried to enter the formula.

Thanks to this logical formula, Works displays *N/A* for the month's principal and balance in row 76, the month after the loan is paid off, because the beginning loan balance is less than 10 cents.

In cell F16, the ending balance is simply the beginning balance (cell C16) minus the principal (cell E16), so the formula here is = C16-E16.

Finally the cumulative interest value in cell G16 is the same as the interest calculated in cell D16 for this month, because this is the first month of the loan. Therefore, cell G16 contains the value = D16.

Calculating the Second Month's Loan Activity

In row 17, the second month of the loan, three new formulas are needed so the spreadsheet will automatically increase the payment number, the payment date, and the cumulative interest from the previous month. All these formulas contain relative references that automatically refer to the cells in the row directly above when the formulas are copied down the spreadsheet to fill out the Loan Activity area.

In cell A17, the formula is = A16 + 1. This simply adds 1 to the value in the cell directly above, increasing the payment number by 1 in each successive row.

In cell B17, the formula uses Works' DATE, YEAR, and MONTH functions to increase the previous month's date by one month. The DATE function's format is DATE(YEAR,MONTH,DAY), and it returns a specific date when values are supplied for the year, month, and day portions of the argument. However, the formula in cell B17 looks like this:

DATE(YEAR(B16),MONTH(B16)+1,1)

Here the YEAR function supplies the year value in the argument by extracting the year value from cell B16 above (YEAR(B16), and the MONTH function supplies the month part of the argument by extracting the month value from cell B16 above and then adding 1 to it (MONTH(B16) + 1. The Day portion of the argument is entered as the value 1. (Works automatically increases the year number when it adds 1 to a December month.)

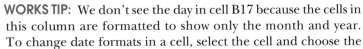

WORKS TIP: We don't see the day in cell B17 because the cells in this column are formatted to show only the month and year. To change date formats in a cell, select the cell and choose the Time/Date command from the Format menu (Alt-T-T).

Finally the cumulative interest value in cell G17 comes from a formula that adds the current month's interest (from cell D17) to the previous month's cumulative interest (from cell G16). So, the formula here is = G16+D17.

Using the Amortization Table

The Loan Amortization template is useful for determining the costs of new loans, or for estimating the remaining balance on any loan you currently have. For new loans, simply enter the original loan amount (principal), annual interest rate, term, periods per year, and start date; Works then calculates the payment for each period and number of payments. By filling out the Loan Activity area for the life of the loan and then scrolling to the final month, you'll see how much total interest you'll end up paying.

To figure out the remaining balance on any existing loan, enter the original loan amount, rate, term, periods per year, and start date; fill in the Loan Activity area; and then check the Ending Balance column for the current month. Some processing or payoff fees might be included in addition to the actual loan balance, but the Ending Balance column will give you a good idea of how much you owe.

 WORKS TIP: This amortization table might not match your actual loan payment to the penny because different banks determine amortization different ways. It makes a difference in the payment, for example, whether the bank assumes that payments come in at the beginning or at the end of each month.

If you want to view parts of the Loan Activity area but keep the Loan Analysis part of the spreadsheet and the Loan Activity column labels on the screen at the same time, you can simply freeze the appropriate area of the screen with the Freeze Titles command:

1. Select cell G16 (the cell that is just below the Cumulative Interest column label).

2. Choose the Freeze Titles command from the Options menu (Alt-O-T). Works freezes the Loan Analysis area and Loan Activity column labels on the screen. When you scroll the window, the Loan Activity rows will scroll up and down but the Loan Analysis area and the column labels won't budge.

WORKS TIP: After you freeze an area of a spreadsheet with the Freeze Titles command, you can't select or modify any of the cells in the frozen area. To select or modify any of these cells, you'll have to first unfreeze them by choosing the Freeze Titles command again.

This concludes our practical look at the Works Spreadsheet's features in action. If you need more information about a specific spreadsheet command or function, consult the *Microsoft Works User's Guide* or check the Help Table of Contents for on-line instructions. As you gain experience with this powerful number-crunching tool, you'll discover a wide variety of tasks that it can handle with ease.

8

Basic Database Techniques

The Microsoft Works Database lets you store, sort, organize, calculate, and otherwise manipulate data using some of the same techniques you use in the Works Spreadsheet to manipulate numbers. Data can be text — such as names, addresses, and product descriptions — or numbers — such as dates, times, part numbers, or prices — or any combination of the two. With the Database, you can store these elements of data and then find them again easily.

FIELDS, RECORDS, AND FILES

Every Database program lets you store and manipulate items of information, called *data*. In an address database, for example, you might want to store each person's first name, last name, street, city, state, zip code, and telephone number.

In a Database file, each type of information (the street address, for example), is contained in its own category, which is called a *field*. Usually a Database file contains many fields. One complete collection of fields is called a *record*. A *file* is a collection of records. Database files can contain many fields that store different types of information.

Before you can begin entering information into a Database file, you must decide on its structure. You set up the file's structure to store the necessary types of data and their specific categories by creating and naming fields. After you create and name fields, you can enter information in the fields to create records. And after you have stored some records, you can search for specific information and rearrange that information or create reports from it that you can print.

CREATING A SIMPLE DATABASE

To see how the Database works, let's create a simple personal database file that contains names, addresses, and telephone numbers. First we create a new Database file and define the fields that will store the types of information we want. Then we enter some information and see how to sort records and how to select a particular subset of them from the database. Finally we format the information in a report for printing.

Using the Database Window

Let's suppose we want to create a file that stores name, address, and telephone information about business and personal contacts.

1. Choose the Create New File command from the File menu (Alt-F-N). Microsoft Works displays the Create New File dialog box in which you can choose the type of new file to create.

2. Choose the Database file type, and then double-click the Standard/ Blank template. Works opens a new Database document on the screen, like the one shown in Figure 8-1.

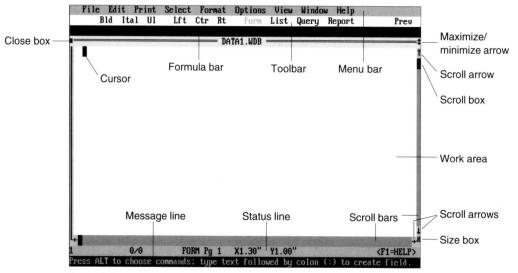

Figure 8-1.

Each Works Database document begins with a blank Form window in which you can enter field names and labels. (A Form window shows the layout of the information in a single record. Because you haven't entered any information yet, the form is blank.)

As you can see, a new Database screen has some of the standard features of every Works window, including a menu bar, a toolbar, a formula bar, a status line, a message line, scroll bars, and a work area. The work area is the space in which we'll enter field names and where we'll later enter the actual data into the file.

Defining Fields

Let's assume we've determined that our file will contain fields with these names: FirstName, LastName, Company, Street, City, State, Zip, and Phone. The cursor is at the upper-left corner of the work area. To enter the first field name, follow these steps:

1. Type *FirstName:* and press Enter. Works displays a dialog box that shows the width and height of the field (the allowed number of characters across and number of lines high), like this:

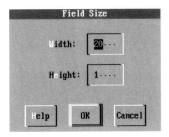

2. Press Enter to accept the default field size values. Works enters the field name on the screen and moves the cursor down to the next line, like this:

Now enter the *LastName:, Company:, Street:,* and *City:* field names and accept the default field sizes in the same way. Be sure to include the colon at the end of each field name. When you finish, the cursor is in the line below the City field.

WORKS TIP: The Database screen examples in this book were made with the screen mode set to Text. (See the Works Settings command on the Options menu.) If your screen mode is set to Graphics instead of Text, the data spaces, or *data entry area,* after each field you define on the Database's Form View screen contain dotted underlines that show the exact size of each field.

Setting Custom Field Lengths

So far we've entered these fields by accepting the default field size values Works has proposed. In the State field, however, we only need to enter a two-letter state code, so we can save a lot of space by specifying a smaller field size.

1. Type *State:* and press Enter. Works displays the Field Size dialog box.

2. Type *2* to indicate a field length of two characters.

3. Press Enter. Works enters the field name and moves the cursor down to the next line.

When we create the Zip and Phone fields, we'll also modify the field lengths so that they are no longer than necessary:

1. Type *Zip:* and press Enter.

2. Type *10* to specify 10 characters as the field length (which allows a 9-digit zip code plus one space for a dash after the fifth digit).

3. Press Enter to enter the field name.

4. Type *Phone:* and press Enter.

5. Type *15* and press Enter. (Using 15 characters allows enough room in this field for area codes, international dialing codes, and the leading 1 or 9 digit for dialing long distance or connecting with an outside line through a company switchboard.)

Now that you have created all the fields for this Database document, the screen looks like this:

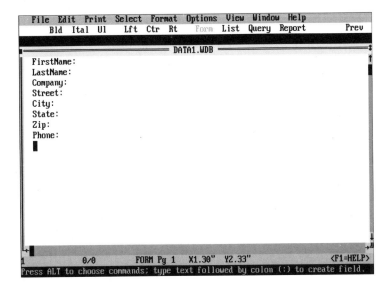

This is the Database's Form view, which shows the data in one record at a time. You can also look at your data in a List view, which shows several records at once in a row-and-column layout, much as data would appear in a spreadsheet. (See "Using the List View," later in this chapter.) There are two other views as well: Query view is for selecting specific groups of records, and Report view is for designing reports for printing.

The status line in Form view shows the following database-specific information (reading from left to right):

■ The number of the record you're currently viewing.

■ The name of the field you currently have selected. (No field name currently appears in the status line in the example above because none is selected.)

■ The number of records included in the current selection you're viewing, out of the total number of records in the file.

■ Whether you're in Form, List, Query, or Report view.

■ Which page of a form you are viewing. (Database forms can have more than one page.)

- The X and Y coordinates of the cursor's current position on the form, or the cursor's distance from the left and top edges of the form.

- Whether you're in a special mode like Move or Copy.

We'll refer to these status line indicators later in this chapter. Now we'll use some of the Database's formatting features to arrange the fields on this screen so that it's more readable.

Moving Fields with the Mouse

As you'll see in a moment, you can enter information in the document by typing data in any individual field. Because this is the screen we'll ordinarily use for viewing or entering original data in each record, we should reformat it so that it's easier to work with.

First reposition the fields so that they are formatted more like traditional names and addresses. You can move fields in the Database's Form view by using the Move Field command:

1. Click the LastName field name to select it.

2. Choose the Move Field command from the Edit menu (F3 or Alt-E-M). Works highlights the field name and the field data space defined for that field. The MOVE indicator appears in the status line.

3. Click the same line as the FirstName field, about an inch to the right of the FirstName field name.

4. Press Enter to move the field. Works displays a warning message, like this:

Works won't let you move a field if doing so would make it overlap another field name or data space. We have just tried to place the LastName field name on top of the FirstName field's data space. This isn't a big problem, however.

5. Click OK to close the warning message, and then click just underneath the *D* at the beginning of the filename in the window title bar.

6. Press Enter. The LastName field moves into place to the right of the FirstName field.

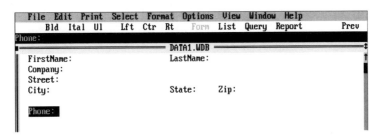 **KEYBOARD TIP:** You can also move a selected field by pressing the arrow keys, which lets you move a field one character at a time in any direction, so it's easier to judge exactly where you're placing a field when you move it. For example, if you know the FirstName field data space is 20 characters wide, you can move the LastName field name 21 characters to the right of the FirstName field name to place it as close to the FirstName field data space as possible without overlapping it.

Moving Fields with the Keyboard

Now you'll see an empty line on the screen where the LastName field used to be. Let's clean up the screen by rearranging the rest of the field names. This time, we'll use the keyboard to move fields.

1. Select the Company field name, press F3, press the Up arrow key once to move the field one line up, and then press Enter.

2. Repeat step 1 for the Street and City field names.

3. Select the State field name, press F3, press the Right arrow key 32 times (or until the selection is lined up below the Last Name field), press the Up arrow key twice, and then press Enter.

4. Select the Zip field name, press the F3 key, move the field 43 characters to the right and three lines up (so that it's about 3/4-inch to the right of the State field), and press Enter.

5. Select the Phone field name, press the F3 key, move the field name up two lines so that there's a blank line between it and the line with the City, State, and Zip fields, and then press Enter. The screen now looks like this:

```
 File  Edit  Print  Select  Format  Options  View  Window  Help
     Bld  Ital  Ul     Lft  Ctr  Rt    Form  List  Query  Report          Prev
Phone:
                             ═══════ DATA1.WDB ═══════
    FirstName:              LastName:
    Company:
    Street:
    City:              State:      Zip:

    Phone:
```

Adding a Label to the Form

Now let's add a label at the top of this form. You add labels to the Form view screen exactly as you add field names, except that you don't type a colon (:) at the end of a label. The colon at the end of a name signals Works that you're creating a field — if you don't put a colon at the end of a word or phrase, Works assumes that it's a label.

1. Click the FirstName field name to move the cursor to the top of the screen.

   NOTE: *When the cursor is in the middle of a form, pressing the PgUp key also moves it to the top of the form.*

2. Choose the Insert Line command from the Edit menu (Alt-E-I) two times to insert two blank lines at the top of the form.

3. Click the top line of the form, three characters to the left of the *D* in the filename in the window title bar. The X coordinate in the status line should read 4.20".

4. Type *ADDRESSES* and then press Enter. Works enters the label.

 WORKS TIP: Unlike the Word Processor tool, the Database tool doesn't let you use the Tab key or centering commands to align text on the screen. However, if you know the width or height of a form, you can calculate the form's center by checking the X and Y coordinates in the status line.

Formatting the Label

To finish this form, let's make the ADDRESSES label underlined and bold. The label is still selected.

1. Click the Bld tool in the toolbar. The text changes color or intensity to indicate that it will be bold when printed.

2. Click the Ul tool in the toolbar, and then click to the right of the form name to remove the selection from it. The text changes color or intensity again to indicate the underline style, like this:

KEYBOARD TIP: You can press Ctrl-B to make selected text bold, Ctrl-U to make it underlined, or Ctrl-I to make it italic. To change styled text back to plain, press Ctrl-Spacebar. See the *Database Formatting Keys* topic in the Database category in the Help Table of Contents for more formatting shortcuts.

You can change the style of any selected text in a Database form this way. You can select field names, labels, or even the data in fields and make them bold, underlined, or italic. Simply select the text or data first, and then click the format tool in the toolbar, press the keyboard command keys, or choose the style you want with the Style command on the Format menu (Alt-T-S). You can only have one font and size for a given database; if you want to change the font and size, choose the Font command from the Format menu (Alt-T-F).

Adding, Deleting, and Renaming Fields

After you've created fields in a form, you can add more fields, delete existing fields, or edit field names anytime you want.

■ To add a field, move the cursor to an unused part of the screen, and type the field name. Be sure to end the field name with a colon. Press Enter. Change the field size settings, if you like, and then press Enter to confirm them.

■ To delete an existing field, you select the field name (not the field data), choose the Delete Field command from the Edit menu (Alt-E-D), and click OK when Works prompts you. When you delete a field, note that Works also deletes all the data you've stored in that field.

 KEYBOARD TIP: You can also press Del, press Enter, and then click OK to delete a selected field name. You can press Del and then Enter to delete a form label or the data in a field. If you delete something accidentally, press Esc immediately after the deletion and the deletion will be canceled.

■ To rename an existing field, select the field name, type a new one (or click in the formula bar and edit the existing name there), and then press Enter when you finish.

Saving the Database File

Although this form contains only a few fields, you can create forms that occupy more than one screen and contain up to 256 fields. In such a large form, you would use the vertical scroll bar or PgUp and PgDn to move around. Before we do more work on this project, let's save this new file as ADDRESS.

1. Choose the Save command from the File menu (Alt-F-S). Because this is a new, untitled document, Works displays the Save As dialog box.

2. Type *Address* and press Enter. Works saves the file as ADDRESS.WDB. (If you created an Address Book with WorksWizards in Chapter 4, Works prompts you to click OK if you want to replace it, which you do.)

So far we've established and positioned field names and data space on the screen. In the next section, we'll enter data in our document using this same screen.

Entering Data in the Form View

For entering or viewing data, Works lets you work in either the Form view or the List view. Let's continue with the Form view for a little longer to see how we use it to enter information and to move from one record to another. Let's enter three records now:

1. Select the FirstName field (the data space, not the field name).

2. Type *John*. As you type, the characters appear in the formula bar above the work area.

3. Press Tab. The name appears in the FirstName field, and the selection moves to the LastName field, like this:

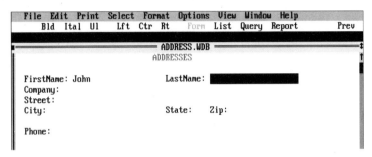

If you make a mistake entering field data, either select the field again and retype the data or select the field, click the formula bar or press F2, and edit the field's contents there.

> **KEYBOARD TIP:** Pressing Tab always enters the data you've typed in the current field and then moves the field selection to the next field in the document. Even if the selection is on a field name when you press Tab, the selection moves to the next field data space and not to the next field name.

- Pressing Tab moves the selection to the next field in the record. If the current field is the last field in the record, the selection is moved to the first field in the following record.

- Pressing Shift-Tab moves the field selection to the previous field in the record. If the current field is the first field in the record, the selection moves to the last field in the previous record (unless you're in the first record, in which case the selection doesn't move).

- Pressing the arrow keys, however, moves the cursor around the form and doesn't necessarily select field names or field data.

MOUSE TIP: You can also select different fields by clicking them with the mouse, and you can move from one record to the next by clicking the vertical scroll bar.

Let's enter some more data.

1. Type *Jones* and press Tab. The name appears in the LastName field's data space, and the selection moves to the Company field.

2. Type *ABC Glass* and press Tab.

3. Type *123 3rd St.* in the Street field, *San Jose* in the City field, *CA* in the State field, and *95111* in the Zip field, pressing Tab after each entry.

After you enter the zip code and press Tab, you'll notice that the zip code is aligned at the right side of the field data space instead of at the left side as all the text entries were. Works recognizes the zip code as a number and stores it as such. As in the Works spreadsheet, numbers, dates, and times are right-aligned in fields, and text is left-aligned.

WORKS TIP: If your database will contain any of the many zip codes that begin with zero, you will probably want to designate your Zip field entries as text in order to display the leading zero. To do so, type a quotation mark (") in front of the zip code when you enter it.

Finish this record by typing *408-555-1111* in the Phone field and pressing Enter. As you can see, pressing Enter enters data in the field, but it doesn't advance the selection to the next field. Also notice that because the telephone number contains dashes, Works treats it as a text entry and aligns it at the left edge of the field data space. All text entries are preceded in the formula bar with a quotation mark ("), which designates them as text.

Because the Phone field is the last field in the record, we can move to the next record by pressing Tab one more time. When the last field in the Form view is selected and you press Tab, Works moves the selection to the first field in the next record, like this:

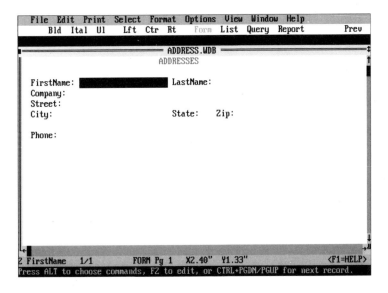

The record-number indicator at the left edge of the status line shows that we're now viewing record number 2 in this file.

KEYBOARD TIP: If you want to browse through records more quickly, you can press Ctrl-PgDn to move to the next record or Ctrl-PgUp to move to the previous record. See the *DB Movement and Selection Keys* topic in the Database category of the Help Table of Contents for more shortcuts.

Enter the next two records on your own, using the following data:

Fred Smith

Ace Vending

234 2nd St.

Clearview CA 94122

415-555-1111

Tom Brown

Brown Mailing

345 Sather Ln.

Barkins CA 94702

510-555-8888

When you finish entering the above data, press Enter. Now you're ready to explore the List view.

 WORKS TIP: If you enter a name that Works recognizes as an abbreviation for a month, you must type a quote mark before it. For example, if you enter the name *Jan*, Works converts it to *January;* to retain the abbreviated form, you must type a quotation mark before the name.

USING THE LIST VIEW

Viewing one record at a time in the Form view is useful if each of your records contains a lot of information and you want to be able to concentrate on that information. But when you want to look at many records at one time, use Microsoft Works' List view:

- Click the List tool in the toolbar to switch to List view, and then press Ctrl-Home. (Ctrl-Home is a navigation shortcut that always moves the selection to the first field in the document's first record. Similarly, Ctrl-End moves the selection to the last field in the last record.)

Works then changes to List view, like this:

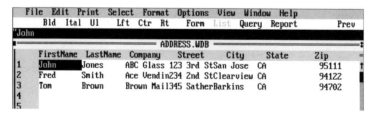

The List view looks like the row-and-column matrix of a spreadsheet. Each record occupies a row, and each column represents a different field, as you can see. You can also see the drawback to the List view: Because the data from each record is arranged in columns, some fields contain more data than can be displayed within the default width of their columns (10 characters). And if you have more than a few fields, you won't be able to see all the fields on the screen at one time. In the above example, the Phone field is off the screen to the right, so you must scroll to the right if you want to see it.

Changing Field Widths

You can, however, make the most of the horizontal space on the screen by changing the field widths to accommodate the amount of data each field contains. For example, the State field is far wider than it needs to be because it will never contain more than two letters. If we make it narrower, more room will be available to display or widen other fields.

1. Select the data in the first record's State field.

2. Choose the Field Width command from the Format menu (Alt-T-W). Works displays the Field Width dialog box, which shows the current width of 10 characters.

3. Click the Best Fit option, and then click OK. The field is narrowed. You can see that some of the State field name at the top of the window is now hidden, and the screen has more room for Zip and Phone fields, like this:

 MOUSE TIP: You can widen or narrow more than one field at a time by holding down the mouse button and dragging the pointer across the fields you want to select, releasing the mouse button, and then choosing the Field Width command to set the width you want.

We could narrow the FirstName and LastName fields to show the Phone field completely here, but let's move on for now.

Scrolling the List View

When the List window is unable to show every field in a document, the other fields are off screen. You can scroll the window to bring them into view.

■ If you're using a mouse, you can simply click the left and right scroll arrows, click the horizontal scroll bar, or drag the scroll box to scroll the window.

■ If you prefer to use the keyboard, keep pressing Tab, Shift-Tab, or the Right or Left arrow keys to scroll other fields into view.

Hiding Fields

Of course, you might not want to look at all of each record's information in this view. Suppose that you want to see only the name and telephone number fields. In that case, you would hide the unwanted fields and make the important ones wide enough to show all their data. Let's hide all but the FirstName, LastName, Company, and Phone fields and then make those fields wider.

1. Select an entry in the Street field, hold down the mouse button, and drag the pointer to the right to select entries in the City, State, and Zip fields as well.

2. Choose the Field Width command (Alt-T-W). Works displays the Field Width dialog box.

3. Type *0* to indicate a field width of 0 characters.

4. Press Enter. The Street, City, State, and Zip fields disappear from the screen.

These fields are now hidden in the List view, but they're still in the document. To see for yourself, click Form in the toolbar to switch back to the Form view, and you'll see the fields reappear. Click the List tool to return to List view when you're finished.

To finish our rearrangement of data in the List view, select an entry in the Company field, set this field's width to 20 characters, and then click a blank record below the three filled records so you can see all three records clearly. Now only the information we wanted appears in the List view, and there's plenty of space around it so we can see all the data in each field:

```
 File  Edit  Print  Select  Format  Options  View  Window  Help
       Bld  Ital  Ul      Lft  Ctr  Rt      Form  List   Query  Report            Prev


                            ADDRESS.WDB
     FirstName  LastName       Company        Phone
  1  John       Jones       ABC Glass         408-555-1111
  2  Fred       Smith       Ace Vending       415-555-1111
  3  Tom        Brown       Brown Mailing     510-555-8888
  4
  5
  6
```

Revealing Hidden Fields

In the next section, we'll see how the List view can speed up data entry. But first we'll reveal all the hidden fields.

1. Press Ctrl-Shift-F8 to select the entire Database document.

2. Choose the Field Width command (Alt-T-W) again, and click the Best Fit option.

3. Click OK. Works sets all the document's fields to the narrowest width that will display all the data in each field. The hidden fields reappear. Press Esc to remove the selection.

Copying Field Data

Copying data rather than retyping it can save you time. In List view, you can see the data in the previous records easily. When you're entering a lot of records in a document and a group of them contains the same information in certain fields, you can copy that information into a group of new records. Works provides two ways to copy data from one or more selected fields in List view.

First we'll copy the contents of a field in one record to the record immediately below it. Suppose we know that the next record in this document is for another person who also lives in Barkins, CA, and who has the same zip code. We can copy the City, State, and Zip data from the record above by using a simple command.

1. In List view, select the City field for record number 4.

2. Press Ctrl-'. Works copies *Barkins* to record number 4's City field, like this:

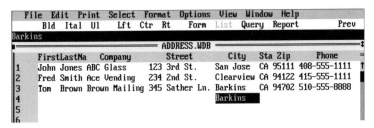

The Ctrl-' command always copies the data from the same field in the record directly above to the currently selected field. When you want to copy data from more than one field at a time into fields in records below, you can use the Fill Down command on the Edit menu. Let's copy the State and Zip data at the same time to see how this works.

1. Click the State field in record number 3, hold down the mouse button, drag the pointer to the right into the Zip field, and then drag it down into record number 4. The State and Zip fields in both records 3 and 4 should now be selected.

2. Choose the Fill Down command from the Edit menu (Alt-E-F). Works copies the data from record 3 into record 4.

Finish entering the data for record number 4 by typing the data in the remaining blank fields, one field at a time.

1. Select the FirstName field in record number 4.

2. Type *Bill* and press the Right arrow key. Works enters the first name data and selects the LastName field.

3. Type *Watson* and press Tab. Works enters the name and selects the Company field.

4. Type *Able Refrigeration*. You'll notice that the name is longer than the field width can completely display, but the formula bar shows the whole name and the field contains the whole name.

5. Select the Street field. Notice that although the Street field appears to be overwritten by the company name, the formula bar is empty when the Street field is selected, indicating that the Street field contains no data.

6. Type *400 University* and press Ctrl-End to select the Phone field.

7. Type *510-555-0000* and press Enter.

Copying Records

The Ctrl-' shortcut command and the Fill Down command are handy when you want to copy only the data from one or more selected fields from the record directly above into the current record, but you can also select rows in the List view to copy entire records. Let's copy the first two records in our document.

1. Click the 1 at the left of the first record to select the entire record, hold down the mouse button, and drag the pointer down to the second record.

2. Release the mouse button. Records 1 and 2 should both be selected.

> **KEYBOARD TIP:** You can also press Ctrl-F8 to select an entire record if you've already selected one field in that record. However, to select more than one record, press Ctrl-F8, press F8 again to extend the selection, and then press the Down arrow key to extend the selection to other records.

3. Choose the Copy command from the Edit menu (Alt-E-C, or Shift-F3). The COPY indicator appears in the status line.

4. Select any field in record number 5.

5. Press Enter. Works copies the two selected records to records 5 and 6, like this:

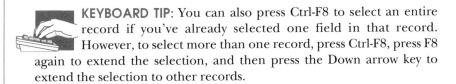

Sorting Records

Let's sort these records so that the names are in alphabetic order. The sorting features of the Works Database are much like those in the Spreadsheet: You can sort Database records on up to three fields of data at a time, in either ascending or descending order. For now, we'll sort the records only on the LastName field.

1. Choose the Sort Records command from the Select menu (Alt-S-O). Works displays the Sort Records dialog box, as shown at the top of the following page.

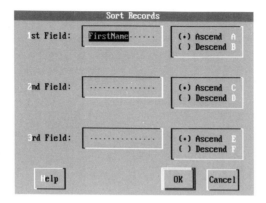

2. Type *LastName* in the 1st Field box. The Ascend option is already selected, so simply press Enter to sort the document in ascending order. Works sorts the records on the LastName field.

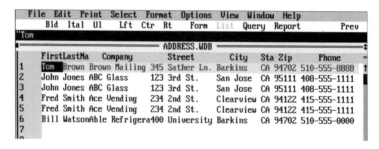

 WORKS TIP: After you've specified field names in the Sort Records dialog box, Works remembers them, so you can sort again on the same field names without having to enter those names again.

For more information about sorting data, choose the Sort Records command and then click Help in the Sort Records dialog box.

Deleting Records

Because we now have duplicate records in this document, let's delete those records before going on:

1. Select records 3 and 4 (the duplicate John Jones and Fred Smith records) by clicking the 3 to the left of the third record and dragging the pointer down to record number 4.

2. Choose the Delete Record/Field command from the Edit menu (Alt-E-D) to delete these records.

FINDING DATA

You can always find information in a document by scrolling through the List or Form views, but you can also use special commands to find specific data quickly. In this section, we'll see how to locate and select information.

Microsoft Works offers two ways to find specific data in a Database document.

- To find only one occurrence of data, such as one person's last name, you can use the Select menu's Search command.

- To find a group of records that matches one or more selection criteria, use the Query view.

Let's explore these two data-finding methods.

Using the Search Command

Use the Search command when you simply want to locate a particular record based on the data in one field. Suppose, for example, that you want to find the record for the person who works for ABC Glass.

1. Click the FirstName field in record number 1, or press Ctrl-Home to move the selection to the beginning of the document. (Works searches from the selection forward in a Database document, so if you want to search the entire document, be sure to select the first field in the first record of the document before you begin. If you start a search in the middle of the document, Works cycles back to the first record after it searches the last record.)

2. Choose the Search command from the Select menu (Alt-S-S). Works displays the Search dialog box, like this:

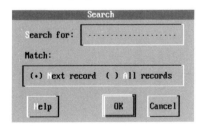

3. Type *ABC* in the Search For box. The Match options in the dialog box are already set to search for the next record that contains this information, which is what we want.

4. Press Enter. Works finds the record that contains ABC and selects the field that contains that string, like this:

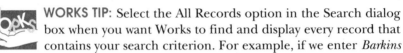

File Edit Print Select Format Options View Window Help
Bld Ital Ul   Lft Ctr Rt   Form List Query Report   Prev

`ABC Glass`

```
═══════════════════════ ADDRESS.WDB ═══════════════════════
   FirstLastNa  Company        Street        City      Sta Zip     Phone
1  Tom  Brown   Brown Mailing 345 Sather Ln. Barkins   CA  94702  510-555-8888
2  John Jones   ABC Glass     123 3rd St.    San Jose  CA  95111  408-555-1111
3  Fred Smith   Ace Vending   234 2nd St.    Clearview CA  94122  415-555-1111
4  Bill WatsonAble Refrigera400 University   Barkins   CA  94702  510-555-0000
5
6
```

> **WORKS TIP:** Select the All Records option in the Search dialog box when you want Works to find and display every record that contains your search criterion. For example, if we enter *Barkins* in the Search For box and then click the All Records option, Works would find and display all the records that contain Barkins in any field. In this case, we would see only the two records containing Barkins in the City field. To redisplay all of a file's records after viewing a selection, choose the Show All Records command from the Select menu (Alt-S-L).
>
> You can also have Works select only records that *do not* contain a certain criterion. Simply use the All Records option to find and display records that do contain the criterion, and then choose the Switch Hidden Records command from the Select menu (Alt-S-W). Works then switches the records that contain the criterion you entered with records that don't contain the criterion. Again, choose the Show All Records command to redisplay all of the Database's records.

Using Query View

The Search command works well if you're looking for only one item of information, but Works has a Query view that lets you search for records using formulas that can match several criteria at once or that can contain logical operators to match data within ranges. To query the Works Database, you need to use Query view to enter the criteria you want Works to match. You then return to Form view or List view, and Works displays only those records that conform to the criteria you specified.

Suppose that we're working with our sample ADDRESS document in List view. We're doing a special mailing and we want to select only the records for companies with zip codes higher than 94200 and for people whose last name doesn't begin with A, B, or C.

1. Click the Query tool in the toolbar to display the Query view. Works displays a screen that's similar to the Form view of the document but that shows only field names. The word Query appears in the status line.

2. Select the LastName field, type >"C" and press Enter. (When you use a logical operator such as >, you must enter any text after it inside quotation marks so Works knows you want the operator to work on text. Otherwise, Works produces an error message when you press Enter.)

   NOTE: *Query formulas are not case-sensitive; you could have typed* >"c" *instead.*

3. Select the Zip field, type >94200, and press Enter.

   What you've typed represents your query formula: You've told Works to display only the records in which the LastName field begins with letters that come after C in the alphabet and the Zip field contains numbers greater than 94200.

4. Click the List tool to display the List view again. Works displays only those records that match the query formula, like this:

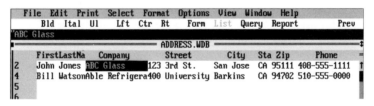

The other records in the document aren't gone, they're only hidden from view because they don't match the query formula. The fraction 2/4 in the status line indicates that two of the four records in the database match these criteria.

To show all the records in the document again, choose Show All Records from the Select menu (Alt-S-L).

After you enter a query on the Query screen, it remains there until you change it. To apply the query again, simply choose the Apply Query command from the Select menu (Alt-S-Q). To show all the records that do not match the query instead of those that do, choose the Switch Hidden Records command from the Select menu (Alt-S-W).

NOTE: *Before you continue with the exercises in this chapter, be sure the List view is showing all four records in the document. If it is not, choose the Show All Records command.*

If you use a query to display selected records, only those records will be included in any report you print. Works will also use only those records to supply data to labels or form letters you create using the Insert Database Field command on the Edit menu in the Works Word Processor tool.

We used a fairly simple query formula in our example above. But formulas can include other elements, such as wildcard characters or other logical operators that you can use to specify the records you want Works to display. For more information, see the *Querying a Database* or *Searching a Database* topic in the Database category of the Help Table of Contents.

DESIGNING A DATABASE REPORT

To print records from the Database, you need to create a report format first. (Unless you're merging database data with a form letter or mailing label in the Microsoft Works Word Processor — in these cases, see Chapter 4.) Just as you can create and view up to eight chart definitions with the Works Spreadsheet, you can create and view up to eight report formats in the Works Database.

Using the Report Generator

Let's create a report that includes customer names, company names, and telephone numbers.

1. Choose New Report from the View menu (Alt-V-N). Works displays the New Report dialog box, like this:

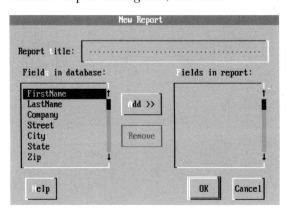

This is the new Report Generator in Microsoft Works version 3.

2. Type *Phone List* in the Report Title box.

3. Works has already selected the first field in the file (FirstName). Click Add to add it to the Fields In Report list. When you do so, the selection automatically moves down to the LastName field.

4. Click Add again to add the LastName field to the report.

5. Click Add again to add the Company field to the report.

6. Scroll down the Fields In Database list until you can see the Phone field, and then select it and click Add.

7. Click OK. Works displays the Report Statistics dialog box, like this:

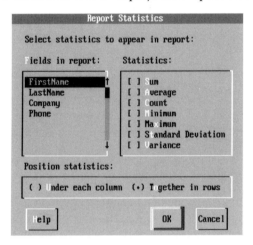

We don't want to include statistics in this report because it's only a telephone list, so click OK. Works displays the Report preview screen next.

Using the Report Preview Screen

The Report preview screen is essentially a preview of the report's appearance when printed, except it doesn't show the correct font or font size, the edges of the page, or the page margins. It looks like the screen shown on the following page.

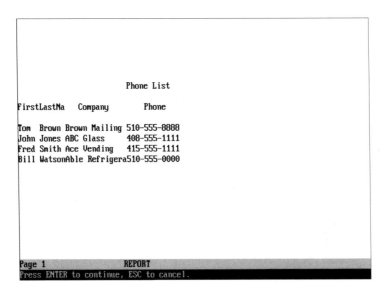

```
                         Phone List

FirstLastNa   Company        Phone

Tom  Brown Brown Mailing 510-555-8888
John Jones ABC Glass      408-555-1111
Fred Smith Ace Vending    415-555-1111
Bill WatsonAble Refrigera510-555-0000




Page 1                     REPORT
Press ENTER to continue, ESC to cancel.
```

This screen shows the fields we selected for the report. Notice that the field names are included as column labels above the actual field data. Each Report preview screen shows several records. When a document contains more records than will fit on one Report preview screen, you can press Enter to view the succeeding pages that contain the rest of the records. Works automatically makes the title bold and field names bold, underlined, and centered.

After you create a new report, Works assigns that report a number and adds the full name to the View menu. The first report you create is Report1, the second is Report2, and so on up to Report8. You can change the name of any report on this menu by choosing the Reports command from the View menu (Alt-V-R) and typing a new name.

Every time you create a new report, Works sets default column widths for the fields in that report. You will probably want to make some adjustments to the layout of any report you create. That's where the Report definition screen comes in.

Using the Report Definition Screen

The data in our report is a little hard to read because the columns are too narrow, but fortunately we can fix things in the Report definition screen.

- Press Esc. Works displays the Report definition screen, as shown in Figure 8-2.

You use the Report definition screen to change a report's format. You can remove fields from the report; make fields wider or narrower; add various titles, headers, or footers to the report page; and, if you didn't specify them in the Report

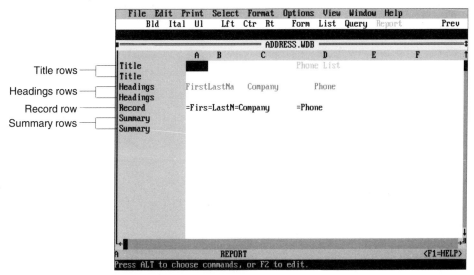

Figure 8-2.
The Report definition screen.

Statistics dialog box, produce various calculations from numeric data in the report. As you can see, the Report definition screen contains several types of rows:

- The Title rows can contain text that will be printed as a main report title on the first page of the report. If you entered a title for your report in the New Report dialog box, Works automatically suggests it as the report title here.

- The Headings rows can contain text that will be printed at the top of each report page. (These rows are usually used to display the field names.)

- The Record row represents the space in the report used for printing actual records. The equal sign plus the field name tells Works to display the contents of that field.

- The Summary rows can contain formulas that calculate totals, averages, or other statistics from data in the report fields. (If a field contains quantities, for example, a Summary row could contain a SUM formula to total all the quantities in that field.)

If we were to print the report using the report definition shown in Figure 8-2, the report title would be Phone List. Each page of the report would contain field names because the first Headings row contains the field names. (The second Headings row is blank, so the report would have a blank line between the field names and the actual data.) Finally the Summary rows contain no entries so the report would include no calculations. Let's make a couple of changes to see how the Report definition screen works.

First let's widen the columns so the data is easier to read.

1. Select the FirstName and LastName columns by clicking the A above column A, holding down the mouse button, and dragging across to column B.

2. Choose the Column Width command from the Format menu (Alt-T-W).

3. Type *10* in the dialog box that appears, if necessary, and then click OK. Works widens the FirstName and LastName fields.

4. Select the Company field (column C).

5. Choose the Column Width command, type *22* in the dialog box, and press Enter. Works widens the Company field.

6. Select the Phone field, choose the Column Width command, type *15* in the dialog box, and press Enter.

   Now we'll view the report format again. We can return to the Report preview screen for this report by clicking the Report tool in the toolbar. Works displays the report format on the screen, like this:

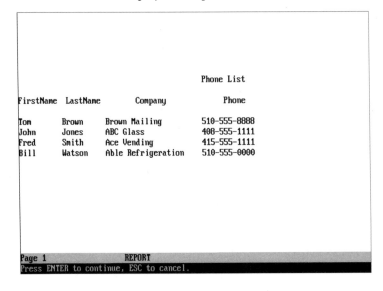

7. Press Esc to return to the Report definition screen.

Adding Rows, Data, or Calculations to a Report

You can add extra Title, Headings, and Summary rows to a report as needed. Simply choose the Insert Row/Column command from the Edit menu, and select the option to insert a row. You'll see a dialog box where you can select the type of row you want to add. After you select a row type and click OK, Works adds the new row in the appropriate part of your report.

Whenever you have selected a row or field in a report, you can choose special commands from the Edit menu to insert field names, field data, or summary calculations in a report. To delete a Title, Headings, or Summary row, select the row, choose the Delete Row/Column command from the Edit menu, and press Enter.

- The Insert Field Name command (Alt-E-N) inserts the field name at the location that is selected. When you choose this command, you'll see a dialog box where you can choose which field name to insert. After you click OK to insert the field name, it looks like those shown in the Headings row in Figure 8-2.

- The Insert Field Contents command (Alt-E-O) inserts the contents of a field. After you choose this command, you can select the name of the field whose contents you want to insert and click OK. Once you insert field contents, Works places a marker — the field name preceded by an equal sign — in the Report definition screen that looks like the ones in the Record row in Figure 8-2.

- The Insert Field Summary command (Alt-E-S) displays a dialog box, like this:

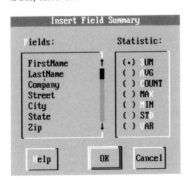

Here you select the name of the field whose data you want to summarize, and then select the type of calculation you want to make. When you insert a summary calculation in your report, Works calculates its result based on the records currently selected for viewing or printing.

243

Finally you can build your own formulas in Database reports to calculate the contents of fields in ways other than summaries. For example, in an order form report, you might multiply the Price field data by the Quantity field data to produce a Subtotal amount in another column in the report. In this case, you would insert a new column in the Report definition screen, add the Subtotal name for the column in the Heading row, and then enter the formula = Price*Quantity in the Record row. This formula would then produce a subtotal in each row (or for each record) in the report.

We'll put some of the reporting options and calculations to work in Chapter 10. For more information about various calculating options in database reports, see the *Working in Report View* topic in the Database category of the Help Table of Contents, or see Chapter 5, "Guide To Database Reporting," in the *Microsoft Works User's Guide*.

Printing a Report

As with other Works documents, you can choose either to print a report on paper or to preview it on the screen. Let's preview this report to see how the data will look when printed. To preview the report, follow these steps:

1. The Report definition screen for the Phone List report should still be showing on the screen. If it isn't, display it by choosing Report1 from the View menu and then pressing Esc. Then click the Prev tool in the toolbar to choose the Preview command. Works displays the Preview dialog box, like this:

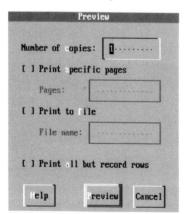

This dialog box contains an option for printing all the information on the report except the record rows. If you select this option, Works prints the report title, the column labels, and any summations or other calculations you have specified, but not the data from individual records. This option is handy when you want to print summaries, such as the subtotals and grand total from an inventory report.

2. Click Preview to accept the defaults. Works displays the report on the screen, like this:

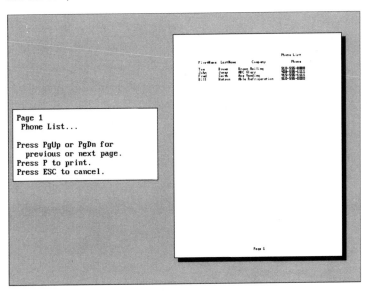

As you can see, the Preview command displays the report with the correct margins for your report, while the Report preview screen does not. Works automatically adds a footer with the current page number to each page.

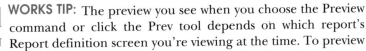 **WORKS TIP:** The preview you see when you choose the Preview command or click the Prev tool depends on which report's Report definition screen you're viewing at the time. To preview a particular report, be sure to display that report first. If you're in List or Form view when you choose the Preview command, you'll see a preview of the records in that Form or List layout.

Between its query features and its report definition features, the Microsoft Works Database has a lot of powerful data-management options that let you work with your data the way you want to. In Chapter 10, we'll explore some different practical ways to put the Database to use. First, however, we'll cover general Database tips in Chapter 9.

9

Making the Most of the Database

The Microsoft Works database offers great flexibility for storing and manipulating various kinds of data. Although it's easy to create a simple address file, as you did in Chapter 8, you'll need to know more about how to use Works' features to their best advantage as your data-handling needs grow. With the right techniques, you can create accounting systems, inventory files, order-entry or reservation systems, and other business and personal data-handling tools. This chapter gives you tips for using the Works Database productively.

Database management involves four areas of activity: designing the Database document, entering and viewing data, manipulating data, and reporting information. We'll look at ways you can more effectively use the Database in each area.

DESIGNING A DATABASE

Before you create a field or enter a record, you need to determine how you want your data document to look based on what types of data you want to store and how you want to retrieve or manipulate the data later. You'll find several ways to get the most out of Microsoft Works' data entry screens as you create the document.

Make a Plan

The most common mistake we make when setting up a new Database document is neglecting to consider how we want to use the data. Often we've already created fields and entered data when we discover that we'd like to divide the data in a different way or that we've arranged the fields in such a way that we can't easily select or report the information we need. Although you can always add new fields, delete fields, change field names, or alter the layout of reports in a Works Database document, it's far easier to design the document properly in the first place.

Start by thinking through the challenge at hand. What types of data will you store, and how will you break up the data into different fields? Make a list of all the types of data you'll want to store, and give each type a suggested field name. Then sit down with your list of names and consider your uses for the Database document. Will you use it only to look up information? If so, how do you want to be able to find or select the data? If you're planning to create reports, what data do you want the reports to show? If you're printing on labels or forms, how do those forms break up the data, and will you be able to break up records in your Database document in similar ways?

> **WORKS TIP:** Instead of making a list of field names on paper, create the field names in a new Database document and review them on the Form view screen before you enter any data. If you need to make changes, you can select field names and rename them or add or delete fields on the Form view screen before you enter any data. Furthermore, if you find that the new file needs too many changes, you can always close it without saving it and start over with a new, blank document.

Suppose, for example, that you're creating an address list for sending out form letters. You create a field called Name, in which you plan to store each person's first and last names. Later, when you want to send out a form letter, however, you discover that because you've combined both names in one field, you have to include both names in the greeting line of a form letter. Your letters must begin "Dear Fred Smith," instead of "Dear Fred" or "Dear Mr. Smith." If you know in advance that you'll want to send such letters, you should create three separate fields: one for the appropriate title (Mr., Mrs., Ms., Dr., and so on), one for the first name, and one for the last name. That way, you can use the information in those three fields independently or in any combination.

Another common mistake when setting up a database is failing to create enough fields for a proper address. Many people and businesses have addresses that include suite numbers, mail stops, divisions, or other designations in addition to a street or post office box number. On a typical mailing label, these pieces of information occupy two different lines of the address rather than one. If you have only one street address field in your database document, you'll probably have a hard time creating mailing labels that show full addresses.

By thinking through the various ways in which you'll want to use your data before you begin creating the Database file, you're more likely to get the document's design right on the first try.

Use Efficient Field Names to Maximize Screen Space

It's tempting to use long, descriptive names when you create fields, but lengthy names use up a lot of space on the screen and in printed reports. Keep in mind that the field name needn't do all the work of identifying the information the field contains. After you enter information in a document or a report, it's fairly obvious which information pertains to which field.

With a little thought, you should be able to come up with a name for each field that is no longer than the longest data entry that the field is likely to contain. In our sample address file in Chapter 8, for example, we used *Phone* as the name for the field containing telephone numbers. If we had used *Telephone Number*, we would have had to make the field wider than its data in the List view just to see the whole field name.

 WORKS TIP: If you really prefer long field names, try to use names that will still make sense when the last part of the name isn't showing in the List view. For example, we used *State* in the sample address file in Chapter 8, and when the field was narrowed to 3 characters in the List view, the field name became *Sta*.

Customize the Form Window to Simplify Data Entry

As we saw in Chapter 8, it's easy to create a stack of fields in the Form view by typing field names and pressing Enter. We also saw that you can easily rearrange fields to suit your needs. The screen-based form for any Works Database can be up to five pages long and over 26 inches wide, and you can arrange fields any way you want over those five pages as long as no two fields overlap.

Knowing how easy it is to create and rearrange fields, you might order your fields to match a printed form you use in your business.

 WORKS TIP: You can change the style of any field name, field data, or form label to more closely match entry blanks on a paper form. Simply select the field name, data, or label and click the appropriate tool in the toolbar, or choose the Style command from the Format menu and select options in the dialog box that appears. If you're working in text mode, the formatted information will appear in a different color or intensity.

You might also use different pages of the screen form if various employees will use groups of fields for different purposes. For example, an order-entry clerk might fill in the customer name, number, address, item number, quantity, and price, and a warehouse employee might fill in the date the item was shipped or indicate whether the item is back ordered. By placing these groups of fields on different pages of the screen form, you'll make it easier for each employee to focus on entering only the applicable data.

 KEYBOARD TIP: Press the PgUp or PgDn keys or the arrow keys to move to different pages (or areas of a page) of a screen form in Form view.

Protect Forms or Data So They Can't Be Changed

When you create a Database file that your employees or other people will use, you might want to prevent them from making changes to the Form or List view layouts or to some of the data in the file.

- To protect a List or Form view, simply display that view and choose the Protect Form command from the Options menu (Alt-O-F). If you try to delete or insert a field, you will see an error message. Choose the Protect Form command again to unprotect the view so changes can be made.

- To protect the data in a field from being changed, select that data in any record and choose the Protect Data command from the Options menu (Alt-O-P). If you try to edit or replace data in that field in any record, you will see an error message. Choose the Protect Data command again to allow changes to that field.

ENTERING AND VIEWING DATA

Microsoft Works offers both Form and List views for entering and viewing data. Each view has features that can make these activities easier. Here are some tips you can use for entering and viewing data in Form view, List view, or both.

Use the Keyboard to Enter Data

Whether you're using Form view or List view, the fastest way to enter data is to type the entry, and then press Tab to move to the next field. (Even when you need to skip a field or two before making the next data entry, it's faster to use

Tab than the mouse.) The following sections offer some other guidelines for deciding whether to use the keyboard or the mouse when you're working with the Database.

Use the Keyboard to Choose Commands

In most cases, it's faster to press Alt-key combination commands from the keyboard than it is to use the mouse to choose commands. The exceptions are when you want to click several options in a complex dialog box, or when you're simply clicking a tool in the toolbar.

Use the Mouse to Select Fields or Records

It's faster and more accurate to point and click with the mouse to select individual records or fields, or groups of records or fields in List view. Clicking the vertical scroll bar moves you from one record to the next in Form view. To jump to the end of a file, drag the scroll box in the vertical scroll bar down to the bottom.

Use the Split Bars in List View

The row-and-column layout of the List view usually prevents you from viewing all your document's fields on the screen at one time. In Chapter 8, we saw how you can hide or decrease the width of fields to maximize the horizontal space on the screen, but you can also use the split bars to divide the window either horizontally or vertically so that you can simultaneously view different parts of the document.

If your document contains two dozen fields, for example, you can use the vertical split bar to divide the screen into two independently scrolling windows or panes. You can then view one set of fields in the left pane and another in the right pane. For example, you might need to view the leftmost fields in a document (because they contain the name information you use to identify each record) while you simultaneously look up order number information located in fields that would ordinarily be off screen to the right. In this case, you could use the vertical split bar to view both groups of fields at one time, like this:

```
 File  Edit  Print  Select  Format  Options  View  Window  Help
      Bld   Ital   Ul      Lft  Ctr  Rt     Form  List  Query  Report              Prev
"510-555-4444
═══════════════════════════ ADDRESS.WDB ══════════════════════════
             Company          FirstName LastName        Phone
  1  123 Catering             Rita      Sandoval      510-555-3409
  2  AAA Answering Svc.       Jack      Ferguson      510-555-6556
  3  ABC Glass                John      Jones         408-555-1111
  4  Able Refrigeration       Bill      Watson        510-555-0000
  5  Accurate Input           Tony      Hodges        415-555-8803
  6  Ace Amusements           Ted       Wilson        510-555-0987
  7  Ace Vending              Fred      Smith         415-555-1111
  8  Acme Glass               Lois      Martin        415-555-2232
```

If you want to view two groups of records in List view, you can use the horizontal split bar to divide the window into upper and lower panes. You can then scroll one group of records into the upper pane and another into the lower pane. You even can split the window into four separate panes in List view.

To restore the window to a single pane, drag either or both split bars back to their original position.

Rearrange Fields in List View

If you want to view only certain fields in List view but they're not in the right order, rearrange them. You can move any field in the List view by selecting the field name, choosing the Move command (F3 or Alt-E-M), pressing the Right or Left arrow key to reposition the field, and then pressing Enter. You can also hide any field that you don't need to see by changing its width to 0 characters with the Field Width command on the Format menu (Alt-T-W). (For more information about hiding and redisplaying fields, see "Hiding Fields" and "Revealing Hidden Fields" in Chapter 8.)

Use Formulas to Enter Standard Data

When you have fields that contain the same data for most or all of the records in your Database document, use a formula to have Works enter that data for you. By using text formulas, you can tell Works to create the same entry in a field for every new record. If your customers are all in California, you can enter the formula = *"CA"* in a document's State field, like this:

This formula will cause Works to enter *CA* in each new record's State field. If one customer moved to a different state, you could enter the new state code without affecting the formula — Works would continue to enter *CA* in other new records. By using formulas for entering standard data, you also reduce data entry errors. For more information on using formulas to enter standard data, see the *Formulas in a Database* topic in the Database category of the Help Table of Contents.

If you're working in List view, you can also use the Fill Down or Fill Series commands on the Edit menu to automatically copy or enter data into new records below. We practiced using the Fill Down command in our sample address file in Chapter 8. To enter a series of numbers or dates in a field in consecutive records, do the following:

1. Select the field in List view in the first record you want to include in the series.

2. Enter the first number or date in the series.

3. Hold down the mouse button and drag down to select the same field in the other records.

4. Choose the Fill Series command from the Edit menu (Alt-E-L), and then choose the type of value you want to enter and the interval by which you want it to increase from one record to the next.

MANIPULATING DATA

Manipulating data means moving data, selecting groups of records, or maintaining the accuracy of data in a Database document.

Sort and Select to Find Records Quickly

After you have stored dozens or hundreds of records, you might want to rearrange the data. You can choose from among several ways to arrange data as well as use Microsoft Works' selecting commands to make data easier to find.

- If you're browsing through records looking for information in a specific field, sort the document on that field using the Sort Records command on the Select menu so that the record you want will be easier to find. If you want to find a transaction record from a certain date, for example, it will be much easier to find the record quickly if the records are sorted on the transaction date field.

- Use the Search command (Alt-S-S) to jump to specific data in a record. The Search command lets you type a word, phrase, or number and then tell Works to find the first record in which that item occurs. To repeat a search for the same entry, press F7.

WORKS TIP: When you search for data, remember that Works searches only from the current selection forward in the document. If you want to search the entire document, press Ctrl-Home to move the selection to the beginning of the document before you choose the Search command. If you begin a search in the middle of a document, Works will cycle back to the first record after it looks at the last record.

■ The Go To command (F5) is useful if you know the number of the record or the name of the field that you want to find. If a file contains dozens of fields and you want to scroll quickly to a certain one that's currently off screen, for example, you can choose the Go To command (Alt-S-G) or press F5 and then enter the field name or select it from the list that appears. You can also jump to a particular record number by entering that number in the Go To command's dialog box.

NOTE: *Neither the Search nor the Go To command is case-sensitive;* CITY, City, *and* city *produce the same result.*

Use Selection Options to Validate Data

One of the weaknesses in the Works Database tool is that it doesn't provide a way to force a certain type of entry in each field. Even though you set a certain field length when you define each field, and even though you can set a numeric, date, time, or text format for each field, these formats and field sizes don't prevent you from entering inaccurate information. A person can enter text in a number field, for example, and Works won't alert the user. Also, Works has no way to check for and warn about the entry of duplicate records. Therefore, you need to validate the data in your file manually by scanning the records and determining that all the entries in the fields are appropriate.

Works offers two ways to use its sorting and selecting features that are designed to simplify the process of manual data validation. To use the sort method, display the List view of the document and sort the document on an important field, such as the LastName field in an address file. After the sort finishes, any records that contain identical information in this field are rearranged so that they're next to each other, making it easier to spot duplicates as you scroll through the document. Try sorting several different fields in List view, one field at a time. After each sort, scroll through the document and scan for duplicate records, missing data, or incorrect entries.

WORKS TIP: If your file contains the same data in a key field such as LastName (you have more than one customer named Smith, for example), sort the file on two fields at once. If you sort an address file on the LastName and Street fields, Works arranges any duplicate records (Smith at 212 Elm Street, for example) next to each other.

You can also use Works' query capabilities to search for specific types of mistakes in certain fields. A query formula can include record-selection criteria for more than one field, so you can build query formulas that search for common mistakes in as many fields as you want at the same time. The following section offers some guidelines.

Use Wildcards and Logical Operators to Create Specific Queries

If you've properly designed a Database document so that the data is arranged in appropriate fields, you can use Works' Query view to locate any record or group of records. We practiced a fairly simple query with the sample address file in Chapter 8. For a more complex query, you can use wildcards and logical operators that let you select records based on ranges of numbers, dates, times, or incomplete strings of text characters.

The wildcards are the question mark (?), which you can use to replace any single character in a text string, and the asterisk (*), which you can use to replace any unspecific group of characters in a text string. To find all the addresses for people named Joe or Jon, for example, you could enter *Jo?* in the file's FirstName field, like this:

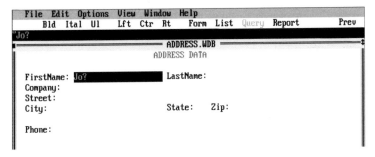

This wildcard causes Works to select records containing any three-letter name beginning with *Jo* in the FirstName field. If you enter *Jo** in the FirstName field, Works displays records containing first names of any length that begin with *Jo*, such as *Joanne* or *Josephine*. To find all the addresses for people whose last names begin with *B*, you could type *B** in the LastName field.

> **WORKS TIP:** After you've defined a query in Query view, Works stores it there until you replace it with another one. If you've chosen the Show All Records command from the Select menu to view all the file's records again and you want to reapply the same query you created before, simply press F10. Clicking the Query tool or choosing the Query command from the View menu (Alt-V-Q) returns you to the Query view screen, where you can change the existing query.

The logical operators you can use in query formulas are as follows:

Equal to (=)

Not equal to (<>)

Less than (<)

Greater than (>)

Greater than or equal to (≥)

Less than or equal to (≤)

And (#AND#)

Or (#OR#)

Not (#NOT#)

Use the Equal to, Not equal to, Greater than, and Less than operators to look for information that does or doesn't exactly match your query or to find ranges of numbers. Use the And, Or, and Not operators to combine query instructions in the same field.

For example, if you have a field called Item# that contains three-digit part numbers between 100 and 400, you could use the Less than, And, and Greater than operators in a query formula that searches for records in which the Item# field contains numbers less than 100 or greater than 400, like this:

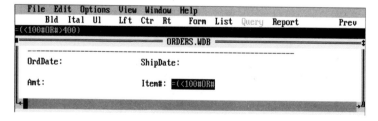

This query prompts Works to locate and display any records that incorrectly contain part numbers outside the range.

For more information about building queries, see the *Querying a Database* topic in the Database category of the Help Table of Contents or Chapter 4, "Guide to the Database," in the *Microsoft Works User's Guide*.

Copy Between Files to Approximate Relational Features

The Works Database is a *flat file database* as opposed to a *relational database*. In a flat file database, each file is separate from every other file, and you cannot merge, compare, or move information between two or more different files. A relational database, as shown in Figure 9-1, is often composed of two or more files, and you can easily combine, extract, or compare information between them.

The ability to work with more than one file at a time and to combine, extract, and compare information between files is often handy. For example, suppose you had a relational personnel database with one file (we'll call it SALARY) that contained current salary information for each employee and another file (we'll call it HISTORY) that contained employment history and educational information for each employee. If you wanted to determine whether a correlation existed between each employee's years of experience and salary level or between each employee's education and salary level, you could extract the education and employment history data from the HISTORY file, the salary information from the SALARY file, and view the information or create a new file that contained both types of data.

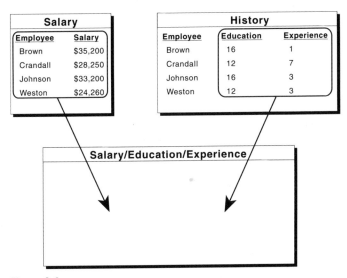

Figure 9-1.

A relational database can contain many database files. Information from separate files can be combined to create new files.

You can accomplish similar comparing, extracting, and merging operations in the Works Database by using Works' copying features and flexible file structure. Let's suppose you have two different personnel database documents called SALARY and HISTORY; both have a common field of LastName, and both documents have the same number of records and the same LastName entries. Let's say you want to merge the Education and Experience fields from the HISTORY file into the SALARY file. To do so, you can copy the fields from one document to another as long as you're careful to sort both documents in the same way so that the record positions in each document match.

1. Open the SALARY file, display the List view, and sort the file on the LastName field.

2. Open the HISTORY file, display the List view, and sort the file on the LastName field. Choose the Arrange All command from the Window menu (Alt-W-A) and click the Salary window. The screen would look something like this:

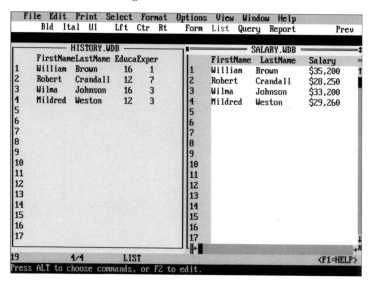

Now, unless your two documents contain a different number of records or different employees' records, you will have two documents in which the records appear in exactly the same order. (Check the left side of the status line in each document's window to determine the total number of records in each document.)

3. Select the Education and Experience field names in the HISTORY document, and choose the Copy command (Alt-E-C or Shift-F3). (If these fields aren't next to each other in List view, use the Move command to move them together before you select them.)

4. Choose the SALARY file from the Window menu, and select a field in the first record.

5. Press End to select the field that's farthest to the right. (You can be sure you've selected the field — rather than the empty column next to it — by checking the status line: The selected field name will appear there.)

6. Press the Right arrow key to select the next (empty) column in List view.

7. Press Enter. Works copies the contents of the Education and Experience fields to the SALARY file, like this:

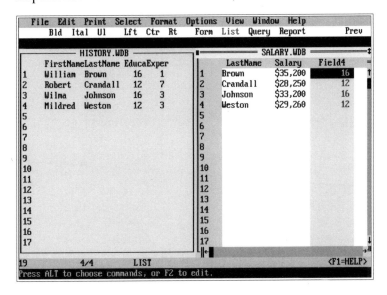

Works initially assigns the next two available field numbers to these two fields. If your salary document contains three fields, for example, these new fields will be named *Field4* and *Field5*. You can rename the fields using the Field Name command on the Edit menu (Alt-E-N).

WORKS TIP: When copying information from one file to another, you might find it helpful to first display the files side by side with the Arrange All command on the Window menu (Alt-W-A).

Split a File for Distribution to Several Users

Multiuser databases allow several users to work with the same file at once. The Works Database doesn't support this feature, but you can use its flexibility to work around this limitation. Suppose you have a large mailing list file called ADDRESS, and you want to make different portions of it available to three salespeople, based on the zip codes in each record. Let's say you want to give the records with zip codes 00001 through 30000 to Jones, the records with zip codes 30001 through 60000 to Smith, and the records with zip codes 60001 through 99999 to Brown:

1. Open the ADDRESS file.

2. Create a new field called Date. (This field will store the date on which each record was last updated.)

3. In List view, type the current date in the first record's Date field. You can also enter the current date by pressing Ctrl-; and then pressing Enter. (You can enter the current time by pressing Ctrl-Shift-: and then pressing Enter.)

   In List view you can use the Ctrl-' shortcut to copy the date from the above record to the current record, so you can move through the document quickly by pressing the Down arrow key and then pressing Ctrl-'. In fact, you can record a macro that will make the repeated copies for you with only one or two keystrokes. See Chapter 1 for more information about macros.

   Now the document shows that all the records were last updated on the day you split up the document for the salespeople.

4. Sort the document on the Zip field.

5. Save the file to preserve the sort order.

6. Using the Query view, select all the records with zip codes greater than 30000. Delete these records from the Database by using the Delete Record/Field command on the Edit menu (Alt-E-D).

7. Choose the Show All Records command from the Select menu (Alt-S-L) to display the remaining records.

8. Using the Save As command, save the document with the name JONESADD, and then close it. (Because you've renamed the file, the ADDRESS file remains unchanged on your disk.)

9. Open the ADDRESS file again.

10. Select all the records with zip codes smaller than 30001 or greater than 60000. (Use the criteria *<30001#OR#>60000* in the Zip field in Query view.) Delete them from the database.

11. Choose the Show All Records command from the Select menu (Alt-S-L) to display the remaining records.

12. Use the Save As command to save the file with the name SMITHADD, and then close it.

13. Open the ADDRESS file again.

14. Select all the records with zip codes less than 60001. (Use the criteria *<60001*.) Delete them from the database.

15. Display the remaining records, and use the Save As command to save the file with the name BROWNADD, and then close it.

Now you have three files (JONESADD, SMITHADD, and BROWNADD) that each contain a subset of records, and you still have the complete, sorted ADDRESS file on disk.

After these files are distributed, Smith, Jones, and Brown can add to them or update them. As they do, they'll enter the dates on which they entered new records or changed existing ones. At some point, you'll want to merge the records again into the ADDRESS file so that it contains the latest information.

1. Open your original ADDRESS file and display the List view.

2. Sort the document on the Date field.

3. Select all the records that were entered on or before the date you distributed subsets of the file, and delete them.

4. Open the JONESADD file, and select all its records by clicking the first record's row label and dragging down to the last row. (Do not use the All command on the Select menu or you will copy over the existing records in ADDRESS.WDB.)

5. Choose the Copy command, and then choose the ADDRESS file from the Window menu.

6. Select the first blank record at the bottom of the list, and press Enter. Works copies all the Jones records to the ADDRESS file.

7. Repeat steps 4 through 6 for the SMITHADD and BROWNADD files.

8. Save the ADDRESS file. It now contains copies of all updated records for Jones, Smith, and Brown and any new records that were entered or updated in the ADDRESS file itself after the distribution.

Enter Formulas in Fields to Calculate Within Records

Works lets you enter formulas in Database fields much as you do in Spreadsheet cells. These formulas can calculate a value based on the values in one or more other fields in the record, or they can automatically enter standard data that will usually be found in a field. In an inventory database, for example, you might have one field called Qty that stores the quantity of an item and another field called Price that stores the item's price. You could enter the formula = Qty*Price in a third field, called Value, and Works would calculate the value of that item by multiplying the number of items by the price. We'll see more of this technique in Chapter 10.

REPORTING

Reporting involves designing report formats, using their features to extract as much information as you can from your data, and then displaying that information in the most useful way. The following are a few tips that you can use when working with Microsoft Works Database reports.

Use Summary Rows to Produce Subtotals and Grand Totals

Because you can calculate Database data in report formats, you can handle many jobs with the Database that you might otherwise have tackled with the Spreadsheet. Any numeric field in the Database can be calculated with the arithmetic operators +, −, *, and /. You can also use the spreadsheet functions SUM, AVG, COUNT, MAX, MIN, STD, and VAR to perform Database calculations.

When you enter a formula containing a function in a numeric field's Summary row (on the Report definition screen), the formula calculates all the values in that field. For example, you might insert a SUM formula in the QTY field's Summary row to determine the total quantity of items in the records the report contains.

If you've sorted a Database document into groups of items, you can produce a subtotal for each group by instructing Works to generate a subtotal whenever the contents of another field change. For example, an inventory document might contain a field called Section that stores the name of each storeroom section and a field called Qty that stores the amount of each item in stock. If you sorted the document on the Section field (so that all the items in each section were grouped together in the list), you could create a formula that tells Works to generate a subtotal whenever the entry in the Section field changes. We'll see this technique at work in Chapter 10.

For more information on using summary formulas, see the *Inserting a Summary Formula* topic in the Reporting category of the Help Table of Contents.

Use Macros to Speed Up Repetitive Operations

Works' built-in macro feature can help speed up report formatting when you use certain types of rows or calculation formulas in more than one report. You can record strings of commands that insert and format special Headings or Summary rows in reports or that handle repetitive data-entry operations. Whenever you have to execute a procedure that requires several commands — whether that procedure involves inserting rows or deleting, inserting, or moving fields — you can automate the procedure with a macro. Be on the lookout for repetitive operations, and try recording a macro to automate those operations. For more information about creating macros, see Chapter 1.

Select Fields, and Use Font and Page
Setup Options to Maximize the Printing Area

As in the Works Spreadsheet, most of your Database documents will contain more fields than you can print across one piece of paper. Also as in the Spreadsheet, however, you can narrow fields, narrow the page margins, and use a smaller font or size to make the most of the horizontal space on a page. Try deleting unnecessary fields from a report to make room for the fields you do want to print.

The Microsoft Works Database can handle most personal and small business jobs with ease. By putting some of the tips presented in this chapter to work, you'll soon be handling data like a pro. Turn to the projects in Chapter 10 to see more of these techniques.

10
Database Projects

Any time you want to store, arrange, select, or calculate collections of information that contain text, numbers, times, or dates, the Microsoft Works Database is the tool for the job. In this chapter, we put the Database through its paces to complete some business and personal data-management projects.

A TAX LEDGER

In this project, you'll use the Database to record income and expense information and to create a simple but effective accounting system. Using this ledger, you'll be able to record taxable income and expenses as they occur. This accounting system is useful for projecting future budgets based on current or past expenditures, and it's a lifesaver at tax time, when you'll want a neat, categorized list of deductible expenses and taxable income.

To create this database, we need to capture the date of each transaction, its expense or income category, a brief description of the transaction, and the amount of the transaction. Because we'll want to determine totals or subtotals of only expenses or income, we'll also include a field called Type. All the transactions recorded will be for tax purposes, so we don't need a field to identify them as such. The List view of the completed tax ledger document looks like the one shown in Figure 10-1 on the next page.

Creating the fields for this document is the simple part. The real secret is in knowing how to select records and create reports to produce useful information.

Creating the Ledger File

To begin, you'll need to create a document like the one shown in Figure 10-1. First create the fields by following these steps:

1. Choose the Create New File command, click the Database file type, and then double-click the Standard/Blank template. Microsoft Works displays a new, blank database file in Form view.

File	Edit	Print	Select	Format	Options	View	Window	Help
	Bld	Ital	Ul	Lft	Ctr	Rt	Form	List	Query	Report		Prev

```
══════════════════ LEDGER.WDB ══════════════════
     Date      Type     Account        Description       Amount
1   4/15/93 Expense   Donation  Jones for Mayor          $5.00
2    5/2/93 Expense   Donation  Heart Association        $5.00
3   5/26/93 Expense   Donation  Church                   $5.00
4   4/14/93 Expense   Interest  VISA bill               $22.65
5   4/16/93 Income    Interest  Savings acct.            $6.03
6   5/15/93 Expense   Interest  VISA bill               $11.15
7   5/17/93 Income    Interest  Savings acct.            $6.16
8    4/1/93 Income    Paycheck  Paycheck             $2,465.00
9    5/1/93 Income    Paycheck  Paycheck             $2,465.00
10  4/14/93 Expense   Taxes     Federal income tax     $350.00
11
```

Figure 10-1.
A simple ledger of taxable income and expenses in List view.

2. Type *Date:* and press Enter; then type *15* (to specify the field size) and press Enter again.

3. Type *Type:* and press Enter; then type *10* and press Enter again.

4. Type *Account:* and press Enter twice.

5. Type *Description:* and press Enter; then type *30* and press Enter again.

6. Type *Amount:* and press Enter; then type *10* and press Enter again.

Entering Data in List View

Next we'll enter some sample expense records, which we can do more quickly in List view because many of the records contain identical Type entries. Before entering the records, however, we'll widen the Account and Description columns in the List view so that we can see most or all of the information in them.

1. Click the List tool in the toolbar to display List view. Works shows the default column widths of 10 characters for each field.

2. Select the Account column by clicking its name, and choose the Field Width command from the Format menu (Alt-T-W).

3. Type *15* and press Enter.

4. Select the Description column and widen it to 25 characters as in steps 2 and 3 above.

Now enter the records shown in Figure 10-1. Be sure to enter the first date and amount entry in the format shown in Figure 10-1; Works then automatically assumes you want the same format for all other entries in this field in other records.

In some cases, you can use the keyboard shortcut Ctrl-' to copy the entry from the field above into the currently selected field. In record numbers 2 and 3, for example, the Type (Expense), Account (Donation), and Amount ($5.00) are the same as in record number 1. So, when the Type field in record number 2 is selected, you can press Ctrl-' to copy the entry from the field above.

> **WORKS TIP:** If you have many recurring entries, such as a monthly paycheck or rent payment, you can insert all the records for the year at once. To quickly create a dozen monthly entries for the same payment, for example, simply enter the first record, select it and the 11 records below it, and then use the Fill Down command to copy the record 11 times. After you've made the copies of the record, you can either change the date entry in each successive copy of the record to match the correct month or use the Fill Series command from the Edit menu (Alt-E-L).

Before moving on in this project, let's save the file as LEDGER by choosing the Save command from the File menu (Alt-F-S), typing *Ledger,* and then pressing Enter to save the file.

Viewing Selected Records

Suppose you want to determine how much money you gave in donations during a year. You can use Works' Search command with the Match All Records option to show all the records that contain donations.

1. Choose the Search command from the Select menu (Alt-S-S).

2. Type *Donation* and click the All Records option.

3. Click OK. Works displays only the records that contain the word *Donation,* like this:

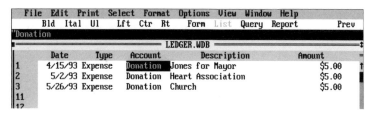

Notice that Works displays all the records that contain the word *Donation,* regardless of where the word appears. If for some reason this word appeared in a record that wasn't a donation, then that record would also appear on the screen.

Using Works' Query feature, you can display an even more specific group of records. Suppose, for example, that you wanted to view only the records that contain expenses for the month of April.

1. Click the Query tool in the toolbar to display the Query view screen.

2. Select the Date field, and type =(month()=4) to indicate that the Date field must contain a month entry with the number *4.*

3. Select the Type field, type *Expense* to indicate that the Type field must contain the word *Expense,* and then press Enter.

4. Click the List tool in the toolbar to return to List view. Works displays only the expense records with dates in April, as shown here:

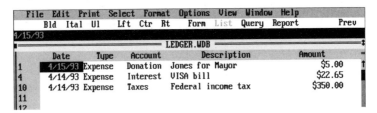

Using these query formulas and some of the calculating features of Works reports, you can spot-check your ledger throughout the year to see how much you've spent in specific expense categories during certain periods. For more information about entering query formulas, see the *Querying a Database* topic in the Database category of the Help Table of Contents.

Creating a Monthly Expense Report

At this point, our Database document shows only the expense records for the month of April. Let's leave this selection of records displayed and make a report that will show a total of the expenses — either on the screen or on paper. We won't need to display the Type field in this report because we know that it will contain only Expense records, so let's set up the report that way with Works' Report Generator.

1. Click the Report tool in the toolbar to display the New Report dialog box, like this:

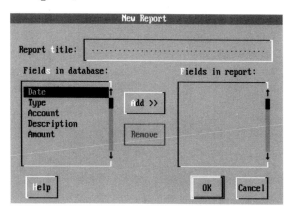

2. Type *April Expenses* in the Report Title box.

3. Click Add once to add the Date field to the report.

4. Select the Account field and then click Add to add this field to the report. Works adds the field and automatically selects the next field in the list.

 MOUSE TIP: If you're adding all the fields in a file to a report, you don't need to select their names in the New Report dialog box. Because Works selects the next field after you add one, you can simply click Add once for each field to add it to the report.

5. Click Add to add the Description field to the report.

6. Click Add again to add the Amount field to the report, and then click OK. Works displays the Report Statistics dialog box, as shown at the top of the next page.

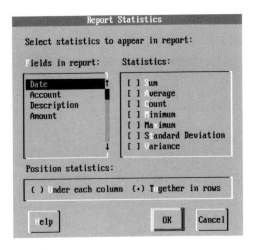

This dialog box lets us select a field on which to perform summary calculations in the report and also lets us select the type of calculation. We want this report to total up the expenses for the month, so we want to sum the contents of the Amount field.

1. Select the Amount field in the list at the left.

2. Click Sum at the top of the list on the right.

3. Click OK to display the report. The Report preview screen appears, like this:

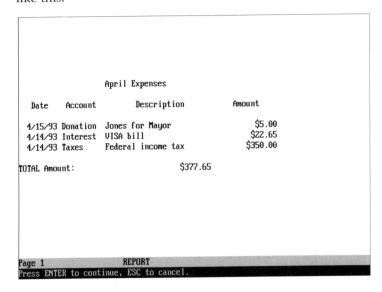

Notice that Works has placed the result of our calculation in a row at the bottom of the report and has automatically added the label *TOTAL Amount:* in the same row to identify the calculated value.

Modifying the Report Format

The Report preview screen shows the total we want, but it would look better if the total were underneath the Amount column. (By clicking the Under each column option in the Report Statistics dialog box, you can have Works put the total in the proper column, but it won't include the field label.) Let's move the summary formula and its label.

1. Press Esc to return to the Report definition screen. Works displays the report's definition, like this:

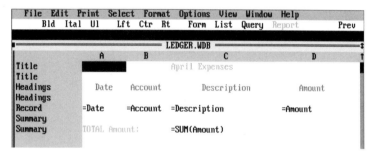

2. Select the formula = SUM (Amount) in the Summary row, and press F3 to choose the Move command. Works displays the MOVE indicator in the status line.

3. Press the Right arrow key once to move the selection over into the Amount column of the report, and then press Enter to complete the move. Works moves the formula.

4. Select the *TOTAL Amount:* label (be careful not to select the entire row), press F3, press the Right arrow key twice, and then press Enter to move this label over two columns.

WORKS TIP: You enter or edit labels and formulas in the Report definition screen just as in a Spreadsheet document: Click a field in any row, and then enter a label or formula by typing it and pressing Enter. You can also use the Insert Field Name, Insert Field Contents, and Insert Field Summary commands on the Edit menu to insert these items.

Changing the Report Name

Before we move on, let's rename this report to identify what it will be used for.

1. Choose the Reports command from the View menu (Alt-V-R). Works displays the Reports dialog box, like this:

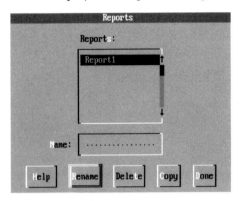

We've only created one report so far, so Report1 is the only report listed, and it's automatically selected.

2. Click the Name box, and type *Mo. Expenses.*

3. Click Rename to rename the report.

4. Click Done to put the dialog box away.

Now we can use this report to determine a month's total expenses at any time. To see and calculate the expenses for a different month quickly, simply click Query in the toolbar or press Alt-V-Q to display the Query view, and then change the formula in the Date field so that it tells Works to find and display the records for the month you want to view. To see records for May instead of April, for example, change the formula in the Date field to =(MONTH()=5). Then click Report in the toolbar or select *Mo. Expenses* from the View menu. Finally press Esc, select the report title on the Report definition screen, and then change it to *May Expenses.*

Selecting Records for an Annual Expense Report

Using the query and reporting features of the Database, we can produce a year-end report that shows expenses by category, subtotals after each category, and a grand total of all expenses for the whole year. The finished report is shown in Figure 10-2.

```
Annual Expenses

  Date     Account     Description              Amount

 4/15/93 Donation  Jones for Mayor              $5.00
  5/2/93 Donation  Heart Association            $5.00
 5/26/93 Donation  Church                       $5.00

                   SUBTOTAL                     $15.00

 4/14/93 Interest  VISA bill                    $22.65
 5/15/93 Interest  VISA bill                    $11.15

                   SUBTOTAL                     $33.80

 4/14/93 Taxes     Federal income tax          $350.00

                   SUBTOTAL                    $350.00


                   TOTAL Amount:               $398.80
```

Figure 10-2.
This annual expense report contains subtotals of expenses by account category.

Category labels and subtotals, as well as a grand total for all its expense amounts, appear on this annual expense report.

The first task in creating this report is to select only the expense records. Remember, a Works report always includes the current selection of records in the file, as specified by the Search or Query command. For this report, we'll query the database to select only expense records.

1. Click the Query tool to display the Query screen. It still shows the query formulas for the April expenses report that we created before.

2. Select the Date field, press Del, and then press Enter to clear the formula from this field. Now the only formula left is the Expense entry in the Type field, which tells Works to show only Expense records. This is the selection of records we want.

3. Click the List tool in the toolbar to display the List view. Only expense records are showing.

Defining the Annual Expenses Report

Next let's create a report that calculates the totals we want.

1. Choose the New Report command from the View menu (Alt-V-N) to create a new report. Works displays the New Report dialog box again.

 WORKS TIP: If you clicked the Report tool in the toolbar instead of choosing the New Report command at this point, Works would display the old April Expenses report you created before. After you've created your first report, you must use the New Report command to create a new report or you must select the name of an existing report from the View menu to display it.

---

2. Type *Annual Expenses* as the report title.

3. Next add the Date, Account, Description, and Amount fields to the report. (See the section titled "Creating a Monthly Expense Report" earlier in this chapter for the detailed steps in this procedure.)

4. Click OK. Works displays the Report Statistics dialog box.

5. Select the Amount field, click the Sum statistics option, and then click OK. Works displays the report format on the screen, as shown at the top of the next page.

```
            Annual Expenses

 Date    Account        Description         Amount

 4/15/93 Donation   Jones for Mayor             $5.00
  5/2/93 Donation   Heart Association           $5.00
 5/26/93 Donation   Church                      $5.00
 4/14/93 Interest   VISA bill                  $22.65
 5/15/93 Interest   VISA bill                  $11.15
 4/14/93 Taxes      Federal income tax        $350.00

TOTAL Amount:                      $398.80




Page 1                    REPORT
Press ENTER to continue, ESC to cancel.
```

As you can see, Works has created a total for all the expense amounts, and because all our yearly expense records are included in the report, this reflects the whole year's expenses.

Sorting Records in Report View

This report now shows the total of annual expenses, but it will be most useful to show subtotals of expenses by each expense account category. To create these subtotals, we'll have to sort the report on the Account field. Within each account category, we'll sort the records to appear in chronological order.

In Chapter 8, we saw how you can sort a Database document from List view. However, you can also sort a Database document from the Report definition screen. Whether you perform the sort from the List or Form view or from the Report definition screen, you always change the order of the records that appear in the document. When you sort from the Report definition screen, though, Works also adds the extra rows that you will need to create category labels and subtotals. Let's see how this works.

1. Press Esc to display the Report definition screen.

2. Choose the Sort Records command from the Select menu (Alt-S-O). Works displays the Sort Records dialog box.

3. Type *Account* to enter this name in the 1st Field text box. The Sort Records dialog box now looks like the one shown at the top of the next page.

275

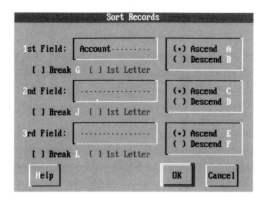

As you can see, the Sort Records dialog box contains two extra options for each sort level when you display the dialog box from the Report definition screen. Works uses the Break and 1st Letter options in this dialog box to create groups of records in a report. If neither of these options is selected, Works prints all the records in a report in one group, with no breaks between them. When all the records are printed in one group, you cannot create category labels or category subtotals.

We want Works to divide the records in our expense report by account category so that all the records for each account will be in a distinct group and will be followed by a subtotal, so we must select the appropriate option.

1. Click the Break option under the 1st Field entry.

   With the Break option selected, Works will break up a new group whenever the contents of the Account field change. Because we're sorting the document on the Account field, Donation expenses become one group of records, Interest expenses become another group of records, and so on. (At the end of this chapter, we'll see how the 1st Letter option works in the inventory project.)

   This is the only set of subtotals we want in this report, but we also want the report sorted by dates within each account category.

WORKS TIP: If you want breaks between sort categories in every report, you must select the Break option in the Sort Records dialog box for each sort level. In our case, we want the report's records grouped by account, but we don't want them grouped by date (or else a break would be included after each different date). Therefore, we only want to select the Break option on the Account sort level. You must select the Break option in order to make the 1st Letter option available.

---

2. Select the 2nd Field text box and type *Date*.

3. Press Enter or click OK to sort the records in ascending order and return to the Report definition screen.

We can now see how sorting the report from the Report definition screen gives us new capabilities. The Report definition screen now looks like this:

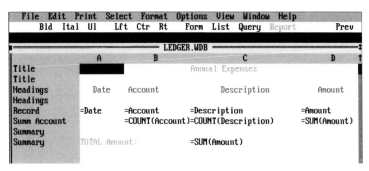

Modifying the Annual Expenses Report

Because we sorted the report and specified a break on the Account field, Works has inserted a Summ Account row below the Record row on the Report definition screen, and it has added the SUM(Amount) formula in the Amount column.

 **WORKS TIP:** If you specify breaks when sorting a report, Works automatically adds a new row type, Summ Account, to the Report definition screen. The new row type is named after the field on which you've broken the sort. You only can add a Summ row if you have a sort break in your report. If you choose the Insert Row/Column command from the Edit menu to insert a row, you also see a new Intr Account row type listed among the types you can choose from. The Intr Account row can contain a special heading that Works inserts before each category on which the sort break occurs. In our current example, you could insert a subheading that falls before each group of sorted account records.

Notice that Works has also inserted COUNT formulas in the Summ Account row's Account and Description columns.

The COUNT formulas calculate the number of records in each group. We don't need that information in this report, so we'll delete these formulas from the Summ Account row.

1. Click the COUNT formula in the Account field, hold down the mouse button, and drag the pointer across to select the COUNT formula in the Description column as well.

2. Choose the Clear command (Alt-E-E) to clear these formulas from the screen.

The SUM(Amount) formula in the Amount column in the Summ Account row should remain where it is, because it produces subtotals for each category of account records in the report. To check this, click the Report tool. Works displays the modified report preview on the screen, like this:

```
                        Annual Expenses

         Date    Account       Description          Amount

         4/15/93 Donation  Jones for Mayor            $5.00
          5/2/93 Donation  Heart Association          $5.00
         5/26/93 Donation  Church                     $5.00
                                                     $15.00
         4/14/93 Interest  VISA bill                 $22.65
         5/15/93 Interest  VISA bill                 $11.15
                                                     $33.80
         4/14/93 Taxes     Federal income tax       $350.00
                                                    $350.00

        TOTAL Amount:                $398.80


        Page 1                  REPORT
        Press ENTER to continue, ESC to cancel.
```

As it is, the report preview shows subtotals, but they're hard to read because there's no space above or below them. Let's add some new, blank rows to this report to separate the subtotals, add a label for the subtotals, and move the grand total label and total over into the Amount column.

1. Press Esc to return to the Report definition screen.

2. Click the Summ Account row's label to select the entire row.

3. Choose the Insert Row/Column command from the Edit menu (Alt-E-I). The Insert Row/Column dialog box appears, and the Summ Account row type is selected there.

4. Click OK. Works inserts the new row above the existing Summ Account row and returns to the Report definition screen.

We now have one blank Summ Account row between the subtotal and the last record in each group, but we need another one between the subtotal and the first record in the following group:

1. Click the upper Summary row's name (the blank Summary row) to select this row.

2. Choose the Insert Row/Column command from the Edit menu (Alt-E-I). The Insert Row/Column dialog box appears, and the Summary row type is selected there.

3. Click the Summ Account row type, and then click OK. Works inserts another blank Summ Account row above the Summary row and returns to the Report definition screen, like this:

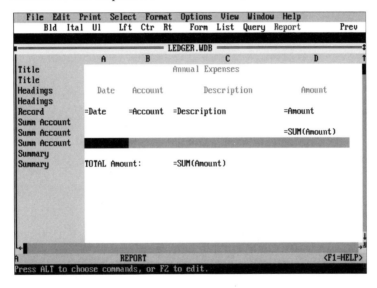

Now let's add a label to identify the subtotal amounts, make some amounts and labels bold, and move the report title, grand total label, and amount into the proper columns.

1. Click the Description column (column C) in the middle Summ Account row, to the left of the SUM(Amount) formula.

2. Type *SUBTOTAL* and press Enter.

3. Drag the pointer across the SUBTOTAL label and the subtotal formula to select them both, and then click the Bld tool in the toolbar to make them bold.

4. Select the Annual Expenses label in column D at the top of the report, and press F3 to choose the Move command.

5. Press Home to move the selection to column A, and then press Enter to complete the move.

6. Select the SUM(Amount) formula in the last row of the report (the bottom Summary row), press F3 to choose the Move command, press the Right arrow key once, and then press Enter to complete the move.

7. Click the Bld tool in the toolbar to make this formula bold.

8. Select the TOTAL Amount: label in the last row, press F3, press the Right arrow key twice, and press Enter to move this label.

Renaming the Report

Finally let's rename this report.

1. Choose the Report command from the View menu (Alt-V-R). Works displays the Report dialog box, which now lists our monthly expenses report along with Report1, which is the current year-end expense report. Report1 is selected because it's the report we're currently working with.

2. Click the Name text box, and type *Annual Expenses.*

3. Press Enter or click OK to rename the report, and then click Done to return to the Report definition screen.

At this point, when you print or preview the report, it should look like the one in Figure 10-2 (see page 273). Works groups the expenses into categories by account name and sorts them within each account category by date, subtotals each category's expenses, and displays the total of expenses for the year at the end of the report.

Using the Ledger

You can use the ledger document you just created to record and print financial transactions for a small business or for your personal finances. The challenge is to divide your expenses and income into meaningful categories (for example, categories that match your tax return so that you can easily transfer them at the end of the year). Then you must be consistent about how you enter the account names you set up. (If you call a donation *Donations* one time and *Donation* the next, for example, you won't be able to include both records in the same category with a database sort. A Database sort does not distinguish between uppercase and lowercase letters, however, so the Works Database groups *donation* with *Donation*.)

At the end of the year, you can validate your data and check to see that you entered account names the same way every time by sorting the file on the Account field and checking for correct spellings of account names. You can also create similar reports for your income, sorting the report on the account categories.

With monthly or quarterly reports, you can see how well you're sticking to a budget or whether your income is meeting your projections. This ledger document has many uses and serves as the basic accounting system for many small businesses.

MODIFYING THE CHECKBOOK TEMPLATE

The tax ledger project in the previous section works well if you only want to track your tax-related expenses and income. However, the Checkbook template that comes with Microsoft Works version 3 allows you to track all of your transactions, tax-related or not. Nevertheless, the Checkbook template doesn't let you categorize expenses and income into different accounts or identify which transactions are tax-related.

In this project, we'll modify the Checkbook template to add fields for identifying transactions by account and for indicating whether or not a transaction is tax-related.

Opening the Checkbook Template

First let's open the template and have a look.

■ Choose the Create New File command, click the Database document type, and then scroll the list of templates and double-click the Checkbook template. Works opens the template in the List view, like this:

```
 File  Edit  Print  Select  Format  Options  View  Window  Help
     Bld  Ital  Ul     Lft  Ctr  Rt    Form  List  Query  Report          Prev
1599.44
══════════════════════════ DATA1.WDB ══════════════════════════
    Num   Date       Description      Check   Deposit   Balance   Clr
1                  Starting Balance                    $1,599.44
2    323  10/1/92  Home Mortgage       566.81           $1,032.63 C
3    324  10/1/92  Service Station       9.50           $1,023.13 C
4    325  10/2/92  Stationery Store     14.90           $1,008.23 C
5         10/2/92  Sewing Machine Sale          100.00  $1,108.23 C
6    326  10/11/92 Electric Company    112.88            $995.35 C
7
8
```

The template has seven fields:

- The Num field stores the check number.
- The Date field stores the transaction date.
- The Description field stores a description of the transaction.
- The Check field stores expense amounts.
- The Deposit field stores income amounts.
- The Balance field contains the formula = *Balance – Check + Deposit*. This formula calculates the current checkbook balance by subtracting the value of the current transaction (the Check amount plus the Deposit amount) from the previous balance. Because each transaction is either a check or a deposit, one of the two values (Check or Deposit) will be zero, and the correct current balance will be calculated.
- The Clr field contains a character that indicates whether the check or deposit has cleared the bank.

You can use this template as it is to record every check you write or deposit you make. When you get a bank statement, you put a C in the Clr field to indicate when a check or deposit has cleared.

Adding Fields

To modify this template so it will help us at tax time, we need to add a field to indicate whether a transaction is tax-related and another field to store account names, so we can sort our records by account category.

When you open this template, the form and the data in it are protected, so you must unlock them before you can add fields. After you do this, you can add the Account field between the Date and Description fields, and then add the Tax field to the right of the Clr field.

1. Choose the Protect Form command from the Options menu (Alt-O-F) to unlock the form itself.

2. Choose the Protect Data command from the Options menu (Alt-O-P) to unlock the data.

3. Click the Description field's name to select the entire column.

4. Choose the Insert Record/Field command from the Edit menu (Alt-E-I). Works inserts a new, empty field column between the Date and Description fields, but the field has no name.

5. Choose the Field Name command from the Edit menu (Alt-E-N). Works displays the Field Name dialog box.

6. Type *Account* in the Name box and press Enter. Works names the new field, like this:

File	Edit	Print	Select	Format	Options	View	Window	Help	
	Bld	Ital	Ul	Lft	Ctr	Rt	Form	List	Query	Report		Prev

DATA1.WDB

	Num	Date	Account	Description	Check	Deposit
1				Starting Balance		
2	323	10/1/92		Home Mortgage	566.81	
3	324	10/1/92		Service Station	9.50	
4	325	10/2/92		Stationery Store	14.90	
5		10/2/92		Sewing Machine Sale		100.00
6	326	10/11/92		Electric Company	112.88	
7						
8						

MOUSE TIP: When you click a field name to select the entire column, Works automatically knows you want to insert a new field when you choose the Insert Record/Field command. If you simply click a field space in one record before choosing the Insert Record/Field command, you must then indicate whether you want to insert a field or a record.

Now select the new Tax field by scrolling the List view to the right and selecting the column to the right of the Clr field name. In this case, we don't need to insert a new field between two others, so we can define this field by naming it. Simply choose the Field Name command from the Edit menu, type *Tax,* and press Enter.

The List view now contains too many fields to show on the screen at one time. However, you can still enter transactions by typing in a field and then pressing Tab to move into the field on the right. When you press Tab to move to a field that's off the screen to the right, Works automatically scrolls the List view to reveal it. If you really want to be able to see all the fields at once in List view, narrow the Description field. You'll still be able to type long descriptions into it — you just won't see them on the screen.

In fact, you could even hide the Description field from view by setting its width to 0 characters. As we'll see, there are other fields in this file that are now hidden from the List view.

Saving the Modified Template

Let's save this modified template as a normal Works Database file so we can use it to store our transactions.

1. Choose the Save command from the File menu (Alt-F-S).

2. Type *Checks* and press Enter. Works saves the file as CHECKS.WDB in the current directory.

Modifying the Form View

To see all the fields in this file on one screen, we'll switch to Form view.

1. Click the Form tool in the toolbar. Works displays the Form view.

2. Click once in the lower part of the vertical scroll bar to display the second record in this file, or press Ctrl-PgDn. Now you can see the second record in the file, as shown in Figure 10-3.

You can see the new Account and Tax fields at the bottom of the Form view screen. When you add a new field to either the List or Form view, the field is also added to the other view as well. Let's move these two fields to a better place on the screen.

1. Select the Account field name and press F3.

2. Click about 2 inches to the right of the Description field entry, and then press Enter. Works moves the field there.

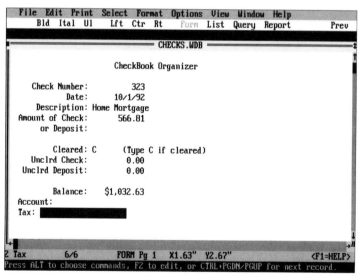

Figure 10-3.
The Form view can show fields that are hidden from the List view.

3. Scroll to the left, if necessary. Select the Tax field name, and then press F3.

4. Click underneath the A in the Account field name, and then press Enter. Works moves the field there.

 MOUSE TIP: If Works displays a message when you press Enter to move the Account field, you're trying to put the Account field on top of part of the Description field data space. Click OK, click half an inch farther to the right of the Description field name, and press Enter again.

Using Label Tricks to Change Field Names

Along with these two new fields, you'll notice that the Check, Deposit, and Clr field names are different than they were in List view. Actually, the Check and Deposit field names simply have extra labels in front of them, and the Clr field name has been hidden and replaced with a label. See for yourself.

1. Click the word *Check* in the Amount of Check field name. Works highlights only the word *Check* and the colon after it. This is the real field name, the same as it is in List view.

2. Click the word *Amount* to the left of the word *Check* on this same line. Works highlights only the words *Amount of.* These words were added as a text label in front of the Check field name on the same line to make the field name appear more descriptive here. (If you click to the left of the word *Deposit* on the line below, you'll find that the word *or* is also a separate label.)

The Cleared label is a special case. This label actually appears on top of the real field name, Clr. To do this, you must first hide the real field name and then enter a label to put on top of it. To see how this was done, let's hide the Tax field name and replace it with the label *Taxable.*

1. Click the data space to the right of the Tax field name.

2. Choose the Show Field Name command from the Format menu (Alt-T-N). The Tax field name disappears, and the field data space is selected.

3. Press F3, press the Right arrow key four times, and then press Enter to move the field data space.

4. Click underneath the A in the Account field name, and type "Taxable:. (You have to type a quotation mark in front of this field label because the label has a colon after it. If you don't type a quotation mark first to indicate that this is a label, Works thinks you're entering a new field name.)

5. Press Enter to enter this label. The screen now looks like this:

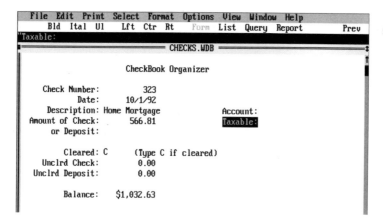

Now the field name appears to be *Taxable*, but this is really a text label that covers up the hidden field name *Tax*.

Using Logical Formulas

Along with these changes in the appearance of field names, this form also shows two other fields we didn't see in List view, the Unclrd Check and Unclrd Deposit fields. Both of these fields contain zero values in the sample above, but these values are produced by logical formulas, as follows:

- The Unclrd Check field contains the formula *IF(Clr > " ",0,Check)*. This formula tells Works to look in the Clr field (which is now labeled *Cleared*). If the Clr field contains any text (anything greater than " ", which is no text), Works puts a zero value in the field (as it has done in Figure 10-3, shown on page 284). If the Clr field is blank, Works inserts the value from the Check field (labeled *Amount of Check* in Figure 10-3).

- The Unclrd Deposit field uses a similar logical formula: *IF(Clr " ", 0,Deposit)*. In this case, Works copies the value in the Deposit field (labeled *or Deposit* in Figure 10-3) if the Clr field is blank, and places a zero value here if the Clr field contains any text at all.

WORKS TIP: These logical formulas look for any text at all in the Clr field, so you don't necessarily have to type a C there to show a check has cleared. You can type any letter or symbol character; Works responds the same way. However, the logical formula is looking for text, not values, so if you put a number in the Clr field, Works won't evaluate the logical formula properly.

Adding Account and Tax Data

Before we create a new tax report with this file, we need to add some data in our new Account and Tax fields.

1. Click the List tool to switch to List view.

2. Scroll to the left, if necessary, and click the Account field's space in record number 2.

3. Type *Mortgage,* and press the Down arrow key to enter this account type and move the selection to the record below.

4. Repeat step 3, and enter the account labels *Gasoline, Ofc. Supp., Misc. Inc.,* and *Utilities* in records 3, 4, 5, and 6, respectively.

5. Click record number 4 (the Stationery Store record), scroll the List view to the right, and click the Tax field.

6. Type *X,* and press Enter to indicate that this record is tax-related.

 WORKS TIP: You can quickly scroll the List view to the rightmost field by pressing End, or to the leftmost field by pressing Home. However, Works only selects the leftmost or rightmost field if that field contains an entry in at least one record in the file. In our example, the Tax field is still empty, so Works would select the Clr field if you pressed End, and you'd then have to press the Right arrow key to select the Tax field.

Making a Tax Report

The Checks file already has an activity summary report that helps you balance your checkbook each month (it's listed as Summary on the View menu), but let's create a year-end report of deductible expenses similar to the one in the tax ledger project at the beginning of this chapter.

1. Choose New Report from the View menu (Alt-V-N).

2. Type *Deductions* in the Report Title box.

   For this report, we only need the Date, Account, and Check fields, so select those and add them to the report.

3. Click the Date field name, and then click Add.

4. Repeat step 3 for the Account and Check field names, and then click OK. Works displays the Report Statistics dialog box.

5. Select the Check field name, and click the Sum option in the Statistics list.

6. Click OK. Works displays the Report preview screen, like this:

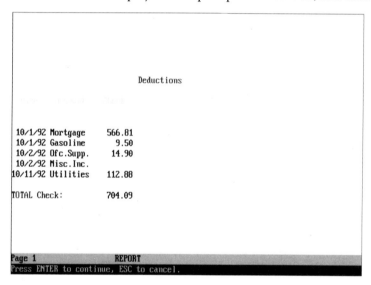

Deductions

```
10/1/92 Mortgage    566.81
10/1/92 Gasoline      9.50
10/2/92 Ofc.Supp.    14.90
10/2/92 Misc.Inc.
10/11/92 Utilities  112.88

TOTAL Check:        704.09
```

Page 1   REPORT
Press ENTER to continue, ESC to cancel.

Selecting Tax-Related Records

As it is, this report contains all the records in the file, including the income record for the sewing machine sale (Misc. Inc. account in the example given earlier), and the first record in the file, which simply contains the label Starting Balance in the Description field. (Because the other fields in the first record are blank, there's an extra blank line in the report to represent them between the field labels and the second record in the example above.)

We want the report to contain only tax-related expenses, so we must create a query to select them.

1. Press Esc to display the Report definition screen, and then click the Query tool in the toolbar. Works shows the Query view screen, which already contains a query formula in the Date field. (This query was stored as part of the original Checkbook template file.)

2. Select the Date field formula, press Del to remove it, and then press Enter.

3. Select the Taxable field's data space, type >"", and then press Enter. This logical condition tells Works to select only records where the Taxable field contains text. Because we've only entered an *X* in the Taxable field for the taxable expense records, this one criterion selects only the records we want to include in the report.

4. Click the List tool in the toolbar. You'll find that only record number 4, the one in which we typed an *X* in the Taxable field, is selected.

Completing the Report

Now that we've selected the records (in this case, a single record) we want, the only remaining tasks are sorting the file so we can produce subtotals of each account category, inserting some rows and adding or moving some labels or formulas on the Report definition screen so the subtotals stand out, and renaming the report so it's easier to identify on the View menu. These procedures were covered in detail under "Sorting Records in Report View," "Modifying the Annual Expenses Report," and "Renaming the Report" in the tax ledger project at the beginning of this chapter.

Using the Checks File

You created this file from the Checkbook template, so don't forget to delete the dummy records that were stored in the original Template file before storing records of your own. The simplest way to delete all the records is to display all the records with the Show All Records command from the Select menu (Alt-S-L), if necessary; choose the All command from the Select menu (Alt-S-A) to select all the file's data; and then choose the Clear command from the Edit menu (Alt-E-E).

A SIMPLIFIED INVENTORY FILE

The Microsoft Works Database is a good tool for creating an inventory file because it allows you to sort, select, and organize items in an inventory. You can use a Database formula to calculate the total value of each item in stock, and you can use subtotal and grand total formulas in a report to calculate total quantities and the value of items in various categories.

Works comes with two different inventory database templates, one for business use and one for personal use. However, each is fairly complex and might require more input than you'll want to provide. In this project, we'll build a much simpler inventory database.

To begin this project, you will create the Database file shown in Figure 10-4. This document isn't yet complete, but it will give us the data we need to begin this project.

Creating the Inventory Document

To create this document, open a new Database file, create the four fields shown, and then enter the records, like this:

1. Choose the Create New File command, and then select the options to create a Standard/Blank Database document.

2. Type *Item#:* and press Enter twice.

3. Repeat step 2 to create the *Name:*, *Qty:*, and *Price:* fields.

4. Click the List tool in the toolbar to switch to List view. Each field is 10 characters wide.

5. Click the Name field in the first record, and then choose the Field Width command from the Format menu (Alt-T-W).

6. Type *20* and press Enter.

Now you can enter the records shown in Figure 10-4. Be sure to enter the first entry in the Price field as shown; subsequent entries in this field will be automatically formatted as currency with two decimal places. When you finish, choose the Save command, and save the file with the name INVENT.

```
 File  Edit  Print  Select  Format  Options  View  Window  Help
       Bld  Ital  Ul      Lft  Ctr  Rt     Form  List   Query  Report        Prev


                            ═══ INVENT.WDB ═══
        Item#          Name        Qty     Price
  1   G001      Small Gizmo         246    $0.30
  2   G002      Medium Gizmo        527    $0.35
  3   G003      Large Gizmo          89    $0.45
  4   W001      Small Widget        340    $0.05
  5   W004      Medium Widget       125    $0.10
  6   W005      Large Widget        189    $0.20
  7
  8
```

Figure 10-4.
A sample inventory document in the Database.

This document now contains information about the item number, name, quantity, and unit cost of each item in inventory, but it won't show us the total value of each item. We'll solve that problem next.

Adding a Calculation Field

To determine the total value of each item in stock, we'll add a new field and then enter a Database formula that multiplies the quantity of each item by its price.

1. Click to the right of the Price field name to select the empty field to its right.

2. Choose the Field Name command from the Edit menu (Alt-E-N), type *Value,* and press Enter. The new name appears at the top of the column.

To calculate the value of each inventory item, we'll enter a formula in this field.

1. Select the Value field in the first record.

2. Type = to let Works know you're beginning a formula. The equal sign appears in the formula bar.

3. Click any entry in the Qty field in the first record. The Qty name appears in the formula bar.

4. Type * to indicate that you want to multiply. The asterisk is entered after Qty in the formula bar, and the selection moves back to the Value field.

5. Click any entry in the Price field. This field name appears in the formula bar, so the formula now reads: = Qty*Price.

6. Press Enter to enter the formula. Works calculates the value for each inventory item, as shown at the top of the next page.

 WORKS TIP: As in the Spreadsheet, you can enter formulas in the Database either by typing their contents or by pointing to and clicking the fields you want referenced in the formula.

```
 File  Edit  Print  Select  Format  Options  View  Window  Help
        Bld  Ital  Ul    Lft  Ctr  Rt    Form  List  Query  Report          Prev
=Qty*Price
============================== INVENT.WDB ===============================
        Item#          Name          Qty      Price      Value
   1   G001      Small Gizmo         246      $0.30       73.8
   2   G002      Medium Gizmo        527      $0.35      184.45
   3   G003      Large Gizmo          89      $0.45       40.05
   4   W001      Small Widget        340      $0.05       17
   5   W004      Medium Widget       125      $0.10       12.5
   6   W005      Large Widget        189      $0.20       37.8
   7
   8
```

The values appear in the default General format. Change the format to Currency by choosing the Currency command from the Format menu (Alt-T-U) and pressing Enter to accept the default value of two decimal places.

Calculating Item Counts and Value Totals

Now let's create a report that calculates subtotals of each category of items by item number. Unlike the sorting we've done in the other projects in this chapter, we'll have to ask Works to break up the sort categories by the first character in the Item# field.

1. Choose the New Report command from the View menu (Alt-V-N).

2. Type *Total Values,* and then click Add five times to add every field in the file to the report.

3. Click OK. Works displays the Report Statistics dialog box. We want to produce two different calculations in this report: a total of the inventory values for each category and for the whole report, and a count that shows the number of different inventory items in each subcategory.

4. Click the Qty field name, and then click the Count statistic option.

5. Click the Value field name, and then click the Sum statistic option.

WORKS TIP: You're not limited to one statistical calculation per field when you define a report. If you like, you can select two or more statistical options for each selected field in the Report Statistics dialog box.

---

6. Click the Under each column option in the Position Statistics area, and then click OK. Works displays the Report preview screen, like this:

```
                        Total Values

   Item#         Name           Qty    Price    Value

G001        Small Gizmo          246    $0.30    $73.80
G002        Medium Gizmo         527    $0.35   $184.45
G003        Large Gizmo           89    $0.45    $40.05
W001        Small Widget         340    $0.05    $17.00
W004        Medium Widget        125    $0.10    $12.50
W005        Large Widget         189    $0.20    $37.80

                         COUNT:            SUM:
                             6                 $365.60




Page 1                    REPORT
Press ENTER to continue, ESC to cancel.
```

Notice that the COUNT formula produces a count of the number of different items (or the number of records), rather than the number of total items in inventory (you would need a SUM formula to do that). The COUNT formula might not make much sense in a Database file that contains only three items in each category, but it would be very helpful in a typical inventory with dozens or even hundreds of different items in each category.

Sorting to Produce Category Subtotals

As it is, the report calculates a count of different items and a sum of values for the whole report, but not for each of the item categories. To have Works create subtotals for the categories, we must sort the report.

Looking at Figure 10-4, you can see that the logical categories for this inventory would be Widget-type items, which have item numbers that begin with the letter *W*, and Gizmo-type items, which have item numbers that begin with the letter *G*. In this case, we want Works to create a new category of items only when the first character in the Item# field changes. So we need to select the 1st Letter option in the Sort Records dialog box to tell Works to create new categories only when the first letter of the Item# field contents changes.

1. Press Esc to display the Report definition screen.

2. Choose the Sort Records command from the Select menu (Alt-S-O).

3. Type *Item#* in the 1st Field box.

4. Click the Break option below the 1st Field box.

   By selecting the Break option, you tell Works to divide each group of items into different categories. With only the Break option selected, however, Works will create a new group of Item records each time the contents of the Item# field changes. Because the item number changes with each record, Works places each record in a separate category.

5. Click the 1st Letter option next to the Break option you just selected, and then click OK. Works returns to the Report definition screen and adds a new Summ Item# row.

6. Delete the formulas in the Item#, Name, and Price field contents in the Summ Item# row. The screen now looks like this:

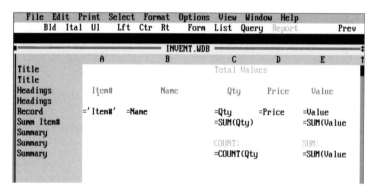

Copying Formulas in Report View

Although it has added a new row for subtotal formulas (the Summ Item# row), Works has also included a Sum formula in the Qty field in the new Summ row, where we really want a COUNT formula. However, because the COUNT formula already exists in the last Summary row on this screen, we can copy it from there:

1. Select the COUNT formula in the last Summary row and then choose the Copy command from the Edit menu (Alt-E-C or Shift-F3).

2. Click the Summ Item# row in the same column — where the Sum(Qty) formula is now — and then press Enter. Works copies the formula there over the existing formula.

You've now entered all the formulas. Let's display the Report preview screen again to see how the calculations look.

- Click the Report tool in the toolbar. Works displays the report with the category subtotals and grand totals, as in Figure 10-5.

Adding Report Labels

The only remaining tasks are formatting adjustments that will make the report look better. Let's add a spacing row between categories and some titles to identify the totals, and then change the alignment of some column headings.

1. Press Esc, and select the name of the topmost Summary row. Works selects the whole row.

2. Choose the Insert Row/Column command (Alt-E-I). Works displays a dialog box that lists the different row types you can insert in the report.

3. Select the Summ Item# row type, and click OK. Works inserts a new Summ Item# row below the existing one. We'll leave this row blank so that it will appear in the report as a blank line.

4. Select the Name field in the last Summary row at the bottom of the report, type *Grand Totals,* and press Enter.

```
                        Total Values

    Item#       Name         Qty     Price    Value

G001        Small Gizmo      246     $0.30    $73.80
G002        Medium Gizmo     527     $0.35   $184.45
G003        Large Gizmo       89     $0.45    $40.05
                              3                $298.30
W001        Small Widget     340     $0.05    $17.00
W004        Medium Widget    125     $0.10    $12.50
W005        Large Widget     189     $0.20    $37.80
                              3                $67.30

                    COUNT:            SUM:
                              6                $365.60


Page 1                  REPORT
Press ENTER to continue, ESC to cancel.
```

Figure 10-5.

After you enter subtotal and total formulas in the Report definition screen, those totals appear in the Report preview screen.

5. Select the Name field in the upper Summ Item# row, type *Subtotal,* and press Enter.

Finishing Touches

Figure 10-5 has only one other formatting problem: The numeric entries in the Qty, Price, and Value fields aren't centered below their titles. Let's change the alignment of the column titles.

1. Select the Qty label in the upper of the two Headings rows.

2. Hold down the mouse button and drag the pointer to the right two columns to select the Price and Value labels.

3. Click the Rt tool in the toolbar to right-align these column headings.

If you like, you can enhance this report in other ways, such as:

- Changing the report name with the Reports command on the View menu

- Making the subtotals and grand totals labels bold

- Adding another Summ Item# row above the one that contains the formulas so there's a space between each subtotal and the records in the category above it

For now, let's add a header to the report.

1. Choose the Headers & Footers command from the Print menu (Alt-P-H). Works displays the Headers & Footers dialog box, and the cursor is blinking in the Header text box. Notice that the option to use header and footer paragraphs is not available; you can only use single-line headers and footers in the Database. Also, Works automatically adds a footer that contains the page number. (The &p&c commands in the Footer box tell Works to add the page number and center it.)

2. Type &*RInventory Value* and then press Enter.

The &R command tells Works to right-align the header on the page. For more information on headers and footers in the Database, choose the Headers & Footers command, and then click Help in the dialog box that appears.

The projects included in this chapter have covered all the major features of the Microsoft Works Database tool. You can now put the Database to work on data-handling tasks of your own.

11

Communications Concepts & Techniques

The Communications tool in Microsoft Works lets you communicate with other computers either over standard telephone lines or through a cable directly linking your computer with another. Works lets you connect your computer to other computers so that you can receive or transmit data. In this chapter, we'll look at how the Communications tool works and at some different ways in which you might want to use it. First, though, we'll look at personal computer communications in general.

HOW COMPUTERS COMMUNICATE

For computers to exchange information, they must first have a physical means of transmission, and they must also be running software that enables them to communicate. Although it's possible for computers to exchange data using radio waves, other means are more common, such as a simple cable that links two nearby computers to each other, a local area network that links several computers in a single office or building, or a telephone system that links computers at great distances from one another.

Although any of these physical means can establish a data path between two computers, you must have a communications program in order to establish the specific method of communication and to select and send data or receive data and store it on your disk. The Microsoft Works Communications tool lets you exchange data with other computers either over telephone lines or through simple cables. (You need a special type of software called a "network operating system" to communicate with other computers over a network.)

How Modems Work

Most telephone systems are designed to carry continuously varying voice-frequency signals rather than discrete bits of computer data. To exchange data over telephone lines, computers must transmit and receive their bit streams through a modem. This device allows them to communicate by impressing (or modulating) computer data onto a voice-frequency carrier signal, in much the same way that a radio transmitter impresses voice signals onto the station's carrier frequency. The modem at the receiving end, like your radio, reverses this process and restores the computer data to its original form. (The name *modem* is short for *MOdulator/DEModulator*.) You connect a modem to a serial communications port on the back of your computer.

You can buy a modem from any computer dealer or through any of dozens of mail-order firms. Modems for the IBM PC and PC-compatible personal computers range in price from less than $100 to over $1,000. All modems perform the same basic modulation/demodulation function, but modems differ in how fast they can transmit data, which sets of software commands they understand, whether they reside inside or outside the computer, and what extra features they have.

Modem transmission speeds are measured in bits per second (bps). Expensive modems can transmit data at much greater rates, but most common modems operate at 1200 or 2400 bps. Any modem that transmits at 1200 or 2400 bps can also transmit at slower speeds, so if you have a 300 bps modem and you call another computer that's using a 1200 bps modem, the faster modem will automatically lower its transmission rate to match yours. Modem prices have dropped dramatically in the last few years, and 2400 bps modems are now available for around $125.

Modems are internally programmed to accept certain commands from the communications software you use on your computer. These commands prompt the modem to adjust its transmission speed, dial a number, hang up, answer the phone when it rings, or perform other tasks. The most common set of modem commands is the Hayes command set. (Hayes Microcomputer Products was the first well-known personal computer modem manufacturer, so its command set was adopted by other makers as the standard.) The Works Communications tool uses the Hayes command set, so your modem should be Hayes-compatible.

If you want to save space and a little money, you can buy an internal modem that plugs into one of your computer's internal expansion slots. An internal modem is usually less expensive than an external modem because it is sold on a circuit board rather than in a cabinet.

Other than the basic consideration of speed, it's the extra features that set one modem apart from another. Some of these features might include extra error-checking circuitry that allows a modem to transmit or receive data more reliably, a facsimile transmission feature that lets your computer communicate with stand-alone fax machines, or a built-in memory buffer that can store data for later transmission or receive data and store it while the computer itself is turned off.

An external modem is usually sold with a data cable that connects the modem to a serial communications port on your computer. If not, you'll have to buy a data cable separately.

How Communications Software Works

After you choose a physical method of linking your computer with others, you still need software to control the computer and modem so that they can properly transmit and receive data. A communications tool like the one in Works translates your commands into instructions that your computer and modem, and the remote computer and modem, can understand. These instructions relate to the following:

- The *baud rate,* or speed at which data is transferred through your modem.

- The *data format,* which controls such matters as the number of bits that make up each character of information in the data you send and the number of bits used to identify the end of one character and the beginning of the next character.

- The *data type.* Communications data in Works is of two basic types, *ASCII* and *binary.* ASCII (text) files contain only characters — letters, numbers, or symbols — without any formatting. Binary files can contain text as well as formatting codes, formulas, graphics, or program instructions. Binary files that you might create and send with Works include Spreadsheet and Database files.

- Special error-correction methods, or *protocols,* that can help to maintain the accuracy of data transmissions. Works supports the XModem, YModem, ZModem, and Kermit error-correction protocols. For more about these protocols, see the *Selecting a Protocol* topic in the Communications category of the Help Table of Contents.

The communications settings established for your communications program must match those in use by the remote computer's communications program or you'll experience problems ranging from an inability to connect to garbled data.

It can be difficult to determine exactly what's wrong if you're having trouble connecting with or transferring data to another computer. If you can't make the connection, for example, the problem could be your software settings; your modem; the physical connections linking your computer, modem, and telephone line; the telephone line itself; or the remote computer, modem, or software. (See "Communications Tips" at the end of this chapter for advice about how to prevent communications problems.)

Even if your telephone line is working, the quality of the telephone line also affects communications. For example, you might get a telephone connection that is noisy. Such background noise makes it harder for computers to interpret the precise signals their modems use to transmit data.

To get a better idea of how this process actually works, let's go through it now.

SETTING UP A MODEM

Because you need both hardware and software to communicate, let's set up the hardware first. Presumably you'll be using a modem to communicate over telephone lines.

Your modem hardware will include the modem itself, a telephone cord with modular connectors at both ends, and a power cable (if it's an external modem). You connect your modem to your computer by following the steps listed here.

1. If you have an external modem, connect one end of the data cable to the modem and the other end to your computer's serial port. (Consult your computer's manual if you can't identify the serial port.) If you have an internal modem, install it in one of your computer's available internal expansion slots.

2. Connect one end of the telephone cable to the modular telephone jack on the modem and the other end to the modular telephone jack in your wall. (If you don't have a modular wall jack, you can buy an adapter from an electronics store.) If your modem has two telephone jacks, be sure to connect the telephone cable to the jack marked "Line." (The second jack, marked "Phone," is for connecting a regular telephone to the modem so that you can have both the modem and the phone connected to the same modular phone jack in the wall.) If the two jacks on your modem aren't marked "Line" and "Phone," you can plug the telephone cable into either jack.

3. If you are using an external modem, connect the modem's power-supply cord to the modem, and plug it into a standard electrical outlet.

4. Check your modem's manual to see if you need to set any switches on the modem.

5. If you are using an external modem, turn the modem on.

After the modem is set up, you must set up a Microsoft Works Communications document to control it properly.

SETTING UP A MICROSOFT WORKS COMMUNICATIONS DOCUMENT

Each time you want to call another computer, you must use a communications document. You choose from several communications settings to specify how to transmit your data, and you set these with the Communications tool's commands. Works stores the settings with the document when you save it, so you can set up and save different documents with different groups of settings.

You have many communications settings to choose from. For two computers to communicate properly, though, the settings on both computers must be the same. So, before you try communicating with another computer, find out what communications settings you should use by contacting the operator of the other computer.

When you know the remote computer's settings, you can select the same settings for your Microsoft Works Communications document. After you select the proper settings, you specify the telephone number you want to call, and then issue a command to make the call (or you can set Works to answer an incoming call if the other computer will be calling you). After you establish the connection, you can transmit or receive information using various Works options.

Now let's run through a typical Works communications session from the beginning.

1. Choose the Create New File command from the File menu (Alt-F-N) to select a new Works file.

2. Click the Communications document type, and then click OK. Works displays a blank Communications document, like the one at the top of the next page.

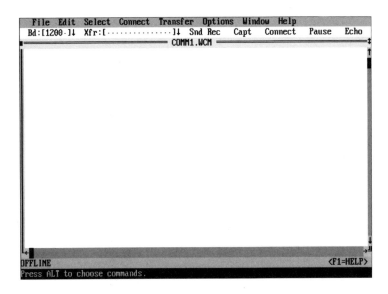

The Communications Screen

Like the screens in other Works tools, a Communications document screen has a menu bar, a toolbar, a work area with scroll bars, a status line, and a message line. Reading from left to right in the toolbar, the tools are as follows:

- The Bd tool lets you select the baud rate. In new Communications documents, the default rate is 1200 bps.

- The Xfr tool lets you select the error-correction protocol. The default here is no error correction.

- The Snd tool tells Works to send a file. (See "Sending Files," later in this chapter.)

- The Rec tool tells Works to receive a file. (See "Receiving Files," later in this chapter.)

- The Capt tool tells Works to capture incoming text on the screen into a file on your disk. (See "Capturing Incoming Text," later in this chapter.)

- The Connect tool begins a connection with a remote computer by dialing the phone number you've stored with the document. If you're already connected to a remote computer, this tool disconnects you.

- The Pause tool tells the remote computer to temporarily pause in its transmission of data to your computer. Pausing a session in this manner gives you time to choose other commands without interfering with your computer's reception of data from another computer.

- The Echo tool lets you select the Local Echo setting for data you type on your own screen. (See "Choosing Terminal Settings," later in this chapter.)

In the status line, you see the message OFFLINE. This means you're not currently connected to another computer. When you're connected, this message changes to ONLINE.

This new Communications document has default settings that determine how it communicates with other computers. In many cases, these settings will be fine for the computer you're calling. However, you should always check them to make sure they match the ones you need for the particular computer you're calling. Works has communication settings, terminal settings, and phone settings. Let's look at these now.

Choosing Communication Settings

To view or change the communication settings, you must display the Communication dialog box.

- Choose the Communication command from the Options menu (Alt-O-M). Works displays a dialog box, like this:

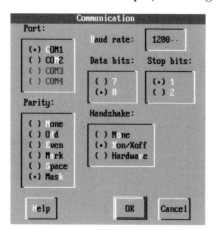

Let's look at these options one at a time:

- The Port setting option tells Works which serial port your modem is connected to if your computer has more than one. If you only have one serial port, it is already selected. If you're using a mouse, the mouse is probably connected to the COM1 port, so you should select COM2 here. Whichever port you select, be sure you have selected the same port in the Modem Port area of the Works Settings dialog box. (For more information on the Works Settings dialog box, see Chapter 1.)

- The Baud Rate setting determines the maximum speed at which your modem will transmit and receive data. The Baud Rate box contains a default value of 1200, but you can type in another rate if you like. The baud rate should match that of the modem on the computer you're calling and should not exceed your modem's limitations. If you are connected by cable to another computer, use 9600 bps.

 MOUSE TIP: You can also change the baud rate with the Bd tool in the toolbar. Click the arrow next to the displayed baud rate, scroll the list that appears until you see the baud rate you want, and then click the new baud rate to select it.

- The Data Bits option is the number of bits used to represent each character of data. The default here is 8 data bits.

- The Stop Bits option is the number of bits used to represent the end of each character of data. The default here is 1 stop bit.

- The Parity setting option checks for transmission errors. Normally both computers must be using the same parity setting, but the Mask option in this dialog box (which is the default option) tells Works to communicate with the other computer no matter how its parity is set. If you know the other computer's parity setting, however, it's better to select the same setting here.

- The Handshake setting option controls how data flows from one computer to another. Use the Hardware setting only when you're communicating over a direct cable connection. The standard

handshake method is Xon/Xoff, which is the default choice here.
If you don't know the handshake, or if Xon/Xoff doesn't work for
some reason, select None.

For now, let's assume the default settings are the ones we want: Click OK
to accept all the default settings.

After you've checked the communication settings and made any necessary
changes, you should check the terminal settings.

Choosing Terminal Settings

To view or change the terminal settings, display the Terminal dialog box.

■ Choose the Terminal command from the Options menu (Alt-O-T).
Works displays the Terminal dialog box, like this:

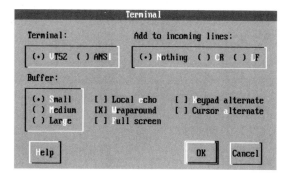

Normally the default settings here are the ones you'll need to communicate properly, but let's run through the groups of options so you'll know
what they do.

■ The Terminal option should be set to the type of terminal required
by the remote computer you're calling. The default setting, VT52,
should work in most cases.

■ The Add To Incoming Lines options tell Works to add a carriage
return (CR) or line feed (LF) character to incoming text if the
remote computer doesn't supply these characters automatically.
The default here is the Nothing option, because most remote
computers supply a carriage return or a line feed at the end of
each transmitted line. However, if the text you receive keeps overwriting the same line on your screen instead of proceeding down
your screen one line at a time, select the CR or LF option.

- The Buffer options set the size of the captured text buffer. When you receive incoming text, it fills your screen, and as a screen fills, it scrolls up automatically to make room for incoming text. Works maintains a *buffer,* or area of your computer's memory, that stores a certain number of lines that have scrolled off your screen. That way, you can scroll the Communications document window up to see the lines again. The approximate sizes of this buffer are 150 lines (Small), 300 lines (Medium), and 750 lines (Large). The default setting here is Small.

WORKS TIP: Because the buffer is part of your computer's memory, a larger buffer means your computer has less available memory for other uses, such as having several large Works documents open at the same time. If you work with large files while you have a Communications document open, select the Small buffer size option to make as much of your computer's memory available for other uses as possible.

- The Local Echo option determines how text is echoed on your screen. If text you type while connected doesn't appear on your own screen, select the Local Echo option. If you see two of each character you type, on the other hand, turn off the Local Echo option here. The fastest way to toggle the Local Echo option is to click the Echo tool at the right edge of the toolbar.

- The Wraparound option should be checked, because it is the default here. This tells Works to automatically wrap text around to begin a new line when it reaches the edge of your screen.

- The Full Screen option is normally not set. This option hides the menu bar, the toolbar, the scroll bars, the status line, and the message line from the screen when you're connected to a remote computer. If you select Full Screen and then want to return to the default display, press Alt-O-T to display the Terminal dialog box, select Full Screen again to deselect it, and click OK.

- The Keypad Alternate option changes the function of your numeric keypad. The numeric keypads on VT52 and ANSI communications terminals send special commands to certain types of remote computers. Choosing this command changes your keyboard's numeric keypad so it will issue those commands when you have the Num Lock key on. This option is useful only when you're familiar with the special keypad commands on VT52 or ANSI terminals and you want to be able to send those commands from Works.

■ If you have the Terminal set to ANSI, the Cursor Alternate option changes the function of the cursor control keys on your keyboard so they're the same as those on an ANSI terminal when you have the Num Lock key turned off. Like the Keypad Alternate option, this option is useful only when you're familiar with cursor movement commands on ANSI terminals and want to be able to use them on your personal computer with Works.

In most cases, you'll be calling a personal computer bulletin board, another personal computer, or a computer information service. If this is the case, the default terminal settings will be fine. Click OK to accept the default settings.

Choosing Phone Settings

The last step before connecting with a remote computer is to set up the phone options. You enter a telephone number and view or select other phone-dialing and connection options in the Phone dialog box.

■ Choose the Phone command from the Options menu (Alt-O-P). Works displays the Phone dialog box, like this:

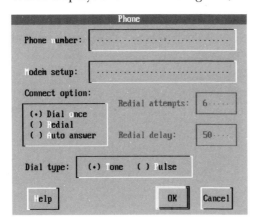

The cursor is blinking in the Phone Number box at the top. You type the remote computer's phone number here, and Works stores it when you save the Communications document. You can store only one phone number for each Works Communications document, so you must create and store a different Communications document for each telephone number you call regularly.

KEYBOARD TIP: You can enter phone numbers with or without dashes between prefixes, or with or without parentheses around area codes. Works ignores dashes and parentheses. However, you can include commas in a phone number to make your modem pause briefly and wait for secondary dial tones. If you have to dial 9 to reach an outside line, for example, you might enter a comma between the 9 and the rest of the phone number so that the modem will pause for a moment to allow for an outside dial tone before continuing to dial. Your modem manual will tell you exactly how many seconds your modem will pause when it receives a comma as part of a phone number.

Now let's look at the other options in the Phone dialog box.

- The Modem Setup box lets you enter commands to set options or special features on your modem, such as turning off the modem's speaker or enabling its built-in storage buffer. You don't need to enter anything here to dial a remote computer's number and connect, however. Check your modem manual for a list of commands that enable its special features.

- The Connect Option settings let you tell Works either to dial the number once only (Dial Once), to redial the number a specified number of times (Redial), or to wait for an incoming call and then automatically answer the phone (Auto Answer). Select the Auto Answer option if you're waiting for a remote computer to call you.

- The Redial Attempts box lets you specify how many times Works redials a number if you've selected the Redial option in the Connect Options area at the left.

- The Redial Delay box lets you tell Works how many seconds to wait between each redial attempt if you've selected the Redial option in the Connect Option area.

- The Dial Type setting lets you select the type of telephone dialing your phone system uses. Most telephone equipment in the United States and Canada uses the newer, faster Tone dial type, but if you are in an area that has older equipment, you might need to select Pulse dialing.

Normally you'll simply enter a telephone number and then press Enter. Let's do that now.

■ Type *5551222* and press Enter. Works stores the telephone number, and the dialog box disappears.

With the settings and telephone number stored, you're ready to make the connection.

MAKING A CONNECTION

To call another computer, make sure your modem is properly connected and turned on. Click the Connect tool in the toolbar or choose the Connect command from the Connect menu (Alt-C-C). (If you've set Microsoft Works to Auto Answer in the Phone dialog box, you now simply wait for the phone to ring.)

Works dials the phone number. If your modem's speaker is turned on, you hear the dial tone as Works takes the phone "off the hook," and then you hear it dialing and see the phone number on your screen. As soon as it dials the number, Works displays and activates a timer in the status line, indicating the duration of the call. When the other computer's modem answers the call, you hear the two modems exchanging high-pitched acknowledgment signals, and then your screen displays the word CONNECT, like this:

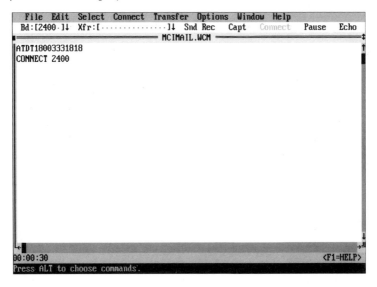

If you dialed the number in this book, or if you dial a wrong number and your modem doesn't automatically disconnect, press Esc and then click the Connect tool to disconnect.

After you are connected to another computer, anything you type on your keyboard is sent to the other computer. If the other computer's operator types a message, you see it on your screen. You can also choose commands to send files from your disk or to receive files from the other computer and store them on your disk.

WORKS TIP: If the number your modem dials is busy, Works will redial as many times as you specified in the Redial Attempts box at intervals of the number of seconds you entered in the Redial Delay box in the Phone dialog box. If you decide you don't want to redial, press Esc and then click OK.

Calling an Information Service

You can use the Works Communications tool to connect your computer to an information service like CompuServe, Dow Jones News/Retrieval, or MCI Mail. These services maintain huge mainframe computers that store thousands of computer files and programs such as magazine articles, stock quotations, and electronic shopping catalogs. You can interact with these mainframe computers to play games, send messages to electronic mailboxes for others to read, or even order merchandise.

To call a commercial information service, you need a subscriber ID number and a password. You get these by contacting the information service in advance and signing up as a member.

Soon after you sign up for a commercial information service, you'll receive your subscriber ID and password. You'll also receive an information kit that explains how to use the service. You'll learn which communications settings to use, how to dial in, and what commands the service provides for looking up information, for sending messages, and for performing other activities. After you browse through the information, you're ready to log on.

The procedure is basically the same as for calling any other computer, except you'll need to enter your user ID and password. Here are the basic steps:

1. Open a new Works Communications document.

2. Choose the Communication command from the Options menu (Alt-C-M), and set the communication settings so that they match those specified in the service's information kit. Click OK when you finish.

3. Choose the Phone command from the Options menu (Alt-O-P), and enter the information service's telephone number. Click OK when you finish.

4. Click the Connect tool in the toolbar to connect with the information service. Works dials the telephone number, the information service's modem answers, and you see the CONNECT message followed by the information service's prompt.

> **NOTE:** *You might have to press Enter after you see the CONNECT message in order to see the information service's prompt.*

Each Communications service has its own prompt. The prompt for MCI Mail looks like this:

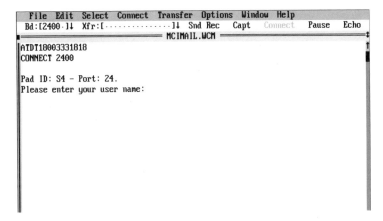

1. Type the user name you received from the information service, and press Enter. The information service presents a second prompt that asks you for your password.

2. Type the password you received from the information service, and press Enter. Usually you can't see the password as you type it on the screen. This prevents anyone from reading the password as you type.

A few seconds after you enter your password, you'll see a greeting message, perhaps some news headlines, and then a command prompt. The MCI Mail prompt is shown in the screen on the next page.

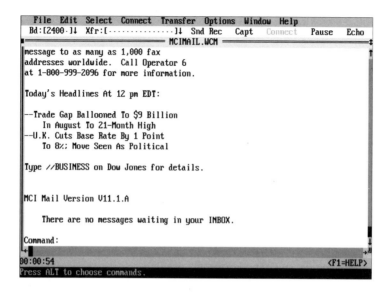

You are now connected to the remote system, and you can proceed to use the system's commands to access information, create electronic mail messages, play games, or take advantage of other services.

Viewing Text on the Screen

While you're connected to another computer, anything you type, anything typed at the other computer's keyboard, and any text transmitted by the other computer appears on your screen.

NOTE: *If you can't see text you type on the screen, click the Echo tool in the toolbar.*

As the screen fills, the text scrolls up out of sight. If you're using the default Small buffer size (as set in the Terminal dialog box), Works stores the first 150 lines of text that you type or receive from the other computer in your computer's memory, and you can scroll up in the Communications document to view them. When your buffer is full, Works discards the oldest text and adds new text to the buffer as you receive or type it.

You can scroll in the Communications document by using the cursor control keys or by clicking or dragging the scroll bar. If you want to scroll up or down in the window while you are still connected to a remote computer, you must click the Pause tool in the toolbar to temporarily halt incoming text before you can scroll the document. (If you're no longer connected to the remote computer, you can scroll the document without clicking Pause first.)

KEYBOARD TIP: For a list of cursor control keys and how they help you move around in a Communications document, choose the *CM Keys* topic in the Communications category of the Help Table of Contents.

 MOUSE TIP: You can also pause a communications transmission by clicking anywhere in the document window. So, to select some text and copy it into another document while you're connected, first click the beginning of the text. Works pauses the transmission so you can then drag the pointer to select all the text and copy it into the other document. To resume the transmission, click the Pause tool in the toolbar.

After you finish viewing the data in the buffer, click the Pause tool again to resume communication with the other computer. The text you receive stays in the Communications buffer after you disconnect from the remote computer. As soon as you close or save the Communications file, however, Works empties the buffer.

Saving Text from the Buffer

Because Works empties the buffer when you close or save the Communications document, you must copy the text from the Communications document into a Works Word Processor document if you want to save it permanently. You can copy text either while you're still connected to the remote computer (by pausing the session, as explained earlier) or after you've disconnected from the remote computer.

You can select all the text in the buffer by choosing the All command from the Select menu (Alt-S-A). To select a portion of the text, hold down the mouse button and drag the pointer across the text you want to save.

> **NOTE:** *After you've selected text in a Communications document, the only thing you can do with it is copy it. You can't delete selected text by pressing Del, and you can't move text elsewhere in the Communications buffer with the Move option.*

After you've selected the text you want to save from the Communications document, follow these steps to copy it into a Word Processor document.

1. Choose the Copy command from the Edit menu (Alt-E-C or Shift-F3).

2. Create a new Word Processor document, or choose an open one from the Window menu to activate it on the screen.

3. Press Enter. Works then copies the text from the Communications document into the Word Processor document.

4. Save the Word Processor file.

5. Select the Communications document from the Window menu to return to it.

 WORKS TIP: You can copy text from a Communications document to Works Database or Spreadsheet documents as well. This is useful if your captured text contains columns of numbers or other data.

Capturing Incoming Text

As an alternative to copying incoming text from the buffer to a Word Processor document, you can set Works to store incoming text directly in a new file on your disk as you receive it — by clicking the Capt tool in the toolbar or choosing the Capture Text command from the Transfer menu (Alt-T-C). Here's how the procedure works:

1. Click the Capt tool in the toolbar. Works displays a dialog box, like this:

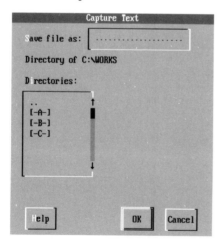

2. Type a name for the new text file, and then click OK. Works will now save all incoming text to that file.

After you open a captured text file, the word CAPTURE appears in the status line and the Capture Text command on the Transfer menu changes to End Text Capture. You can stop capturing text to the file at any time by clicking the Capt tool again or choosing the End Capture Text command (Alt-T-E). If you close the Communications file, Works automatically closes the captured text file.

Notice, however, that Works starts saving captured text in a file only after you open a captured text file using the Capture Text command. When you choose Capture Text, Works will not save any text that is already in the buffer (or on the screen). To save text that was on the screen or in the buffer before you began capturing text, you must select it and copy it into another Works document.

The file Works creates when you capture text is a plain text file. You can open such a file in Works in the Word Processor, the Spreadsheet, or the Database.

RECEIVING FILES

You can also receive text or other data as a complete file. To receive a file, follow these steps:

1. Verify in advance which file transfer protocol you need to use. Both the remote computer and your computer must use the same protocol.

2. Choose the Transfer Options command from the Transfer menu (Alt-T-O), and select the file transfer protocol that matches the one used by the remote computer.

 MOUSE TIP: You can also select a file transfer protocol by clicking the arrow to the right of the Xfr tool in the menu bar and then selecting a protocol from the list that appears.

3. Press Alt-T-R to choose the Receive File command from the Transfer menu. If you choose the XModem/CRC protocol, Microsoft Works displays a dialog box, like the one at the top of the next page.

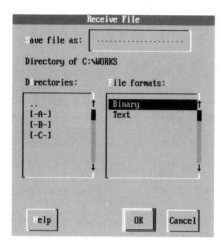

As you can see, you must specify the name of the file you want Works to create in the Save File As text box when you use the XModem/CRC protocol. (The YModem, ZModem, and Kermit protocols automatically save the received file with the same name it had on the remote computer.)

4. Type a filename if necessary.

5. If you are using the XModem/CRC or YModem protocols, you must also indicate whether the file you are receiving is a text or a binary file. Select a file format option, and click OK. (For more on these options, see the *Receiving a File* topic in the Communications category of the Help Table of Contents.) Works displays a status box on the screen, like this:

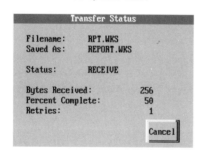

This box shows you the progress of the receive operation. The remote computer begins transmitting the file and displays messages in the status box about the status of the file transfer. When you have received the whole file, the status box indicates that the transfer is complete and the file is safely stored on your disk. Then click OK to resume the communications session. The files you receive in this way can be text files, or they can be binary files that contain program code, graphics, or other information that can't be stored in text format.

To cancel the receive operation before it is completed, click Cancel in the status box, and then click OK to verify that you want to cancel.

The Receive File option sends special signals to the remote computer, telling it when to begin transmitting the file. Because you are receiving a whole file, Works receives a signal when the transmission is complete. This is the advantage of receiving text files with the Receive File option: You don't have to watch the screen to know when you have received the whole file.

SENDING TEXT

To send text from a Microsoft Works Communications document, you have three alternatives: typing at the keyboard, sending a text file, and copying text from another Works document.

Sending Text from the Keyboard

Typing at the keyboard is the alternative to use when you first establish a connection and you want to determine whether the other computer is properly receiving your data. When you connect your computer with a friend's computer, for example, you might type *Hello* after you see the CONNECT message. If everything is all right, your friend will see your "Hello" message and respond. After you know that you can read your friend's message and that your friend can read yours, you can proceed to transfer larger amounts of text from files.

Using the Send Text Command

The second alternative is to send a file in Works' text format using the Send Text command on the Transfer menu. Here's how the process works:

1. Verify in advance with the person running the remote computer which file transfer protocol you will use.

2. Establish a connection with the remote computer.

3. Type a message telling the other user that you are about to send a text file so that he or she will know to set up a capture text file.

4. Click the Down arrow to the right of the Xfr tool in the toolbar, and select the correct file transfer protocol.

5. Choose the Send Text command from the Transfer menu (Alt-T-T). Works displays a dialog box, like this:

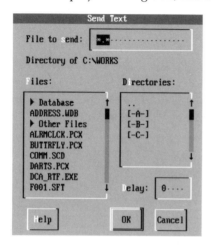

6. Select a file to send from the list.

7. Select the options appropriate for sending your file with the protocol you've chosen. (For more information, see the *Sending a File* and *Sending Text* topics in the Communications category of the Help Table of Contents.)

8. Click OK. The dialog box disappears, and Works displays the contents of the text file on the screen as it sends it to the remote computer.

The Delay option in this dialog box causes Works to pause after sending each line of text for as many tenths of a second as you enter. This option is sometimes necessary when the remote computer can't receive and process your data as quickly as you can send it.

To cancel the Send Text operation before Works has sent the whole file, press Esc and click OK.

The Send Text dialog box shows you all the files in your current directory. When you use the Send Text command, however, Works sends only text-formatted files properly. If you select a Word Processor, Spreadsheet, Database, or other formatted file and try to send it with this option, Works will include a lot of meaningless characters as it tries to interpret formatting commands, formulas, and other information as text. So, to send a Works Word Processor file, Database file, or Spreadsheet file with the Send Text command, you should first save the file in text format by choosing the Save As command and selecting text format from the File Formats list.

Copying Text from Another Works Document

As long as you are connected to another computer, Works sends anything you copy into the Communications document, exactly as if you had typed it from the keyboard. For example, if you began a communications session and then decided to send a paragraph from a Word Processor document, you'd follow these steps:

1. Open the Word Processor file that contains the text you want to send.

2. Select the text you want to send.

3. Choose the Copy command from the Edit menu (Alt-E-C or Shift-F3).

4. Select the Communications document from the Window menu. Works displays the Communications document.

5. Press Enter. Works then copies the text you selected from the Word Processor document into the Communications document and transmits it to the remote computer.

You can also select data or numbers in Database or Spreadsheet documents and then copy them to a Communications document. (See Chapter 12 for more information.)

SENDING FILES

If you want to send entire formatted Word Processor, Spreadsheet, or Database files to another computer, or if you want to send other programs or graphics files, you can use the Send File command (Alt-T-S). Here's the procedure:

1. Establish a connection with the remote computer.

2. Click Snd in the toolbar, or choose the Send File command from the Transfer menu (Alt-T-S). Microsoft Works displays a dialog box, like the one on the following page.

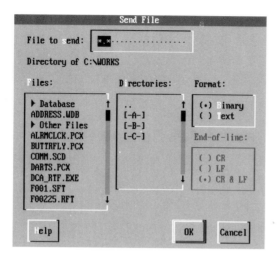

Like the Send Text dialog box, this dialog box offers a list of files that you can choose to send. Because you can send binary as well as text-formatted files, however, you must select the type of file that you want to send. These are the options in this dialog box:

- The Format options let you specify whether the file is text or binary. You must select the Binary option to send Spreadsheet, Database, graphics, or program files.

- The End-of-Line options tell Works whether to add a line feed or carriage return or both at the end of each line in the file. Usually you'll want to select the default CR & LF option as this is the normal format for files.

After you choose a file and click OK, Works displays a progress dialog box like the one you see when you use the Receive File command. After the entire file has been sent, the progress dialog box disappears.

To cancel the sending operation before it is complete, click Cancel in the status box, and then click OK to verify that you want to cancel.

ENDING A COMMUNICATIONS SESSION

Hanging up the phone and finishing your computer call is simple. If the remote computer terminates the call, you're disconnected, but the timer in the status line on your screen continues running. To stop it, you must tell Microsoft Works that you're disconnected.

1. Click the Connect tool in the toolbar, or choose the Connect command from the Connect menu (Alt-C-C). Works displays a dialog box asking if you want to disconnect.

2. Click OK. Works disconnects the phone line. The timer in the status line stops and the OFFLINE message replaces it.

Because telephone calls using a computer cost money in the same way that voice calls do, you'll want to be sure to disconnect from the remote computer as soon as you're finished. Works' integration allows you to open and work with other documents while you're still connected to a remote computer, so it's important to disconnect when you finish to avoid inadvertently maintaining the connection while you work with another document.

RECORDING AND PLAYING SCRIPTS

The Microsoft Works Communications tool has a *scripting feature* that remembers and stores sequences of commands you frequently use, so you can play back those sequences later. These sequences can include operations such as typing the subscriber ID and password information to log on to an information service or issuing groups of commands to navigate to a certain area of an information service or bulletin board.

Sign-on scripts store the commands that connect you with a remote computer and store your user ID, password, and any other information you need to type. You can save only one sign-on script with each Communications document. After you create a sign-on script, Works stores it on the Connect menu under the name *Sign-on*.

Other scripts can perform sequences of commands after you're connected to a remote computer. You can create several of these scripts in each Communications document, but you must be connected to a remote computer at the time. You give each script a name, and Works adds the name to the Connect menu so you can play the script by choosing its name there.

After you've created scripts, you can edit, delete, or rename them.

Recording Scripts

Despite the difference in script types, you record all scripts the same way.

1. Open a Works Communications document if you don't have one open.

2. Choose the Record Script command from the Connect menu (Alt-C-R). Works displays a dialog box, like the one on the next page.

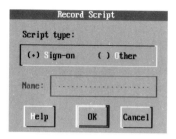

3. Click Sign-on if you want to record a sign-on script, or click Other if you want to record a script that stores other procedures. If you choose the Other script type, the Name box becomes active, and you must click it and type a name for the script.

4. Click OK. The status line shows RECORD to indicate you're recording.

5. Perform the operations you want to record. If you're recording a sign-on, connect to the remote computer and then respond to the prompts for your user name and password. Otherwise, type the commands or text you want to record in the Other script type.

6. Choose the Record Script command again from the Connect menu to end the recording.

WORKS TIP: Works can't record mouse actions in a script. If you want to record commands (such as the Connect command), you must press Alt-key combinations to choose them instead of choosing commands or clicking tools with the mouse.

If you want to cancel a recording session when you're in the middle of it, choose the Cancel Recording command from the Connect menu (Alt-C-A), or press Esc and click OK.

Playing Scripts

Works stores a recorded sign-on script when you save the Communications document and then offers to play it automatically each time you open the Communications document after that. As you watch, Works dials the remote computer's telephone number, waits for the remote computer to prompt for the user ID and password, and then supplies the log-on information you recorded. You don't have to do a thing.

To play a script at other times, choose its name from the Connect menu. When you play such a script, however, make sure you play it back from the same place in a communications session as where you recorded it. For example, if you record a script to issue commands to check your mailbox on an information service, make sure you're at the proper command prompt before you play back that script.

If you begin playing a script and want to cancel it before it finishes, press Esc. Works displays a warning asking you to confirm that you want to cancel the script. Click OK or press Enter to confirm the cancellation.

Editing, Deleting, or Renaming Scripts

You can edit, delete, or rename any script you've stored in a Communications document. If you want to change a short script containing only a few keystrokes, the simplest method is to delete the old script and record a new one. If the script is long and complex, however, you can add, change, or delete keystrokes.

To perform these operations, choose the Scripts command from the Edit menu (Alt-E-S). Works displays the Scripts dialog box, like this:

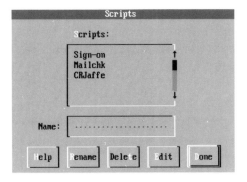

To delete a script, select its name and click Delete. Works displays a warning box to double-check that you really want to delete the script. Click OK, and then click Done to close the dialog box.

To rename a script, select its name in the list, type a new name in the Name box, and then click Rename. Click Done to return to your document.

To edit a script, you do the following:

1. Click the name of the script you want to edit, and then click Edit. Works displays the Edit Script dialog box, as on the next page.

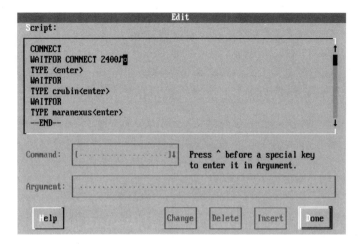

As you can see, the Edit Script dialog box shows the commands you recorded in the order you recorded them. Some commands, like TYPE, have arguments after them, and you must specify the text or a value to complete the argument. To edit or delete a command from a script, you must select its name in the list.

2. Select the command you want to edit or delete. The command name appears in the Command box, and the argument (if any) appears in the Argument box. To delete a command or argument, click Delete.

3. To change a command, click the arrow at the right edge of the Command box and select a new command name from the list that appears, or click the box itself and type a different command name there.

4. To change the argument for a command, click the Argument box and edit its contents. (You must type a caret (^) before typing special keys such as Ctrl, Enter, or Alt.)

5. To insert a new command, select the command below where you want to insert the command, type the command and argument (if needed) in the Command and Argument boxes, and then click Insert.

6. Click Change to store the changes you've made, and then click Done to close the dialog box when you're finished making changes.

For more information on editing Communications scripts, see the *Changing a Script* topic in the Communications category of the Help Table of Contents.

These are the basic procedures for using the Works Communications tool. Now let's look at a few tips for using the tool to its best advantage.

COMMUNICATIONS TIPS

Although the Microsoft Works Communications tool has fewer commands and is simpler to use than the other Works tools, it presents its own challenges because of the various levels of interaction possible between you and the remote computer. The following sections provide some tips for trouble-free communications using Works.

Check Your Setup

If you have trouble initiating a communications session, be sure your modem is properly connected and turned on. Improper hardware setup is the cause of many communications problems. Here are some steps that will minimize your chances of trouble:

- If you have an external modem, it should have an indicator light that tells you the modem is on and ready to go. If the light isn't on, the modem isn't turned on, its switches (if any) aren't set properly, it isn't plugged in, or the electrical outlet is dead.

- If the modem is turned on but it doesn't respond to the Connect command, check the data cable or slot connection to be sure it's secure. Also be sure you've chosen the right COM port for connecting the modem, both in the Works Settings dialog box (Alt-O-W) and in the Communication dialog box (Alt-O-M).

- If your modem's speaker is turned up, you can hear the dial tone and the actual dialing of numbers when you choose the Connect command. If you can't hear a dial tone, check your telephone line connection. If the connection seems secure, check the line itself by temporarily plugging a regular telephone into it and listening for a dial tone.

- If you can hear a dial tone but you can't hear the modem dialing, be sure you've entered a telephone number in your Communications document.

Get the Remote Computer's Settings

Your data format, parity, speed, and other communications settings must match those of the remote computer you're calling. Be sure to get the settings of the other computer before you try communicating with it, and be sure to select the same settings in the Communication dialog box (Alt-O-M).

If you can make contact with the remote computer but the data you receive on your screen is garbled, you might have the wrong parity setting. Try changing the Data Bits, Stop Bits, Parity, and Handshake settings in the Communication dialog box. Works automatically transfers data with Xon/Xoff handshaking, for example, but the remote computer might not support it. If so, changing the Handshake setting to None should solve the problem.

If you can't make contact with the remote computer, you'll usually hear the two modems trying to establish the connection, and then you'll be disconnected. This problem is usually the result of different Data Bits, Stop Bits, or Parity settings, or possibly incompatible Baud Rate settings between yours and the other computer.

Try Redialing

If the problem is a noisy telephone line, you might get a clearer line by redialing. You can check the line condition by lifting the handset of a phone connected to the same line — if the line is noisy, you'll hear the static. Modems themselves normally make a roaring noise, but the noise is distinctive, and you can learn to distinguish between the modem's noise and a noisy line.

A noisy line occasionally causes garbled characters to appear on your screen. You might see most of a line of text, but then you'll see some symbols instead of characters in certain words or sentences. If the line is particularly noisy, it can cause a disconnection.

Check the Local Echo Setting

Most computers transmit in what's called *full duplex mode*, which means that as you send text to the other computer, the text is echoed to your screen so that you can see it. If you find that you can't see your own outgoing text when you type, send text, or copy text into a communications document, click the Echo tool in the toolbar.

If, however, you see double characters on your screen (two occurrences of each character for each one you type or transmit), turn off the local echo by clicking the Echo tool.

When you call an information service, it's normal for the password you type not to appear on your screen. This is a security feature. If you can see the password you type, you will probably see double characters for anything else you type. Again, the solution is to click the Echo tool to turn off the local echo feature.

Reformat Data in the Word Processor

When you receive data in the Communications buffer or when you capture a text file, no formatting is included. To reformat the text easily, copy the buffer to a Word Processor document (or open the captured text file as a Word Processor file), and then use the formatting commands to format the text.

You can have trouble with transmitted files when extra carriage returns are inserted in the file, causing lines to break in odd places. Use the Word Processor's Replace command to search for and replace paragraph markers, which you can delete to eliminate extra carriage returns.

1. Move the cursor to the beginning of the Word Processor document by using the mouse or pressing Ctrl-Home.

2. Choose the Replace command.

3. Type ^{p} in the Search For text box.

4. Click OK. Works searches for paragraph markers, stopping at each one and giving you a chance to replace it. Click Yes at each occurence. Because you didn't enter anything in the Replace With box in the Replace command's dialog box, Works replaces the paragraph marker with nothing and deletes the extra carriage return.

You can also search for extra tab stops and spaces in the Word Processor. See the *Searching and Replacing in the WP* topic in the Word Processor category of the Help Table of Contents.

Use the Template Feature to Store Common Settings

If you normally use the same group of communication settings to call other computers, and they're not the default settings that you get when you open a new Works Communications document, you can create a Template file that will allow you to open new documents with your custom settings. To set up a Template file, do the following:

1. Open a new Communications document.

2. Select the terminal, communication, and phone settings you want.

3. Choose the Save command from the File menu (Alt-F-S).

4. Click the Save As Template option, and click OK.

5. Type a name for the template, and then click OK. Works saves the file as a template, and the next time you open a new Communications document using this template, the custom settings will be selected.

You can store as many Template files as you like, so you could set up different Communications templates for each of several sets of custom communication settings.

Save a Different Document for Each Remote Computer

If you regularly communicate with several different computers, create a different Communications document for each one and save it. If you use both MCI Mail and CompuServe, for example, create a document for each service. Each document will contain one service's telephone number, communication settings, and log-on procedure, so you'll be able to connect to the computer simply by opening the file and clicking the OK button to connect and play your sign-on script. Although the Communications document's screen fills with lines of text while you exchange data with a remote computer, the buffer clears when you close the file. So each time you open a stored Communications document, its screen will be blank and its buffer will be empty, ready for the current session.

Use Special Software When Appropriate

The Works Communications tool is a good basic terminal program, but sometimes it pays to use another software package for communications. If you need to connect your computer to a mainframe computer at your company, for example, you might need a special mainframe communications program that offers menus of mainframe-specific commands. Some information services, such as Lexis or Dow Jones News/Retrieval, also offer special software that makes it easier to navigate their systems. If you have a specialized communications need, check on the availability of software that can make your communications job easier.

By allowing you to connect with other computers and exchange data with them, the Microsoft Works Communications tool offers extra power that you can use to your advantage. By capturing or receiving data from other computers, you can include data from other sources in your Works Word Processor, Spreadsheet, or Database files. Receiving the data and copying it into another Works document is much faster than typing it. In Chapter 12, we'll see how the Communications tool can help you to capture and use data created on other computers.

12

Integrating the Microsoft Works Tools

Microsoft Works is an excellent software value because it combines in one program Word Processor, Spreadsheet, Database, and Communications tools. So far we've focused on using these tools individually, but this chapter shows you how you can use the Works tools together.

You can easily move data between the tools — or between Works and other programs — to work with your data in the format and with the specific features you need at a given time. Using the Communications tool, for example, you can access numeric data on another computer and save it as a text file on your computer. If you need to perform calculations on the data, you can open that text file as a Spreadsheet file; but if you only need to format the data, you can open the text file as a Word Processor file. In this chapter, we'll look at the basics of moving data to and from Works and among its four tools. Then we'll tackle some projects that take advantage of these data-interchange capabilities.

MANIPULATING DATA WITH MICROSOFT WORKS

Microsoft Works lets you manipulate data in several ways.

- You can copy data from tool to tool.
- You can move Database data into a Word Processor document.
- You can insert a Spreadsheet range in a Word Processor document.
- You can import text files from or export text files into other programs.
- You can import or export files in other file formats.

You'll want to use different data-interchange capabilities in different situations. Let's look at these options one at a time.

COPYING DATA WITH MICROSOFT WORKS

In the same way as you can select and copy data from one place to another in the same document, you can select and copy data from any Microsoft Works document to any other Works document. The procedure is simple.

1. Select the data you want to copy.

2. Choose the Copy command from the Edit menu (Alt-E-C or Shift-F3).

3. Open the destination file, or select one that's already open from the Window menu.

4. Move the cursor to the place where you want the copied data to appear, and press Enter. Works copies the data into the specified location in the destination document.

What makes this procedure tricky is how the destination document treats the incoming data. The following sections include some guidelines for determining what will happen when you copy data into each of the four types of Works documents.

Copying Data into Word Processor Documents

Word Processor documents are the most logical destination for copied data because they're usually the place where you integrate various types of data for presentation in a report, article, or other printed document. Here's what happens when you copy data into a Word Processor document:

- Works inserts copied data at the current cursor position. If the document already contains text after the cursor position when you perform a copy operation, Works inserts the copied data in front of that text.

- The margin and indent settings in a Word Processor document always determine the length of its lines. If your Word Processor document is set for 6-inch text lines and you copy 8-inch lines into it, the incoming lines will wrap around to fit the shorter line length. This is an issue particularly when you select and copy records from a Database document or rows from a Spreadsheet document, because Database and Spreadsheet documents are often wider than 6 inches.

■ Works inserts tab stops to separate columnar data. When you copy columnar data (such as database records or spreadsheet rows) into a Word Processor document, Works inserts tab stops to maintain the column formatting in the Word Processor.

Here's an example of what you can expect when copying data into the Word Processor:

```
 File  Edit  Print  Select  Format  Options  Window  Help
Fnt:[Courier······]↓ Pt:[12·]↓   Bld Ital Ul   Lft Ctr Rt Jus   Sp Th   Prev
▪══════════════════════ ADNOTES.WPS ══════════════════════↕
 [L········1········2··R····3··R····4··R····5··R····]·········7·····
» The following table shows the performance of our                    ↑
  advertisements in four different magazines during the summer
  months.
  Magazine          June     July     August    Totals

  Young Modeler       11        8         9        28
  Kit Craft           17       14        15        46
  Model Maven         13       28        19        60
  Car Modeling        25       35        45       105

  Totals              66       85        88       239
```

```
As you│ File  Edit  Print  Select  Format  Options  View  Window  Help
overall│ Bld  Ital  Ul    Lft  Ctr  Rt   $  %  ,    Sum   Width   Chart    Prev
the com│▬
may wel│▬════════════════════ ADVANAL.WKS ════════════════════↕
   ◆   │        A          B         C         D         E        F        =
       │1  Magazine        June      July      August    Totals            ↑
       │2
Pg 1/1 │3  Young Modeler     11         8         9        28
Press ALT│4  Kit Craft        17        14        15        46
       │5  Model Maven       13        28        19        60
       │6  Car Modeling      25        35        45       105
       │7
       │8  Totals            66        85        88       239
       │9
```

Works copied the data from the ADVANAL.WKS spreadsheet into the ADNOTES.WPS Word Processor document. Because the cursor was located between the two text paragraphs, Works inserted the data there when it completed the copy operation. In this case, the rows of spreadsheet data fit within the Word Processor document's margins, so that each row looks as it does in the original spreadsheet. Notice that Works has inserted tab stops in the Word Processor document to maintain the data in columns.

Copying Data into Spreadsheet Documents

A spreadsheet is a number-handling tool, so the data you copy into a Spreadsheet document will usually be data or text in columns. Here are the considerations for copying data into a Spreadsheet document.

■ Works copies data into a spreadsheet beginning at the selected cell and moving down and to the right. For example, if you copy six records (each containing five fields) from a database and then select cell A1 as the destination in the spreadsheet, Works fills the range A1:E6 with the data, as in Figure 12-1.

Figure 12-1 also shows that Works converts database fields and records (shown in the file at the bottom of the screen) to spreadsheet columns and rows (shown in the file at the top of the screen). It copies the contents of each Database field into one column in the spreadsheet, and each record becomes one row in the spreadsheet.

■ Database formulas won't copy into the spreadsheet, but the values of those formulas will. If you've inserted formulas in a database file to calculate results, the database displays those results on the screen. When you select database data from such a screen, you select the displayed results (and not the formulas), and Works copies the displayed results (but not the formulas) into spreadsheet cells.

■ Database formatting is copied intact to the Spreadsheet. The Value field in the database file in Figure 12-1 was formatted as Currency, for example, and it remains in the Currency format after it is copied into the spreadsheet shown here.

```
  File  Edit  Print  Select  Format  Options  View  Window  Help
   Bld  Ital  Ul      Lft  Ctr  Rt    $  %  ,    Sum   Width       Chart        Preu

  ═══════════════════════════════ SHEET1.WKS ═══════════════════════════
        A          B         C        D          E          F          G
   1   G001     Small Gizm    246    $0.30     $73.80
   2   G002     Medium Giz    527    $0.35    $184.45
   3   G003     Large Gizm     89    $0.45     $40.05
   4   W001     Small Widg    340    $0.05     $17.00
   5   W004     Medium Wid    125    $0.10     $12.50
   6   W005     Large Widg    189    $0.20     $37.80

  ═══════════════════════════════ INVENT.WDB ═══════════════════════════
        Item#        Name       Qty      Price     Value
   1   G001     Small Gizmo      246     $0.30     $73.80
   2   G002     Medium Gizmo     527     $0.35    $184.45
   3   G003     Large Gizmo       89     $0.45     $40.05
   4   W001     Small Widget     340     $0.05     $17.00
   5   W004     Medium Widget    125     $0.10     $12.50
   6   W005     Large Widget     189     $0.20     $37.80
   7
   8

  E13                                                              <F1=HELP>
  Press ALT to choose commands, or F2 to edit.
```

Figure 12-1.
When you copy data into a spreadsheet, Works fills the spreadsheet cells down and to the right of the cell you select.

■ Unlike the Word Processor, the Spreadsheet won't move existing data out of the way to make room for the data you're copying into the spreadsheet. If you select a cell in the middle of a block of filled cells as the copy destination, Works replaces the existing data below and to the right of it with the copied data. As a result, you must be careful to select an empty area of a spreadsheet as the destination for copied data if you want to avoid destroying existing data.

 WORKS TIP: If you mistakenly write over data in a spreadsheet by copying in new data, close the spreadsheet file without saving the changes, and then open it again. Your old data will reappear.

■ Works places text separated by tab stops in separate columns. When you copy data that's separated by tab stops from the Word Processor, Works positions the text in separate cells in the spreadsheet. So, if you copied three columns of names or numbers (separated by tab stops) from a Word Processor document, the columns would be placed in three separate spreadsheet columns, as shown here.

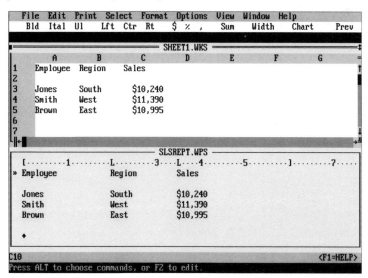

■ In this case, the tab stops in the Word Processor document at the bottom of the screen were set so that there would be only one tab stop between each column in every line of the document. This illustration also shows that Works places text lines separated by carriage returns in separate rows of a spreadsheet (which is why there's a blank row between the column labels and the data in the spreadsheet) and that dollar-formatted numbers in the Word Processor copy into the Spreadsheet in Currency format.

■ Spreadsheet cells won't hold more than 254 characters. When you copy text into a spreadsheet, Works inserts all the text between tab stops and carriage returns in one cell. Works copies only the first 254 characters of text in the selection into the spreadsheet cell. Any text after the 254th character is lost.

Copying Data into Communications Documents

You copy data into Communications documents to transmit that data. Here are the considerations for copying into a Communications document:

■ You can't complete a copy operation in a Communications document unless your computer is connected to a remote computer. If you press Enter to complete a copy operation when the OFFLINE message is showing in a Communications document's status line, Works displays a warning that says you must first be connected.

■ Works immediately transmits text or data copied into a Communications document to the remote computer.

■ Works copies and transmits columnar data in columns. If you copy data in text columns or from spreadsheet columns or database fields, Works transfers it to the Communications document in columns as well. Because Works transmits such data as text, tab stops that would normally separate columnar data are replaced with space characters.

■ Data that is too wide to fit within the Communications document's window wraps around to the next line and is still transmitted. In this respect, the Communications tool treats text as the Word Processor does, wrapping it down to the next line when it's too wide.

MERGING DATABASE DATA INTO A WORD PROCESSOR DOCUMENT

As explained in Chapter 4, you can merge data from a Database file into a Word Processor document. Such merges take place off screen when Microsoft Works is printing a document or writing it into a file. You can use either the Print Form Letters or the Print Labels command to effect the merge.

WORKS TIP: Don't forget: WorksWizards can help you create form letters and mailing label documents. If you already have the Database file from which you're merging data, you can use a WorksWizard to create the Word Processor document that will contain the merged data.

This merging capability is useful for creating form letters, labels, or other documents in which you want to format Database data in a way that Database reports themselves don't allow.

The following steps recap the basic procedure for merging Database data with a Word Processor document:

1. Open the Database file from which you want to merge data.

2. Open or create a new Word Processor file.

3. Move the cursor to the place in the Word Processor document where you want merged data to appear.

4. Choose the Insert Database Field command from the Edit menu (Alt-E-F). Works presents a dialog box that lists the Database files you currently have open.

5. From the list, select the Database file you want. Works displays a list of the fields in that Database file.

6. Select the field whose data you want to merge, and click OK. Works places a field marker in the Word Processor document.

7. Repeat steps 3 through 6 to specify other Database fields to merge in different places in the document, and finish entering and formatting the other text in the document.

8. Choose the Print Form Letters (Alt-P-F) or Print Labels command (Alt-P-L) from the Print menu to print the document. If you specify one copy in the Print dialog box, Works prints one copy of the Word Processor document for each record currently displayed in the Database document, merging the data in the merged fields from one record into each copy of the printed document.

   NOTE: *If you use the regular Print command, Microsoft Works prints one copy of the document, showing the field merge markers rather than the actual merged data.*

For more information about how to merge data from the Database into the Word Processor, see Chapter 4, or choose the *Form Letters (WP)* topic in the Word Processor category of the Help Table of Contents.

INSERTING A SPREADSHEET RANGE IN A WORD PROCESSOR DOCUMENT

Unlike simply copying a range of cells into a Word Processor document (as covered earlier), inserting a Spreadsheet range creates a live data link between the range you insert and the original Spreadsheet file. When you change values or formulas in the range in the original spreadsheet, the inserted range in the Word Processor document changes as well.

You can only insert named Spreadsheet ranges in a Word Processor document, so you must name the range in the Spreadsheet document before you can select that range and insert it in a Word Processor document. When you insert a range, Microsoft Works inserts a placeholder in the Word Processor document to indicate it, in the same way as it inserts placeholders for database fields, pictures, or spreadsheet charts you insert. To see the actual spreadsheet data, you must preview or print the Word Processor document.

Selecting and Inserting a Range

Let's see how this works. We'll assume we want to insert a range called Summary from a spreadsheet.

1. Open the Spreadsheet document that contains the Summary range.

2. Create a new Word Processor document or open the one in which you want to insert the range, and then move the cursor to the place where you want the range to appear.

3. Choose the Insert Spreadsheet Range command from the Edit menu (Alt-E-R). Works displays a dialog box, like this:

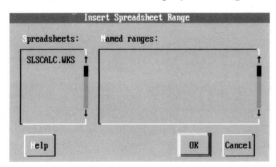

4. Click the name of the spreadsheet in the Spreadsheets list. The names of the defined ranges in that spreadsheet appear in the Named Ranges list at the right.

5. Double-click the name of the range you want to insert (Summary in this case). Works inserts a placeholder for the range in the Word Processor document, like this:

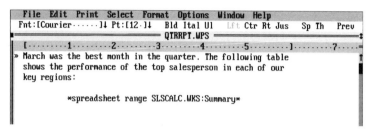

As you can see, the placeholder for a spreadsheet range looks like the placeholders Works inserts when you insert a picture or a spreadsheet chart in a Word Processor document. As with other placeholders, you can select the range placeholder and delete it, move it, or copy it into another location if you like, in the same way as you would any other text in the document.

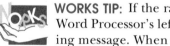

WORKS TIP: If the range you insert is too wide to fit within the Word Processor's left and right margins, Works displays a warning message. When you click OK, it inserts the range, but you still will have trouble printing it on the page. To remedy this problem, either make the Word Processor document's left and right margins smaller or change the font, size, or column width of the range in the Spreadsheet document so that more data will fit into the same horizontal space.

Previewing or Printing a Document with an Inserted Range

To see the actual data from an inserted spreadsheet range in a Word Processor document, you must preview or print the document, and the spreadsheet that contains the range must also be open at the same time. Otherwise, Works won't be able to locate the data.

When you examine the font and size tools in the toolbar or print the Word Processor document, you'll see that the spreadsheet range has the font and style settings that were in the original spreadsheet, not the settings from the surrounding paragraphs in the Word Processor document.

WORKS TIP: If you move, delete, or rename the spreadsheet from which you inserted the range, or if you rename the range or delete the range name inside the Spreadsheet document, Works won't be able to print or preview the range, because it won't be able to locate it.

Formatting an Inserted Range

If you don't like the placement of the spreadsheet data in your Word Processor document when you preview it, you can change the alignment, indent, or spacing between the range and the paragraphs of text above or below it.

1. Click the spreadsheet range marker.

2. Choose the Spreadsheet Range command from the Format menu (Alt-T-A). Works displays the Spreadsheet Range dialog box, like this:

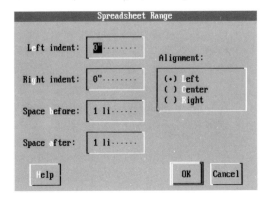

3. Type the left or right indent or line spacing values you want, click the alignment option you want, and then click OK to change the range format.

MOUSE TIP: You cannot change the formatting of a spreadsheet range by clicking the format tools in the Word Processor's toolbar. You must change the font, size, or column width in the original Spreadsheet document to change these formats.

Changing the Data in an Inserted Range

Because you only see a placeholder for a spreadsheet range when you insert it in a Word Processor document, you must return to the spreadsheet that contains the range in order to change the range's data. You can do this by simply opening the Spreadsheet document, using the Go To command on the Select menu to select the range, and then making the changes you want.

 MOUSE TIP: To quickly open the spreadsheet that contains a range you've inserted, double-click the range placeholder in the Word Processor document. Works then opens the Spreadsheet file and selects the range in it.

For more information on inserting spreadsheet ranges, see the *Inserting a SS Range (WP)* topic in the Word Processor category of the Help Table of Contents.

IMPORTING OR EXPORTING TEXT FILES

Whenever you choose the Open Existing File command from the File menu, Microsoft Works displays a list of the files in the current disk directory. The files are displayed in categories by the names of the Works tools that were used to create them. The category called Other Files, however, shows all the other files in that directory. You can select and open any of these Other type files with Works, but unless the files are text format files, you won't be able to make much sense of what you see. If you open one of the Works program files as a Word Processor document, for example, you'll see a screen of meaningless graphics symbols and other characters.

Text files are files that contain only text characters, without any formatting, formulas, macros, or other information. Most word processing, spreadsheet, database, and communications programs that run on any personal computer can create text files, so this format allows you to import data that was created with a different MS-DOS program or with another personal computer, such as the Macintosh.

You can open a text file as a new Word Processor, Spreadsheet, or Database document. When you select an Other type file to open, a dialog box appears in which you choose the type of Works file to create. Each of the Works tools treats text-format data differently.

Opening Text Files in the Word Processor

When you open a text file with the Word Processor, Works shows you all of the file's text. Many other word processing programs create text files that are one continuous stream of data, so your Works screen might show the text without any carriage returns after the lines or breaks between the paragraphs.

If you're opening a text file that was created by a spreadsheet or database program, the text will probably be arranged in columns or with tab stops or commas between the entries that are in different columns or fields. (In order to see the tabs, you might need to select Show All Characters in the Show dialog box.)

Communications programs and some word processors end each line in a text file with a carriage return. If such a text file's line is wider than the 6-inch default format of a new Word Processor document, Works displays the first 6 inches on one line and then displays the rest of the text on the following line.

Opening Text Files in the Spreadsheet and Database

The Works Spreadsheet and Database tools recognize incoming text separated by tab stops as different cells or fields. They treat each carriage return in a file as the signal to begin filling a new spreadsheet row or database record.

Most text files that you'll want to import into the Spreadsheet or Database will have been created by other spreadsheet or database programs, and the data in them will be properly separated by tabs (or commas) and carriage returns. If the text isn't separated by commas or tabs, Works places up to 254 characters of text in the first cell or field, deletes the remaining text from that point to the first carriage return, and then fills the first cell or field in the second row or record with up to 254 characters, and so on.

Saving Microsoft Works Files in Text Format

In the same way as you can open text files from other programs, you can save Works Word Processor, Spreadsheet, and Database files as text so that they can be opened by other programs. The basic procedure is the same with each tool:

1. Choose the Save As command from the File menu (Alt-F-A). Works displays the Save As dialog box.

2. Type the name of the text file.

3. Select the desired text format for the file in the File Formats box.

4. Press Enter.

The text-file format options in the Word Processor are different from those in the Spreadsheet and Database. In the Word Processor, you can select either Text format or Printed Text format. The Text format saves the file as a stream of characters with carriage returns and line feeds separating paragraphs. The Printed Text format inserts a carriage return and a line feed at the end of each line. Some word processing programs can use files in this format more effectively than in plain Text files.

In the Spreadsheet and Database, you can select either the Text & Commas format (to separate the columns or fields in the file with commas) or the Text & Tabs format (to separate columns or fields with tabs). Some programs recognize only commas or only tabs as the means of separating data, so Works gives you a choice.

OPENING OR SAVING FILES IN OTHER FORMATS

In addition to the text formats, Microsoft Works can open and save files in formats used by certain other programs. The formats in which Works opens or saves files depends on which tool you're using.

- The Works Word Processor can open or save files in the format used by Microsoft Word version 5.0 or later or by WordPerfect versions 5.0 and 5.1. Works can also open or save files in RTF and DCA format. RTF, or Rich Text Format, is used by Microsoft applications for both MS-DOS and Macintosh computers. DCA, or Document Content Architecture, is an IBM file format used by DisplayWrite and other programs. Finally, the Works Word Processor can also open files created with Microsoft Word for Windows.

- The Works Spreadsheet can open or save files created with Lotus 1-2-3 version 1.x or 2.0. It can also open files in Microsoft's SYLK format, as well as files created in Microsoft Excel version 4.0 that were saved from that program in the .WKS format.

- The Works Database can open or save files in dBASE III or dBASE IV formats.

Keep in mind that when you share files with other programs, the main point is to avoid having to retype the data. It's quite possible that when you use a Works tool to open files created by another program, some of the features in the original program won't be supported in Works. Conversely, when you save files from

Works in another program's format, you won't be able to use some Works-specific features once you open the file in that other program. For example, macros created in Works won't work in another program.

INTEGRATION PROJECTS

Now that we've covered the various ways in which you can move data from one Microsoft Works tool to another, or between Works and other programs, let's try two projects that show some of these capabilities at work. The instructions for these projects aren't quite as detailed as those in earlier chapters. Here we assume you already have experience with each Works tool and that you don't need keystroke-by-keystroke instructions. If you run across an instruction you don't understand, refer to Chapters 1, 2, 5, 8, and 11 for help, or check the appropriate category's topics in the Help Table of Contents.

Making a Labels Database from a Captured Text File

For this project, let's suppose a colleague in another office has compiled a mailing list file using a different MS-DOS program, and you need to print some mailing labels from that data immediately. Your colleague could send a disk that contains the file via overnight courier, but let's assume that you both have modems on your computers and that you can't wait a day to get the data. So you'll use the Communications tool to receive the file as text, open the text file as a Database file, and then create a Word Processor document to produce labels from the data.

To begin this project, you'll need to create a text file that simulates the one you would receive from your colleague. If you completed the exercise in Chapter 8, you can use the ADDRESS.WDB file you created there. If you did not complete that exercise, create the ADDRESS.WDB file now, or use the Address Book WorksWizard to create one. (If you follow the steps in Chapter 8, it isn't necessary to do the copying, reporting, and sorting exercises; simply create the new file, create the fields, enter the data, and save the file as ADDRESS.WDB.)

1. Open the ADDRESS.WDB file.

2. Choose the Save As command and select the Text & Tabs format option. Works automatically changes the filename to ADDRESS.TXT.

3. Click OK or press Enter to save the file in text format. Works asks you to confirm that you want to save the file without formatting.

4. Click OK and then close the ADDRESS.WDB file.

Now we'll simulate connecting with the remote computer.

Receiving the Text File

Before you perform these steps, you should call your colleague on the telephone and agree on the communication settings you'll use, the time you'll make the call, and which of you will call the other. Also, you should confirm that your colleague has saved the mailing list file in text format before you attempt to receive it. The following steps show how communication might actually proceed:

1. Open a new Communications file.

2. Choose the Communication command from the Options menu. In the Communication dialog box, enter the communication settings you've agreed on, and then press Enter.

3. Choose the Phone command from the Options menu, type the telephone number for your colleague's computer, and press Enter. (We'll assume that you're the one making the call and that your colleague is prepared to receive the call.)

4. If you're using an external modem, turn it on and ascertain that it's properly connected.

5. Click the Connect tool. Works dials the remote computer's number, and when the other computer answers, the word *CONNECT* appears on your screen.

6. Type *Hello* and press Enter. Your colleague sees the message on the screen and types *How are you?* You see that response on your screen.

7. Type *Ready to receive in ten seconds* and press Enter. Your colleague types *Okay,* and you see it on your screen. (This response gives you time to open a captured text file before your colleague begins sending.)

8. Click the Capt tool in the toolbar, type *DATA* as the name for the captured text file, and click OK to begin saving incoming text on your disk. Your colleague begins sending the data file, and you see it as it comes in on your screen. Works saves it on disk.

9. Click the Capt tool again to close the captured text file when you receive the last of the data. (You'll know when the last of the data has arrived because no more new text appears on your screen.)

10. Type *Thanks* to acknowledge your receipt of the data.

11. Click the Connect tool again to disconnect from the remote computer.

At this point, the data file from your colleague would be stored as text on your disk. Because we haven't actually communicated with a remote computer, however, we'll use the dummy text file (ADDRESS.TXT) we created from the ADDRESS.WDB file.

Creating a New Database File

The next step is to open the text file as a Database file and name the data fields properly.

1. Choose the Open Existing File command, select the file named ADDRESS.TXT — listed under Other Files — that you created and stored on your disk, and then click OK.

2. Double-click the Database file option. Works opens the file and displays it, like this:

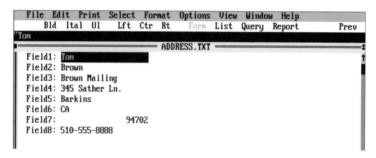

Notice that the field names are generic, and all the field sizes are the standard 20 characters. We'll rename the fields in this document and then save the document as a standard Database file with the name LIST.WDB.

1. Select the Field1 field name.

2. Type *FirstName:* and press the Down arrow key to enter the new field name, and then select the field name below it.

3. Repeat this process to name the rest of the fields as shown in the following table:

Old Field Name	New Field Name
Field1:	FirstName:
Field2:	LastName:
Field3:	Company:
Field4:	Street:
Field5:	City:
Field6:	State:
Field7:	Zip:
Field8:	Phone:

After you rename the fields, use the Save As command to save the file with the name LIST.WDB in the Works DB format. After Works saves the file, leave the file open — we'll need it in a moment.

Making Labels with a Microsoft WorksWizard

The last part of this project is to create a Word Processor document that contains the merged data for mailing labels. The fastest way to do this is to use the Mailing Labels WorksWizard.

1. Choose the WorksWizards command from the File menu, click the Mailing Labels option, and then click OK. You'll see the introductory screen for this WorksWizard.

2. Follow the directions on the screen to select the LIST.WDB file as the source of data, to select fields of data to match the standard ones on the label, and finally to preview or print the labels.

As you follow the instructions, watch for the chance to add the Company field to the label. The WorksWizard assumes you want only the first and last names, street address, city, state, and zip code. After you add these fields to the label, however, Works gives you a chance to add extra fields. When it asks if you want to add more fields, be sure to choose the Company field from your Database file.

After you've finished merging fields, the WorksWizard gives you the option of printing the labels.

This project shows how you can capture data from another computer and manipulate it in Works. The Communications tool helps you access on-line information services and data on other colleagues' computers, and the Works-Wizard for mailing labels lets you easily convert the data to a useful format.

A COMPLEX REPORT

In this project, we'll combine data from various sources into one Word Processor document for final formatting. We'll include in the finished report some Spreadsheet data, a Spreadsheet chart, and a selection of Database records.

Creating the Source Files

We need two data source files for this project. The Spreadsheet file is called FINANCES.WKS, as shown in Figure 12-2. The Database file is the INVENT.WDB file created in the exercise at the end of Chapter 10. If you haven't yet created that file, you can do so by following these steps and entering the data shown in Figure 12-3.

	A	B	C	D
1	Apex Widget Sales - 1st Quarter Finances			
2				
3	Income	January	February	March
4				
5	Products	3500	4500	6000
6	Services	1500	1200	2000
7	Interest	50	45	52
8				
9	Total Inc.	5050	5745	8052
10				
11	Expenses			
12				
13	Material	500	700	900
14	Utilities	150	175	180
15	Leases	750	900	900
16	Salaries	2000	2000	3000
17	Benefits	400	400	400
18	Insurance	260	260	260
19				
20	Total Exp.	4060	4435	5640
21				
22	Cash Flow	990	1310	2412

Figure 12-2.
The FINANCES spreadsheet shows one quarter's expenses and income for a small business.

```
 File  Edit  Print  Select  Format  Options  View  Window  Help
      Bld  Ital  Ul      Lft  Ctr  Rt    Form   List  Query  Report          Prev

====================================  INVENT.WDB  ========================
       Item#           Name              Qty      Price    Value
  1   G001      Small Gizmo              246     $0.30    $73.80
  2   G002      Medium Gizmo             527     $0.35   $184.45
  3   G003      Large Gizmo               89     $0.45    $40.05
  4   W001      Small Widget             340     $0.05    $17.00
  5   W004      Medium Widget            125     $0.10    $12.50
  6   W005      Large Widget             189     $0.20    $37.80
  7
```

Figure 12-3.
The INVENT file shows the current inventory levels for the same business.

1. Create a new, blank Spreadsheet file, and type the labels and numbers in the cells, as shown in Figure 12-2.

2. Save the spreadsheet as FINANCES, and leave the file open.

3. Open a new Database file, create the fields, and enter the records shown in Figure 12-3.

4. Save the Database file as INVENT, and leave the file open.

Beginning the Report Document

This report is only two pages long, but the data-copying techniques used here will serve you well for reports of any size. To begin, open a new Word Processor file and enter the title and introductory text shown here:

Quarterly Report

The first quarter of 1993 was a good one for Apex Widget Sales. We experienced rising income, relatively steady expenses, and calm waters on the competitive front.

Financial Highlights

Our first quarter financial summary shows increasing cash flow with rising sales and manageable expenses. Here are the numbers for total income, total expenses, and cash flow:

After you enter the above text, save the document as Q1REPT. That document name will appear on the Window menu, which will make it easier to select this document again as we copy data from the other two files.

Copying Spreadsheet Data

At the end of the second paragraph in the Q1REPT document, we want to copy in some rows of data from the FINANCES spreadsheet.

1. Press Enter two times to move the cursor two lines below the last sentence in the second paragraph.

2. Select the FINANCES.WKS spreadsheet from the Window menu. Works displays the spreadsheet.

3. Select the Total Inc. label and the three values to the right of it in row 9 of the spreadsheet, and then choose the Copy command from the Edit menu.

4. Select Q1REPT from the Window menu. Works displays the document.

5. Press Enter. Works copies the spreadsheet data into the document, as shown here:

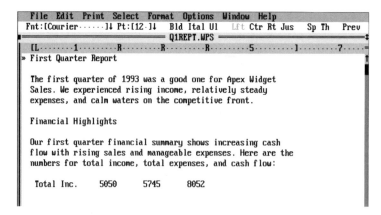

Each column of spreadsheet data is separated by a tab stop, and the cursor is at the beginning of the copied line of numbers. Now let's copy more data.

1. Press the Down arrow key to move the cursor to the next line of the Word Processor document.

2. Select the FINANCES spreadsheet from the Window menu.

3. Select the Total Exp. label and the three values to the right of it in row 20XC, and then choose the Copy command.

4. Select the Q1REPT document, and press Enter.

5. Press the Down arrow key again to move the cursor down a line.

6. Select the FINANCES spreadsheet from the Window menu.

7. Select the Cash Flow label and the three values to the right of it in row 22, and choose the Copy command.

8. Select the Q1REPT document, and press Enter.

Now we have the data in our report document, but the document contains no column labels to indicate to which months the numbers refer. We'll copy these labels from the Spreadsheet document:

1. Click in the blank line between the last line of the text paragraph and the Total Inc. row of numbers, and then press Enter once.

2. Select the FINANCES spreadsheet from the Window menu.

3. Select the three month labels from row 3 of the spreadsheet, and choose the Copy command.

4. Select the Q1REPT document from the Window menu, and press Enter. Now all the data and labels we need are in the Word Processor document, like this:

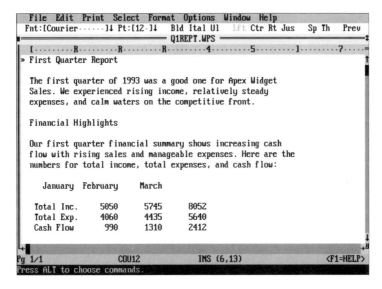

You'll notice that the column labels don't line up above the columns. That's because the first three lines we copied contained four columns of data, but there are only three columns of data formatted here. To move the labels over, press Tab.

Creating a Chart

Now let's continue with the text. Move the cursor to the line below the Cash Flow row of data, press Enter, and then enter the following paragraph:

> Although our cash flow has steadily increased, expenses have climbed rapidly as well. As the following chart shows, salary and benefits costs accounted for just over sixty percent of our monthly expenses in March.

When you reach the end of the paragraph, press Enter twice to move the cursor down. At this point, we want to insert a chart that shows how each expense contributes to the total monthly expenses for March. We'll have to create a pie chart from the appropriate data in the spreadsheet, and then we'll insert the chart in this document.

1. Select the FINANCES spreadsheet from the Window menu.

2. Select cells D13 through D18, and then click the Chart tool to display a chart of this data. Works displays a color bar chart.

Works has used the default bar chart type, and it always formats charts to fill a whole page. We need to change this chart to a pie, add the expense category labels from column A so that each pie slice is identified, add a title to the chart, change the font size of the title and labels, and change the chart's printing options to black and white.

1. Press Esc to display the Chart mode screen.

2. Click the Pie tool in the toolbar.

3. Select cells A13 through A18, and then choose the X-Series command from the Data menu (Alt-D-X).

4. Choose the Titles command from the Data menu (Alt-D-T), type *March Expenses* in the Chart Title box, and then press Enter.

5. Choose the Title Font command from the Format menu (Alt-T-F), and change the font size to 14.

6. Choose the Other Font command from the Format menu (Alt-T-O) and change the font size to 12.

7. Choose the Format For B&W command from the Print menu (Alt-P-F).

This chart is now ready to go. Click the Chart tool in the toolbar again, and Works displays it, like this:

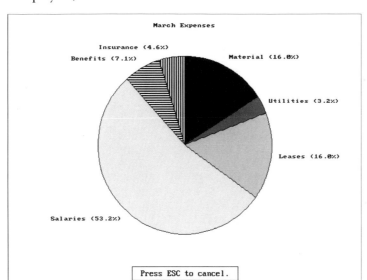

Inserting the Chart in the Report

Now let's insert this chart in the report document.

1. Press Esc to return to the Chart mode screen, and then select the QIREPT document from the Window menu.

2. Choose the Insert Chart command from the Edit menu (Alt-E-I). Works displays the Insert Chart dialog box.

3. Click the FINANCES spreadsheet name in the Spreadsheets list, and then double-click Chart1 in the Charts list. Works places a chart marker in the document.

You can't see charts in the Word Processor, so let's preview the document to find out how the chart will look on the page at this point:

1. Click the Prev tool in the toolbar. Works displays the Preview dialog box.

2. Click the Preview button. Works displays the report page, like this:

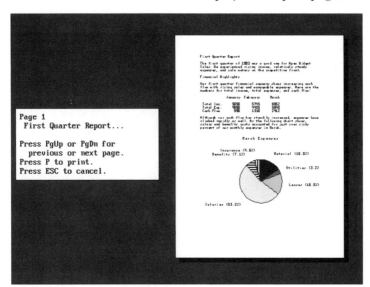

 WORKS TIP: If Works displays a message telling you that the current printer can't print a chart, the chart won't show on the Preview screen. To remedy this situation, select a different printer with the Printer Setup command (Alt-P-S). If necessary, run the Works Setup program from your set of program installation disks, and install the printer driver you need. See Appendix A for more information on installing printers.

The page looks all right for now, but we can see that most of the space on this page is now used. Let's begin a new page and move on.

Inserting a Page Break

1. Press Esc to return to the document.

2. Click in the line below the chart marker, and choose the Insert Page Break command from the Print menu (Alt-P-I, or Ctrl-Enter). Works inserts a page break marker and moves the cursor to the line below it.

3. Type the following:

Inventory Update

We've been trying to minimize our finished goods inventory to better manage expenses, but our stocks of some items are still a bit high, as shown in the following table:

When you finish entering this text, press Enter twice.

Copying Database Data

Now we want to copy some records from the INVENT Database file:

1. Select the INVENT document from the Window menu.

2. Select the List view (if the document isn't already displayed in this view).

3. Sort the records on the Item# field (if they aren't already in that order).

4. Select the Item#, Name, and Qty fields by dragging the pointer across these field names.

5. Choose the Copy command from the Edit menu.

6. Select the Q1REPT document from the Window menu, and then press Enter. Works inserts the records in the document, like this:

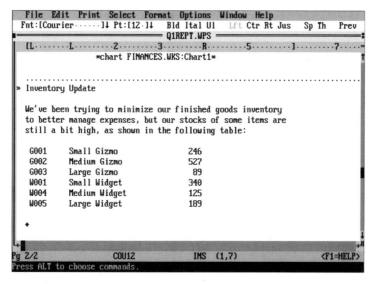

Works has copied the data from the fields, but not the field names themselves. We'll enter those by hand.

1. The cursor should be blinking at the beginning of the first database record. If not, move it there.

2. Press Enter twice to add two blank lines above the group of records, and then press the Up arrow key twice.

3. Type *Item* and press Tab.

4. Type *Description* and press Tab.

5. Type *Quantity* and press Tab.

Now the columns of data have titles. To finish the project, go to the bottom of the document, press Enter, and type the text in the following paragraph:

> In the coming months, we hope to reduce our levels of widgets and gizmos so that there are no more than 200 of any single item in stock.

Let's assume that this is the end of the report. At this point, you could spice up the format by using bold section titles, selecting a larger font size for the report title, indenting the first lines of the text paragraphs, and adding a cover page and a table of contents. See the monthly report project in Chapter 4 for tips about such topics as creating a title page and a table of contents.

DOING IT YOURSELF

The examples in this chapter have shown you how you can move data among Microsoft Works tools to apply the unique strengths of each tool to the problem at hand. Armed with these techniques, you can use Works to capture, convert, format, calculate, sort, select, and otherwise manipulate data to suit nearly any business or personal computing need. As you explore the possibilities for using Works to tackle your own projects, you'll find that you're only at the beginning of a long and productive relationship with Works.

A

Installing & Running Microsoft Works

Microsoft Works will run on any IBM PC, PC/XT, PC/AT, PS/2, or 100 percent compatible computer running PC-DOS or MS-DOS version 3.0 or later and using either a fixed disk or two floppy disk drives. It will also work with every widely used PC-compatible display adapter card, printer, and mouse.

Before you can use Works on your machine, however, you must install it. Thanks to the Works Setup program and Setup disk, Works is easy to install. The procedure is explained in Chapter 1 of the *Microsoft Works User's Guide*. By following a few simple steps, you can have Works installed on your machine and running in a few minutes.

In this appendix, we'll take a thorough look at the installation process. You'll find out what happens during the installation and what to do if something goes wrong. You'll also find out how to start Works and load one or more Works files at the same time and how to modify the AUTOEXEC.BAT file on your startup disk so that Works loads whenever you start your computer.

MS-DOS BASICS

You're probably eager to dive into Works, but if you take a few minutes to learn some fundamental MS-DOS techniques and concepts now, you'll save yourself a lot of frustration and head-scratching later. Before you can begin using Works properly, you need to understand some basics about MS-DOS, the operating system that manages files and programs on every IBM PC and PC-compatible computer. This section will tell you enough to get Works installed and running, but you should also study the MS-DOS tutorial that most likely came with your computer. Trying to run a computer without knowing MS-DOS is like trying to drive a car without knowing the traffic laws: You can do it, but the situation can get sticky.

Your computer is only an inert hunk of hardware until you insert an MS-DOS disk and turn on the computer. When you turn it on, a built-in set of instructions (stored in one of the computer's memory chips) tells the computer to look for an MS-DOS disk in one of the disk drives. If your computer doesn't find MS-DOS, you'll see a message on the screen telling you so.

If you have only floppy disk drives in your computer system, you'll need to insert an MS-DOS disk before you turn on the computer in order for MS-DOS to start up properly. If you have a hard disk, MS-DOS will load from the hard disk when you turn on the power, provided the floppy disk drive is empty.

As part of the startup sequence, MS-DOS performs commands stored in a file called AUTOEXEC.BAT. See "Starting Microsoft Works Automatically from a Hard Disk," later in this appendix, to learn how to change the AUTOEXEC.BAT file to make Works load automatically each time you start your PC.

After your computer locates and loads MS-DOS, your screen displays a command prompt, like this:

A>

The letter in the prompt indicates the current disk drive, which is the drive from which MS-DOS was loaded. In most computers that are MS-DOS–compatible, the first (the leftmost or uppermost) floppy disk drive is designated as drive A. The second (the rightmost or lowermost) floppy disk drive is designated as drive B. The hard disk drive is called drive C.

Along with disk drive names, you'll also find named subsections, called directories, on any disk. When you first prepare (or format) a floppy disk for use with MS-DOS, for example, the root directory represents all the space on the disk. If the disk is in the A drive, the root directory is designated as *A:*. Exactly as you can subdivide the space in a file drawer with labeled folders, you can subdivide a disk directory into named subdirectories. A subdirectory name can be up to eight characters long, and it is always identified at the MS-DOS prompt with a backslash that separates it from other directories. A subdirectory called BUDGETS on the disk in drive A, therefore, would be referenced by the name *A:\BUDGETS*. A subdirectory called SALES located inside the BUDGETS subdirectory would be referenced by the name *A:\BUDGETS\SALES*.

To run a program, format a disk, copy a file, erase a file, or perform any other system activity, you must type the correct command at the MS-DOS prompt, and then press Enter on your keyboard. You usually need to type only the program's name to run a program. MS-DOS assumes that any command you type refers to the current drive and directory showing at the prompt, so if you type the name of a program on a floppy disk in drive B when the prompt reads

A>, MS-DOS won't be able to find and load the program because MS-DOS will be looking for the program on a floppy disk in drive A. Unless you know you want to work with a file located in the current directory, you must type the directory name along with the name of the program or command.

To change the current disk drive from the MS-DOS prompt, you simply type the new drive name followed by a colon. If you loaded MS-DOS from drive A and the current prompt is *A>*, for example, and you wanted to work with files on a disk in drive B, you would type *b:* and press Enter to change to drive B.

The MS-DOS command to change the current directory is *cd*. If you were at the *C>* prompt and you wanted to change to the \DATA subdirectory on the hard disk, you would type *cd\data.*

You can also tell MS-DOS to look on a different disk and run a certain program there at the same time. If you were at the *A>* prompt and you wanted to run the Start program from the root directory of a disk in drive B, you could type *b:\start.* MS-DOS would find the program on drive B and run it.

Navigating among directories to locate files and programs and creating new directories in which to store groups of files are fundamental MS-DOS activities. Other common tasks include formatting blank floppy disks, listing the files in a directory, copying files, renaming files, and erasing files. The following are some examples of basic MS-DOS commands and their functions. The command listings include the MS-DOS prompt so that you can see the current directory name.

Basic MS-DOS Commands

Command	Description
A>*b\:start*	Run the Start program from the root directory on the disk in drive B.
C>*cd \data*	Change the current directory to C:\DATA.
A>*dir*	List all the files in the current directory on drive A.
C>*mkdir \budget*	Make a new directory called BUDGET in the current directory of drive C.
C>*del \budget\fall89*	Delete the file FALL89 from the subdirectory \BUDGET in the current directory of drive C.
B>*ren report q1rept*	Rename the file REPORT on drive B to Q1REPT.
B>*copy report c:\data*	Copy the file REPORT from the current directory on drive B into the directory \DATA on drive C.

These examples give you an idea of how to structure MS-DOS commands. MS-DOS isn't sensitive to whether you use uppercase or lowercase letters in commands, but it is particular about spaces in commands. If you don't include the spaces between the parts of the commands as shown in the table, you'll get an error message. For more information about MS-DOS commands, check the MS-DOS manual that came with your copy of MS-DOS, or see *Running MS-DOS* by Van Wolverton, also published by Microsoft Press.

INSTALLING MICROSOFT WORKS

Microsoft Works comes on several floppy disks that contain the following:

- The Works program
- Dictionary and Thesaurus files
- Help files
- Template files
- Clip art files
- Printer and display card drivers
- Other miscellaneous files

The Setup program on the Works Setup disk simplifies the process of installing these files. These are the steps you take:

1. Turn on your computer and boot MS-DOS. (If you don't have a hard disk, insert an MS-DOS disk in drive A, and then turn on the computer.)
2. Insert the Works Setup disk in drive A.
3. Type *setup* and then press Enter. Works starts the Setup program. (If you have a hard disk and the A drive is not the current drive, type *a:\setup* instead.)
4. Press Enter to move past the welcoming screen.
5. Answer the questions displayed on your screen, and insert the appropriate Works disks as instructed. (Answer the questions by pressing the Up arrow key or Down arrow key to highlight the answer you want and then pressing Enter to select the highlighted answer.)

As you go through the Setup program, you'll answer questions and follow directions to perform the following tasks:

- Indicate whether you're installing a new copy of Works or modifying an existing installation

- Indicate whether you want to make each installation choice yourself or have Setup make the best choices, based on its analysis of your computer hardware

- Choose the hard disk, directory, or floppy disk drive on which you'll install a working copy of Works

- Select and copy a video card driver onto your hard disk or working floppy disk so that your monitor can display Works using all the capabilities of the particular video display card installed in your computer

- Select a printer driver and copy it onto your hard disk or working floppy disk so that Works can print documents using all of the capabilities of your printer (or printers)

Although you can create a working copy of Works by making all these choices yourself, it's best to have Setup make educated guesses about what you want; you can always change the settings later if they turn out to be wrong. Let's assume you've selected the option to have Setup make the best choices, and then let's look at each of the setup tasks to see what really goes on and why.

Choosing a Disk and a Directory

Before it presents you with any options, the Setup program scans your computer system and tries to determine your hardware setup. It checks to see how many disk drives your system has and what kind of video card is installed.

After you decide whether you're installing a new copy of Works or modifying an existing copy, your first Setup task is to select the disk drive where the new copy of Works will be installed.

- If you have a floppy disk system, select either drive A or drive B. The Setup program tells you when to insert the formatted blank floppy disks on which to install a copy of Works.

- If you have a hard disk, select drive C. The Setup program copies the necessary Works files into a directory on drive C so that you can run the program from there.

The Works program is really several separate files that are loaded at various times as you use Works. When all the necessary files are stored on your hard disk, these program files load much more quickly, and you'll be able to get your work done faster. If you're running Works from floppy disks, the program asks you to insert a different floppy disk at times, such as when you check a document's spelling, so that the program can access the extra files it needs in order to continue.

When you copy Works onto a hard disk, the Setup program asks you to name a directory in which to store the program files. (The default directory is C:\WORKS.) After you type a directory name, the Setup program creates the directory — if it doesn't already exist — and then stores all the Works files there. It's more convenient to store all the Works files in their own directory so that they're not mixed in with files from MS-DOS or with other programs on your hard disk.

Typically you'll want to name your directory WORKS — the name the Setup program proposes. If you want to type a new name, delete the proposed directory name by pressing Backspace five times, and then type the new name. MS-DOS directory names can be up to eight characters long.

After you begin using Works, you'll want to create other directories in which to store your data files on your hard disk. It's better to separate data files from program files on your hard disk because it makes it easier to find and work with the data files later. You can use the Create Directory option in Works' File Management command dialog box to create additional directories on your hard disk or floppy disk. (See Chapter 1 for more information.)

If you have only floppy disk drives in your system, it's best to install a copy of Works on a new set of disks and then to store your original Works disks in a safe place because floppy disks can be damaged in a variety of ways. You can then use the copy of the program in your daily work. If your working copy becomes damaged, you can always make another copy from the originals.

When running Works from floppy disks, you'll want to store your data files separately from the program. It will be easier to find and select your data files if they're stored on their own floppy disks rather than jumbled together with Works program files on the same disk.

Choosing a Video Card

After you select a disk and (if necessary) name a directory, the Setup program copies the main Works program files into that directory. Next you're asked to specify which video card is installed in your system. You'll see four bars in different colors or shades on your screen, and the Setup program asks you to select an option based on which colors or intensities you see. Selecting an option helps the Setup program fine-tune Works to display text and graphics as well as possibly using your video card.

Choosing Printers

To print a Works document, you must install the proper printer driver file on the same disk or in the same directory as your working copy of Works. The Works package comes with dozens of printer driver files for various brands and models of printers.

When running the Setup program, you can choose drivers for more than one brand and model of printer. No matter how many drivers you select, the Setup program copies them into your working copy of Works. When you have more than one printer driver installed in Works, you can use Works' Printer Setup command to select the printer you want to use. (See Chapter 1 for more information about the Printer Setup command.)

After you choose a printer, Works asks you to indicate where the printer is connected. The Setup program highlights the first parallel printer port, LPT1, because it's the most common. If you know your printer is using a different parallel port, however, or if your printer has a serial interface and is therefore using one of your computer's COM ports, choose the correct port here. For information about these printer issues, see the manuals that came with your computer and your printer. You will also find information about these topics in *Running MS-DOS* by Van Wolverton.

If you make a mistake on this screen and choose the wrong port, you can always correct your error by using the Printer Setup command after you start running Works. (See "The Printer Setup Command," in Chapter 1.)

Completing the Installation

After you have made all the installation decisions, the Setup program prompts you to insert various floppy disks as it installs the files it needs.

At the end of the installation, Setup modifies your AUTOEXEC.BAT file to include a PATH command for the new WORKS directory it created. (The PATH command tells DOS to look in the Works directory when it tries to execute commands.) When it modifies your AUTOEXEC.BAT file, Setup attempts to save your old AUTOEXEC.BAT file with the name AUTOEXEC.OLD, but if you already have a file by that name on your disk, Setup asks you to supply a different name. After this, Setup quits and returns you to the MS-DOS prompt.

If you have a hard disk, C:\WORKS (or the directory name you chose for it) is now your current directory. If you use floppy disks, the MS-DOS prompt will indicate drive A. To start Works with a floppy disk, type *cd\works,* and press

Enter. Next, with either floppy disks or a hard disk, type *works,* and press Enter. The Works program loads, the Works Quick Start screen appears, and you can begin working in the program.

This procedure is the one you'll follow if you want to run Works immediately after installing it using the Setup program. When you start Works in the future, you'll use slightly different steps.

STARTING MICROSOFT WORKS MANUALLY

To start Microsoft Works, you must type the program name. If you're using floppy disks, you must first insert the floppy disk that contains the Works program. If you type *works* with the wrong floppy disk inserted, you'll see an error message saying that the file was not found.

If you have a floppy disk system, the complete startup procedure is this:

1. Insert an MS-DOS disk in drive A, and turn on your computer. MS-DOS loads, and you see the MS-DOS prompt.

2. Remove the MS-DOS disk and insert the Works program disk in drive A.

3. Type *works* and press Enter. Works starts up.

If you have a hard disk, you can simply type *works* at the MS-DOS prompt that appears after you turn on your computer. The PATH statement in the AUTOEXEC.BAT file tells MS-DOS to look in the \WORKS subdirectory for the Works program file.

If you want to load Works from your hard disk each time you start up your computer, you can modify your AUTOEXEC.BAT file to do this. The next section explains how.

STARTING MICROSOFT WORKS
AUTOMATICALLY FROM A HARD DISK

This procedure for automating the Microsoft Works startup assumes that Works is installed on your hard disk. Each time you turn on your computer, MS-DOS looks for a file on your startup disk called AUTOEXEC.BAT. This file contains instructions about how MS-DOS should display its command prompt (the PROMPT command), which subdirectories MS-DOS should look in for program files when you type a command (the PATH command), which directory should be the current directory (the CD command), and even which programs to load. By adding the Works program name to this file, you can have Works load automatically at startup.

Opening AUTOEXEC.BAT

AUTOEXEC.BAT is stored in your root directory as a text file. You can open this file with the Microsoft Works Word Processor, make the changes you want, and then save it back to the same place on your disk. The next time you start up your computer, MS-DOS will read the modified instructions from the AUTOEXEC.BAT file. Here's the procedure, assuming the Works program file is located in the \WORKS directory on your hard disk.

1. Start your computer.

2. Type *works* and press Enter to start the Works program. The Works Quick Start screen appears.

3. Click the Open Existing File button (or press O). Works displays the Open Existing File dialog box, like this:

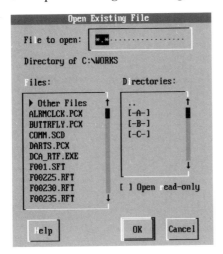

4. You want to open the AUTOEXEC.BAT file, so you must type the name of the directory in which the file is located, followed by the filename itself. Type *c:\autoexec.bat* and then press Enter.

   You can open text files with the Works Word Processor, Spreadsheet, or Database tool. When Works finds the text file you want to open, it displays a dialog box that asks which Works tool you want to use to open the file. The Word Processor option is selected as the default.

5. Press Enter to open the file as a Word Processor document. Works opens the file and displays it in a new Word Processor document window, as shown in Figure A-1.

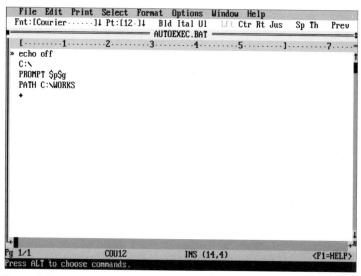

Figure A-1.
The AUTOEXEC.BAT file in a new Word Processor document window.

For more information about using the Word Processor and its document window, see Chapter 2. For now, let's make a backup copy of this file and then modify the current version.

Backing Up the AUTOEXEC.BAT File

First, we'll save a copy of this file so we'll have a copy of the original version in the event that we want to revert to using it.

1. Choose the Save As command from the File menu (Alt-F-A). Works displays the Save As dialog box. The current directory should be the root directory of your hard disk, and the file name AUTOEXEC.BAT should appear in the Save File As box.

2. Click at the right edge of the Save File As box to move the cursor there, then press the Backspace key three times to delete the BAT suffix from the file name.

3. Type *BA1* as the new suffix and press Enter. Works saves a copy of the current version of this file as AUTOEXEC.BA1. If you ever want to restore the original version of your AUTOEXEC.BAT file, you can open the AUTOEXEC.BA1 file and then save it as AUTOEXEC.BAT, overwriting the existing, modified version.

Modifying AUTOEXEC.BAT

Now, we'll modify the current AUTOEXEC.BAT file, which is still open on the screen.

Your AUTOEXEC.BAT file probably contains different commands from those shown in Figure AA-1. For instance, the PROMPT command shown on the third line might be different. The PROMPT command controls the way the MS-DOS prompt appears on your screen. For instance, if you have a hard disk, the default prompt is C>. The PROMPT pg command tells MS-DOS to display both the drive and the current directory at the prompt. For example, if you made \WORKS on drive C the current directory, the prompt would be C:\WORKS>. This book assumes that you have this prompt command in your AUTOEXEC.BAT file, so you may want to add it yourself. (See step 3 below.)

Follow these steps to modify the AUTOEXEC.BAT file:

1. Hold down both the Ctrl key and the End key (Ctrl-End). The cursor moves to the end of the text in the document.

2. Move the cursor down to the next line in the document by pressing Enter.

3. You are now ready to type new instructions. If you want to add the prompt command mentioned above, type *prompt pg* now, and then press Enter to move down another line.

4. Type *works* and then press Enter.

The command *works* on a line by itself tells MS-DOS to load the Works program. Since the PATH command in this AUTOEXEC.BAT file instructs MS-DOS to look in the \WORKS directory when attempting to execute commands, your computer will find the program file called WORKS.EXE there and will load the program.

Now that you've typed the new instructions, you're ready to save the modified file.

Saving the Changes

When you open a disk file, make changes to it, and then save the file with the same name in the same disk location, the new version of the file replaces the old version. This is what we want to do now.

- Choose the Save command from the File menu (Alt-F-S). Works saves the changed version of the AUTOEXEC.BAT file to the same location on the disk.

You've replaced the old AUTOEXEC.BAT file with a new version that will load the Works program each time you start your computer. If you added the PROMPT command, you've also changed the way your prompt will appear. The changes to your AUTOEXEC.BAT file won't take effect, however, until you restart your computer.

If you later decide you don't want Works to load at startup, you can open the AUTOEXEC.BA1 file and save it as AUTOEXEC.BAT, thus replacing the modified version of the file with the original version. As an alternative, you can simply open the AUTOEXEC.BAT file, delete the instructions you just added, and then use the Save command to save it again.

Exiting Works

Once you've modified and saved the AUTOEXEC.BAT file, you may want to exit the Works program. To do this, simply choose the Exit command from the File menu (Alt-F-X). You'll be returned to the MS-DOS prompt.

CHANGING THE MICROSOFT WORKS SETUP

As time goes by, you might acquire a new printer, mouse, or video card for your computer, and you'll want Microsoft Works to take full advantage of it. Every time you change your hardware setup, you need to modify your working copy of Works to take advantage of the changes. You use Setup to do this.

To make changes using Setup, do the following:

1. Insert the Setup disk in drive A.

2. Type *a:\setup* to start the program. Press Enter to move past the welcoming screen. The screen now displays a box that asks whether you want to create a new Works installation or modify an existing one.

3. Select the option to modify an existing Works installation. You'll then see a dialog box that asks you to identify the disk drive where you want to modify the installation.

4. Press the Down arrow key, if necessary, to select the disk drive on which your Works program is installed.

    If you choose drive A or drive B, Setup prompts you to insert the appropriate program disk as needed, depending on which setup option you want to modify. If you choose drive C, Setup prompts you to accept or to enter the name of the directory that contains your installed copy of Works.

After you identify the copy of Works that you want to modify, the screen displays a list of options for installing a different video driver, printer driver, and mouse.

5. Press the Down arrow key, if necessary, to select the option that you want to modify, and then press Enter to confirm this choice. Setup next displays that option as it appeared during the initial installation. (If you're installing a mouse driver, Setup installs it without any further input from you.)

6. Select the new video or printer driver, and then press Enter. Then select the Continue with Setup option that's highlighted in the list of choices. Setup then asks you to select another setting for modification or to complete the setup with the options you've now selected.

7. Select the Complete Setup and Modify Works option, and press Enter. The Setup program prompts you for any disks it needs, makes the selected modification to your installed copy of Works, and then tells you it's finished. Press Enter to exit Setup and return to the MS-DOS prompt.

NOTE: *If you want to quit the Setup program without making any changes after all, press Ctrl-X, and then press Enter.*

RUNNING MICROSOFT WORKS ON A LAPTOP

When you're using a laptop computer (or even a desktop model) and you're pressed for available disk space, you can trim down the Microsoft Works installation without affecting the program's basic features. A full Works installation with one printer driver occupies a little over 4 MB of space on your disk. However, after you've installed all the Works files, you can delete some of the ones you probably won't need every day (if at all). If you delete all the files suggested here, you can fit Works into half as much disk space.

The files you might want to delete are the clip art files, Template files, the Learning Works tutorial and its related files, and the Thesaurus files. You can copy the clip art and Template files to a floppy disk, so you'll have them if you want them without wasting space on your hard disk. You can complete the Learning Works tutorial lessons and then delete them from your hard disk — you probably won't need the lessons again anyway. And as for the thesaurus, see if you can get along without it. If you find you can't, you can always reinstall the two Thesaurus files — they only account for about 360 KB of the over 2.2 MB you'll save if you follow the whole slimming-down process.

Deleting Unnecessary Files

To delete the files mentioned above, you should be at the MS-DOS prompt with the Works directory selected. The command to delete a file is *DEL* followed by a space and then the name of the file you want to delete. However, you can delete whole groups of files at once by using the asterisk (*) wildcard, which is what we'll do now.

First we'll delete the clip art files. These are the only files in the Works directory that all have the extension PCX, so we can delete them as a group.

- Type *del *.pcx* and press Enter. MS-DOS deletes all the clip art files and returns you to the MS-DOS prompt.

Now we'll delete the Template files, using the wildcard in a different way. All the templates are named TEMPLATE followed by number designations, so we can use the name as the beginning of the filename and follow it with the wildcard.

- Type *del template.** and press Enter. MS-DOS deletes the Template files and returns you to the MS-DOS prompt.

Next we'll delete the Learning Works files. There are several of them: one called LEARN.EXE, and three each whose names begin with WORKSONE, WORKSTWO, WORKSTHR, and WORKSFOU.

1. Type *del LEARN.EXE* and press Enter.

2. Type *del WORKSONE.** and press Enter.

3. Type *del WORKSTWO.** and press Enter.

4. Type *del WORKSTHR.** and press Enter.

5. Type *del WORKSFOU.** and press Enter.

Nice work! Typing these five commands just freed up nearly 1.9 MB of space on your hard disk.

Finally we'll delete the Thesaurus files.

- Type *del thesaur.** and press Enter. MS-DOS deletes the two Thesaurus files.

Running a Slimmed-down Version of Microsoft Works

Now you can run Works just as you learned earlier in this chapter. The only difference is that you won't be able to run the Learning Works tutorial, use the thesaurus, or use any clip art files or templates.

Even though you've deleted the Template files, their descriptive names still appear in the Works Open Existing File dialog box. But if you try to open one of these files, Works will display a message saying the Template file can't be found. (See "Opening Templates" and "Changing Templates" in Chapter 1.)

B
Microsoft Works Specifications

A program's *specifications* define its physical limitations. This appendix lists the specifications of both the Microsoft Works program as a whole and for each of its tools. You might want to refer to this list as you approach various data-handling problems. For example, if you know that a Database field can contain no more than 254 characters, you might choose to create two or three separate fields to store lengthy notes in Database records. Specifications are of six types: general (pertaining to the Works program as a whole), Word Processor, Database, Spreadsheet, Chart, and Communications.

GENERAL SPECIFICATIONS

Type of extended memory supported: EMS
Maximum extended memory supported: 4 MB
Maximum number of files open at one time: 8
Maximum number of screen windows per open file: 1
Maximum paper height: 22 inches
Maximum paper width: 22 inches
Minimum paper height: 1 inch
Minimum paper width: 1 inch
Range of page numbers: 1–32,767
Default paper size: 8.5 by 11 inches
Default top and bottom margins: 1 inch
Default left margin: 1.3 inches
Default right margin: 1.2 inches
Maximum length of one-line headers or footers in Word Processor, Spreadsheet, and Database: up to 255 characters, limited by page size and margin settings

WORD PROCESSOR SPECIFICATIONS

Maximum file size: limited by available disk space

Default line length: 6 inches

Default tab settings: every 0.5 inch

Maximum length of search-and-replace strings: 63 characters

Maximum length of header or footer paragraph lines: limited by page size and margin settings

Maximum height of header or footer paragraphs: one page, limited by top and bottom margin settings and other text on the page

Range of numbered pages in a document: 1–32,767

Maximum number of merged database fields in a document: up to 128 fields or 2,048 bytes, whichever comes first

Maximum length of bookmark names: 15 characters

SPREADSHEET SPECIFICATIONS

Maximum file size: up to 8 MB, depending on available memory

Maximum spreadsheet size: 16,384 rows by 256 columns

Maximum number of displayed decimal places in a value: 7

Maximum viewable column width: 79 characters

Maximum length of text in a cell value: 254 characters

Maximum length of a formula: 254 characters

Maximum length of search-and-replace strings: 63 characters

CHART SPECIFICATIONS

Number of chart types: 9

Maximum number of chart definitions per spreadsheet: 8

Maximum number of Y-series: 6

Maximum length of legends: 19 characters

Maximum length of chart titles: 39 characters

DATABASE SPECIFICATIONS

Maximum file size: up to 8 MB, depending on available memory

Maximum number of fields per file: 256

Maximum size of Form view screen: 256 characters by 256 lines

Maximum number of records per file: 32,000, depending on record size and amount of available memory

Maximum length of field names: 15 characters plus the colon (:)

Maximum length of database fields: 254 characters
Maximum length of database formulas: 254 characters
Maximum number of database formulas: 256
Maximum number of database reports per file: 8
Maximum length of search-and-replace strings: 63 characters

COMMUNICATIONS SPECIFICATIONS

Buffer sizes: Small (150 lines); Medium (300 lines); Large (750 lines)
Default buffer size: Small (150 lines)
Maximum size of a captured text file: limited by disk space
Data formats supported: text and binary
Default handshake mode: Xon/Xoff
Default data bits setting: 8
Default stop bits setting: 1
Default parity setting: Mask
Default COM port: COM1
Default terminal type: VT52
File send/receive error-checking protocols: Kermit, XModem/CRC, YModem, ZModem.

Index

References to figures and illustrations are in italics.

Charles Rubin

Charles Rubin grew up in Los Angeles, California. He attended Antioch College, the University of Southern California, and San Francisco State University. He holds both a bachelor's and a master's degree in English. He has been writing about minicomputers since 1981, and his work has appeared in publications such as *PC Week, InfoWorld,* and *The Wall Street Journal.* He has written over a dozen books about personal computer hardware and software, including *Running Microsoft Works 3* from Microsoft Press. He lives with his wife and son in Sedona, Arizona.

The manuscript for this book was prepared and submitted to Microsoft Press in electronic form. Text files were processed and formatted using Microsoft Word for Windows.

Principal word processor: Sean Donahue
Principal proofreader: Bridget Leahy
Principal typographer: Peter Whitmer
Interior text designer: Kim Eggleston
Cover designer: Rebecca Geisler
Cover color separator: Color Service, Inc.

Text composition by Editorial Services of New England, Inc. in ITC Baskerville with display type in Avant Garde Demi, using Ventura Publisher and the Compugraphic 9600 imagesetter.

Printed on recycled paper stock.

Great Resources for MS-DOS® Users

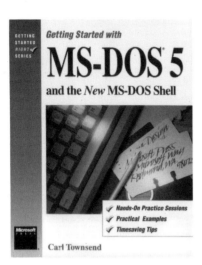

Getting Started with MS-DOS® 5 and the *New* MS-DOS Shell
Carl Townsend

If you are a new or occasional PC user, you'll quickly pick up just what you need to know with this straightforward, task-oriented introduction. It focuses on the features of the enhanced MS-DOS Shell—the graphical user interface that offers point-and-click alternatives to hard-to-remember MS-DOS commands and procedures. Learn how to:

- Manage files and directories
- Use the built-in Editor
- Run applications
- Manage your hard disk
- Print text files
- Protect your data
- Customize your system
- Use shortcuts to find files

ISBN 1-55615-353-8   208 pages $17.95 ($22.95 Canada)

Running MS-DOS,® 5th ed.
Van Wolverton

"Excellent guide for computer novices. Features are clearly defined and illustrated. Good one-book reference." **Computer Book Review**

This is the classic, definitive guide on MS-DOS—for novice to experienced computer users. Beginners will find a wealth of easy-to-understand examples, tutorials, and exercises; experienced users will find an unmatched source of complete and up-to-date information on all major versions of MS-DOS through version 5.

ISBN 1-55615-337-6   592 pages $24.95 ($31.95 Canada)

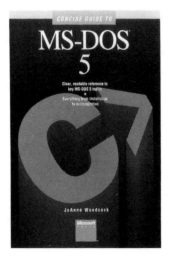

Concise Guide to MS-DOS® 5
JoAnne Woodcock

A readable reference for time-pressed individuals. If you want the MS-DOS essentials but you don't want to read a full-length book, this is the reference for you. Arranged alphabetically by topic, this guide features down-to-earth text and quick access to the key features of MS-DOS 5.

ISBN 1-55615-495-X   176 pages $12.95 ($17.95 Canada)

Microsoft Press books are available wherever books and software are sold. To order direct, call
1-800-MSPRESS *(8am to 5pm central time). Please refer to* **BBK** *when placing your order.* Prices subject to change.*

* In Canada, contact Macmillan Canada, Attn: Microsoft Press Dept., 164 Commander Blvd., Agincourt, Ontario, Canada M1S 3C7, or call (416) 293-8141.
In the U.K., contact Microsoft Press, 27 Wrights Lane, London W8 5TZ. All other international orders will be forwarded to the appropriate distributor.